Ribcage

Israeli Women's Fiction

Ribcage

Israeli Women's Fiction

A Hadassah Anthology

edited by

Carol Diament and Lily Rattok

Printed on Recycled Paper

Contents

Acknowledgments

We would like to single out Claudia Chernov, the Associate Editor/Writer of Hadassah's National Jewish Education Department, whose editing and writing skills have improved virtually every page of this collection. Claudia made the Introduction to this anthology lively and readable, prepared the Questions for Discussion, and obtained permission to reprint and to translate from the original Hebrew when no translations were available.

Doris Oxenhorn, our Production Editor and Administrator, read every word in this volume and saved us from numerous errors. As in the past she put the manuscript into its final form.

The *Ribcage* cover itself speaks for the artist, Jeffrey Schrier.

We owe a special intellectual debt to Roberta Barkan, Professor of Jewish Studies at SUNY Purchase and co-author of *Ivrit la Hadassah*, who provided linguistic and literary insight into Amalia Kahana-Carmon's "N'ima Sassoon Writes Poetry" and Orly Castel-Bloom's "Ummi Fi Shurl," and wrote a number of the Questions for Discussion for these two units.

Sylvia Barack Fishman, Assistant Professor of Contemporary American Jewish Life at Brandeis University, prepared literary analyses, and Peninnah Schram, storyteller, devised dramatic readings of excerpts from several stories for Hadassah's 1994 Convention.

Esther Kustanowitz, the Hebrew Studies Secretary, translated Carol's notes on Haya Ester's "Liar," which provided clues to the meaning of this beautifully crafted, impressionist tale.

The Executive Committee of Hadassah voted to give Carol the opportunity for study and intellectual regeneration on sabbatical at Tel Aviv University. Without their vision and largess, our anthology would not have been produced.

We are indebted to many people for information, ideas, criticism, and encouragement. The following persons merit special mention: Professors David Zisenwine and David Schers, Directors of the Aleph Aleph Program, for greeting this project with interest and for giving us support and approbation; Margalit Mendelssohn, Adviser to the Aleph Aleph Program, for her literary criticism; Hayyim Zohar of the L.A. Pincus Fund, Rabbi Henry Skirball and Rafi Bannai of the Department of Education of the World Zionist Organization, for championing this project; Ruth Grinspan, a student in Lily's class, who shared her notes and thoughts with Carol and represents what is loveliest in Israeli womanhood; Roberta C. Neblett, who wisely insisted that we include a piece on attitudes toward Arabs and who will be the facilitator of a "model" study group in Richmond, Virginia; Professor Zvia Ginor of the Jewish Theological Seminary, for urging Carol to include a story by Orly Castel-Bloom; Rochelle Furstenberg, for suggesting "A Room on the Roof"; and finally Riva Hocherman of the Institute for the Translation of Hebrew Literature and Hany Moshe of ACUM, who expedited permissions to reprint, offered valuable suggestions, and followed up on difficult cases.

Three Chairs of Hadassah's National Jewish Education Department deserve Carol's everlasting gratitude: Ruth G. Cole, 1988-1992, who continued to lead the Department in Carol's absence with strength and wisdom; Belle H. Simon, 1992-1993, who read the stories and contributed wise comments and practical advice; Barbara B. Spack, 1993-present, whose combination of constructive criticism and literary insight was a constant stimulus.

We thank the gifted authors in this book and the extraordinary translators who honed the English versions of the authors' work. We know that their combined efforts and words speak eloquently for them; their biographies are included in the pages that follow.

Carol Diament
Lily Rattok

We gratefully acknowledge permission to use the following copyrighted material:

"Excision" by Dvorah Baron, © copyright for the original Hebrew version by The Bialik Institute, Israel. Permission to translate granted by ACUM, Israel.

"Wedding" by Esther Ra'ab, permission to translate granted by ACUM, Israel.

"Aphia's Plight" by Nehama Pukhachevsky, © copyright for the original Hebrew version by Ruth Arbel.

"N'ima Sassoon Writes Poems" by Amalia Kahana-Carmon, © all rights for the original Hebrew version are reserved by the author, c/o ACUM, Israel. English translation by Arthur Jacobs reprinted by permission of Amalia Kahana-Carmon.

"Apples from the Desert" by Savyon Liebrecht, © all rights for the original Hebrew story are reserved by the author, c/o ACUM, Israel. English translation reprinted by permission of Barbara Harshav.

"Liar" by Haya Ester, the Hebrew original was first printed in *Soft Stones: Stories* © copyright 1983 by Eked Publishing. Used with permission of the publisher and the author.

"Shrinking" by Ruth Almog, © all rights for the original Hebrew version are reserved by the author, c/o ACUM, Israel.

"Loneliness" by Shulamith Hareven, © all rights for the original Hebrew version are reserved by the author, c/o ACUM, Israel. The English translation is reprinted from *Twilight and Other Stories* © copyright 1992 by Shulamith Hareven, translated from the Hebrew by Hillel Halkin. Published by Mercury House, San Francisco, CA, and reprinted by permission.

"A Slight Delay" by Dahlia Ravikovitch, © all rights for the original Hebrew version are reserved by the author, c/o ACUM, Israel.

"White Lines" by Dorit Peleg, Hebrew original and English translation © copyright by the author.

"La Promenade, Triptych" by Michal Govrin, © all rights for the original Hebrew version are reserved by the author, c/o ACUM, Israel. English translation by Dalya Bilu © copyright by the Institute for the Translation of Hebrew Literature.

"A Room on the Roof" by Savyon Liebrecht, © all rights for the original Hebrew version are reserved by the author, c/o ACUM, Israel. The English translation by Jeffrey M. Green of Savyon Liebrecht's "A Room on the Roof" was first published in *ARIEL: The Israel Review of Arts and Letters*, no. 77-78, 198. Reprinted with permission.

"Ummi Fi Shurl" by Orly Castel-Bloom, Hebrew original © copyright by the author. English translation by Dalya Bilu © copyright by The Institute for the Translation of Hebrew Literature.

"Apples in Honey" by Yehudit Hendel, © all rights for the original Hebrew version are reserved by the author, c/o ACUM, Israel.

Foreword

Carol Diament

Ribcage, the collection of stories before you, is meant to be representative of the literature created by contemporary Israeli women authors. Hence, it might be expected that a one-dimensional, homogeneous product would emerge. As the stories themselves will attest, this is not at all the case. Israeli women authors express themselves in many and varied voices. They reflect a mosaic of cultural backgrounds and political and social attitudes of significant breadth and scope.

The idea that led to *Ribcage* began during my sabbatical in the Aleph Aleph Program for Diaspora Jewish Educators at Tel Aviv University, August 1991 to January 1992. There, I met and studied women's Hebrew fiction with Lily Rattok, Professor of Modern Hebrew Literature, and we held discussions before, during, and after class on a number of intriguing questions: What is distinctly Jewish about these short stories—either religiously, ethically, or culturally? In what ways, if any, does this fiction differ from short stories written by an American author (or an author from Sweden, Argentina, etc.)? What is distinctly female or feminist about the short stories? Through our literary discourse, there emerged with clarity and urgency the need to translate for the American Jewish reader stories written by Israeli women.

In January of 1992, as my sabbatical was ending, I was invited to take part in a University symposium entitled "Israeli Women: Issues and Challenges." Lily and I had already begun working on *Ribcage—Israeli Women's Fiction*, and I offered to share my impressions of the stories. I began by asking the audience some of the questions that Lily and I had discussed and some others that had been troubling me as an American Jewish woman. Why do Israeli authors —men as well as women—avoid one of the most prominent themes of American Jewish fiction: the search for spiritual meaning within the Judaic tradition. Israelis, unlike their American counterparts, rarely write about choosing one's level of religious observance or about coming to terms with one's religious heritage. Accordingly, is it the role of Hadassah's Jewish Education Department to translate this literature?

The answer from my listeners was a resounding: "Yes! Translate and write and tell your women about us. This is the only way to build bridges of understanding between Israeli and American Jews, between Israel and the world." We followed up on this plea to translate and disseminate Israeli women's literature, producing the present anthology. Eight of the fifteen English translations were commissioned especially for Hadassah. The project also helped me to fulfill one of the requirements of the Aleph Aleph Program, that participants complete an educational project at their home institution.

When Lily and I divided the tasks associated with the Foreword and Introduction, we decided that she would concentrate on feminist themes and I on the American Jewish reader and how she or he might react to *Ribcage*.

A well-known American Jewish professor of Hebrew literature has argued that "Israeli literature is not Jewish literature." He claims that most contemporary Israeli authors have turned away from traditional Jewish literature, creating instead a new type of foreign literature, written in Hebrew.

The secular Israeli, who considers the State to be a nation among nations and rejects the connections to a religiously-centered diaspora predecessor, is well represented in this anthology. For this type of writer, the Hebrew language and the Israeli nation are a medium of expression and a locale that should be depicted as might any other society, unencumbered by its religious underpinnings and history.

The normalcy of the country and of its inhabitants—be they heroes, heroines, or underworld denizens—is an essential aspect of these writers' work. The denial of Judaic values and behaviors loftier than those of other peoples has often been difficult for American Jewish readers to assimilate and accept.

American Jewish readers often cringe when Israeli writers portray their country and its citizens in any but the best light. In the past Americans cheered literary descriptions of the birth of Israel and the struggle against all odds to establish the Jewish state, but today they are distinctly uncomfortable with depictions of ordinary, fallible Israeli antiheroes. As this anthology reflects, modern Israeli writers tend to depict characters who are lonely and troubled, isolated and estranged from their society, even dysfunctional. Of course, such characters may be found in the fiction written by both men and women of nearly any nation on earth, but perhaps such characters are disproportionately present in the fiction of Israeli women writing in the eighties and nineties. An American reader who clings to the view of the Jewish home as a warm, safe, supportive haven for the family, and by extension regards Israel as a warm, safe, supportive haven for world Jewry, is apt to be dismayed by the harsh, jarring depictions in these stories.

Literary dialogue between the Israeli and American Jewish communities reflects this cultural tension. Israeli writers deplore American readers' preference for an idealized, heroic view of Israeli life over that depicted by Israel's most prominent writers and artists.

Is this tension legitimate? Is it necessary? Judaism has always encompassed a spectrum of viewpoints, traditions, rituals, social structures, themes, and interpretations of life. We should be receptive to the full gamut of these attitudes, if we are to recognize, enjoy, and benefit from the astounding diversity of Jewish creativity—whether from earlier millennia or from our own day.

Today, Jewish women are expressing their creativity in various forms, including remarkable contributions to literature. Judaism's voices include those of the prophets, of the rabbis, of the Hasidim and of the *mitnagdim*, of the religious and the assimilated, of the men and the women—now more and more of the women, encompassing an ever-greater variety of writers. Israeli women with religious backgrounds and milieu are contributors to this collection, as are the writers who portray characters of Middle Eastern origins. Each author brings a different viewpoint and cultural baggage to the depiction of her subject. Each is an important representative of the varied trends in today's Israeli women's literature.

Dvorah Baron, with whom this anthology begins, contrasts the peaceful setting of her father's Rabbinical Court in a small town in Eastern Europe with the emotional turmoil engendered by enforcement of the traditional Jewish *get*. In contrast, Dorit Peleg depicts a predatory female, a prostitute in an Israeli hotel. Elisheva, a Russian poet who, in the early twentieth century, was attracted by the Zionist movement and immigrated to Palestine with her Jewish husband, juxtaposes illusion and reality in depicting the unfulfilled life of a spinster. Esther Ra'ab portrays feminine heroism in war. Nehama Pukhachevsky, an Ashkenazi writer, portrays the tribulations of a Yemenite woman in the latter's encounter with Ashkenazic values. Hannah Trager explores the myth of women's equality in her depiction of the struggle of Israeli women for a political voice on a socialist kibbutz. Amalia Kahana-Carmon combines the holy and the profane in "N'ima Sassoon Writes Poems," weaving sensuality with Jewish religious metaphors. As the stories unfold, you will find that much of Israeli literature, in fact, lies somewhere between *kodesh v'hol*, between the sacred and the secular. Savyon Liebrecht explores the conflict between mother and daughter over the relative merits of a religious and a secular life. In a second story, she portrays the relationship between an Israeli woman and an Arab worker. Ruth Almog exposes women's low self-esteem as they sacrifice themselves for others, while she criticizes secular Zionist society. Haya Ester's heroine constructs fantasies to escape the constricting world of the ultra-Orthodox. Shulamith Hareven depicts the eroded self-image of a woman driven to lesbianism by her husband's neglect. Dahlia Ravikovitch weaves a tale of sexual harassment in the Israeli army, where women are often reduced to useless objects. Michal Govrin invokes the Holocaust in her story of well-to-do survivors who feel secure in Israel but grow uneasy during a trip to Europe. Orly Castel-Bloom raises questions about class distinctions, homelessness, and neglect of one's neighbor—from which Israel is not immune. Hers is a type of fiction that often confuses and angers American readers. The anthology ends with Yehudit Hendel's wrenching portrayal of the widow of a fallen soldier, a reflection of Israel's perpetual state of siege.

Each of the many women's voices in the stories of the collection has a legitimate claim to be heard and to be regarded as a vital part of the rich mosaic of Jewish literature. Together, they comprise an Israeli chorus of intense political and social commentary and of vivid symbolism. American Jewish readers need reorientation to accept Israel and its diversity, with all its flaws as well as all its glories.

Among other profound literary insights, Professor Rattok will show in her Introduction how Israeli women, through their fiction, are attempting to release their souls from the cage imposed upon them by Jewish tradition and by contemporary Israeli life. As an American Jewish educator, I am attempting to disseminate the beautifully crafted poetic imagery and the diverse, vibrant societal attitudes, which also need release from the cage imposed by the limited readership able to enjoy and admire the original Hebrew language, idiom, resonances, and allusions.

The stories offered in this collection can be enjoyed as casual reading but also merit careful study.

Introduction: The Other Voice

Lily Rattok

The Missing Profile: Portrait of Women as Israeli Writers

Israeli women's fiction has not yet reached the scope, variety, and independence of Israeli women's poetry. One reason is the absence of an image of women as story-tellers. That is, though Hebrew poetry encompasses a consolidated, female "poetic I" that is different from the male "poetic I," no image of a woman writer of fiction is available for the female author. The creator in Israeli fiction is almost always a man, just as the fictional protagonist is almost always a man. What force is responsible for this situation, and why have Israel's women authors failed to invent an image of a woman creator that will give expression to their decision to write?

My basic position is that women's literature can be understood as a systems crossroads: a meeting point between the system of literary production and the system of sexual belonging. When these two systems meet, tension arises between the conception of female identity on the one hand and the conception of creativity as a male realm on the other. Women's literature often reflects the individual's attempt to mediate between the commands of feminine identity (which she learns through her every interaction within society) and the dictates of the masculine literary system.

Women writers of Hebrew fiction did not aim to capture the literary territory of men, nor did they seek to revolutionize the production of literature. Instead, women writers sought only to join with their compatriots in the literary arena, and they emphasized the modesty of their demands. This modesty was forced on women by Jewish culture, claims Amalia Kahana-Carmon.[1] Throughout history, women have been barred from the role of public representative in the synagogue. The private realm is assigned to the Jewish woman, while the Jewish man occupies the public realm. The woman writer internalizes the status demanded by religion, Kahana-Carmon argues, and consequently is unable to picture herself as a figure of central importance in the community. Unlike the male writer who, in the words of Amos Oz, assumes the role of "tribal magician,"[2] the female writer does not dare demand such a position of authority.

Devorah Baron—The First Birth of Women's Hebrew Fiction

Hebrew literature may be unique among world literature in that its women's fiction was born twice, and more than fifty years separate the two births. The first birth occurred in 1902 with the publication of Devorah Baron's first short stories in literary journals. Though Baron was forced to wait 25 years for the publication of her first book, the collection *Stories*, her earliest pieces had generated enormous excitement, with the literary community welcoming the young writer as if she were a *wunderkind*. Her embrace by the male establishment was indeed wonderful—and within a short time she had been granted a special status within Hebrew letters.

How do we account for this spectacular reception? In the late nineteenth and early twentieth century, secular Hebrew literature sought to include women. Eliezer Ben-Yehuda, the founder of modern Hebrew, wrote, "the demand of the moment is that women penetrate Hebrew literature."[3] And in 1905 the critic M. M. Feitelson

---

1. Amalia Kahana-Carmon, "Songs of Bats as They Fly," 1989 (Hebrew).
2. Amos Oz, "In Bright Blue Light," 1979 (Hebrew).
3. Cited by Yaffa Berlovitz, "The Writings of the Daughters of the First *Aliyah*: Afterword," *Stories by Women: Daughters of the First Aliyah* (Israel: Sifriat Tarmil, 1984) (Hebrew).

wrote an article entitled "The Liberated Woman In Our Literature." Hence, the Hebrew literary establishment took great pride in its first woman writer, who had—in addition to talent—both beauty and a rabbinic lineage.[4] She was adored as the token female presence.

The young Devorah Baron was an independent personality, and she strove for the freedom that Jewish men were granted. She insisted on an education parallel to men's, and she studied first in *heder* (religious school for younger children) and later in high school. She supported herself by teaching Hebrew, and she worked as a counselor for Zionist youth.

In her early stories Baron dared to protest the neglect of women by Jewish religious law, and she did not shy away from erotic subjects. Though she knew the risks involved, she did not censor her fiction. Her only defenses against malicious gossip were her distant behavior and her exceedingly modest dress. Her nun-like image, however, did not protect her. One particularly suggestive passage in "A Quarreling Couple" led writers and editors to gossip that she was no virgin, and this gossip damaged her relationship with her fiancé, the writer Moshe Ben-Eliezer. But Baron did not let the gossip deter her from writing.

Devorah Baron broke off her engagement in 1910, after five years, and left Russia for the land of Israel. She began working as the literary editor of the newspaper *Hapoel Hatzair*, and in 1911 she married the paper's editor, Yosef Aharonovitch, already a renowned Zionist labor leader. They and their daughter were exiled to Egypt during World War I. Upon returning to Palestine, the couple resumed editing and writing, but Aharonovitch resigned in 1922 to become director of Bank HaPo'alim (The Workers' Bank). Baron also resigned her position with the newspaper. For the next fifty years, no Israeli woman would work in literary editing.

Baron continued writing fiction and translating literary works into Hebrew, but in 1936 suffered an illness which was to keep her bedridden until her death in 1956. She broke off almost every physical contact with the outside world, participated in no public activity, gave

4. A detailed description of her reception by the literary world is found in Nurit Govrin, "The First Half: Devorah Baron and Her Work 1887-1923" (1988) (Hebrew).

no interviews, and met only a small number of people. She did not even attend the funeral of her husband. Dov Sadan, a contemporary literary critic, wrote that on the day of Aharonovitch's funeral he saw Baron take three steps outside the house, and then return inside.

Baron apparently imprisoned herself in her home willingly, giving up freedom of movement and the enjoyment of physical life, in order to win spiritual freedom and the right to create literature with absolute dedication to her craft. Her reclusive life released her from women's customary roles. Sandra Gilbert and Susan Gubar in the ground-breaking *The Madwoman in the Attic* argue that illness expresses women's social weakness in a world whose rules are created by men, yet this weakness gives a woman the only power available to her: the power of refusal.[5] Devorah Baron did indeed refuse with all her strength: she refused to eat regular food and she starved herself; she refused to move freely and she stayed in bed; and she especially refused to meet the world as it was.

Gilbert and Gubar emphasize that self-starvation (anorexia), confinement to the home (agoraphobia), and other predominantly female illnesses, are in fact more than protests or refusals. They are also desperate expressions of the woman's desire to control her life. Though she has only the power to refuse, she has one realm where she remains in control: her body. This results in the paradoxical situation whereby women hurt their bodies to prove their power. The other reason why women damage their bodies is to conquer female physicality. The woman is thus able to attain transcendentalism and to rise to spiritual spheres. Gilbert and Gubar make clear that a woman recoils from the physical because patriarchal society views the female body as tempting, provocative, and monstrous.[6]

Devorah Baron may in fact have recoiled from her body when she took away from it almost every physical enjoyment. Nonetheless,

5. Sandra M. Gilbert and Susan Gubar, *The Madwoman in the Attic: The Woman Writer and the Nineteenth Century Literary Imagination* (New Haven, CT: Yale University Press, 1979).

6. Gilbert and Gubar note the instructive comment by Adrienne Rich that every thinking woman is liable to see herself as captured within her hideous body and to recoil from it.

she made sure to maintain her body at the level required to carry out her spiritual mission. In effect, Baron enslaved her body for one aim—artistic creation. Only by removing herself from mundane existence could Baron create an alternative reality, where she alone would dictate the rules. Baron lived in this closed world mainly with her daughter, Zipporah, and various housemaids. Her world, therefore, was a women's world, and male strictures were outside its boundaries.

Devorah Baron's rules were similar to those of a monastic order: sexual withdrawal, the lack of any bodily enjoyment, dedication to literary/spiritual creation, and the abandonment of selfhood. Nurit Govrin describes the writer as someone who "while still alive became a fairy tale—the tale of the captured princess." Baron, though, was not a tender heroine of romance, and only death rescued her from her self-imposed prison.

The Second Birth of Women's Hebrew Fiction

The second birth of women's Hebrew fiction occurred in 1956 with the publication of Amalia Kahana-Carmon's first short story. Her acceptance as a central Israeli writer, however, alongside the men who were members of her literary generation like Amos Oz and A. B. Yehoshua, took place ten years later with the publication of her first book.

The entrance by Amalia Kahana-Carmon into the literary community took place in an era that differed radically from Devorah Baron's. By mid-century, women poets writing in Hebrew were relatively commonplace, with Rachel, Yokheved Bat-Miriam, and Leah Goldberg among the most renowned, so there was no need for a token representative of womanhood. In addition, Israel was a young country and its existence was in danger, so it valued its masculine foundations—wartime bravery, independence, aggressiveness, self-reliance (all seen as male traits)—and as a corollary devalued women's achievements. Therefore no publishers knocked on Amalia Kahana-Carmon's door in 1956. On the contrary, her unusual works inspired great opposition. A number of editors refused to publish her collection of stories, even though she had won the prestigious Amot prize for "N'ima Sassoon Writes Poems." Only after many rejections were the pieces accepted for publication. The collection, *Under One Roof*, won outstanding praise from the critics, and in the late sixties Kahana-Carmon assumed her place among the central creators of Israeli fiction.[7]

Yet the mid-century retreat from earlier demands for female equality does not adequately explain why so few women between the turn of the century and the late fifties published Hebrew fiction. If Jewish women of 1900 had really been granted the historic opportunity to join with Jewish men in the Hebrew literary re-awakening, why were almost no women fiction writers published except for Devorah Baron? If at the first birth of Hebrew women's fiction the only voices were those of supporters and admirers, why was a second birth necessary?

The answer to these questions is complicated. The Jewish literary establishment of the early twentieth century indeed wanted to accept women, but the openness was toward the writer herself rather than toward her work. In other words, beautiful slogans of equal opportunity misled Jewish women writers, who believed that their stories would find wide acceptance, but who found the reality to be entirely different. The Hebrew literary establishment was no more open to the feminine voice than was the English, French, Russian, or any other literary establishment. Male rejection was hidden behind a facade of admiration for women.

In the case of Devorah Baron, the early twentieth-century male literary world relished the existence of a female writer in its midst, but male editors directed her stories to a separate and marginal place within the publishing hierarchy, and male writers never perceived her as a worthy competitor.[8] Her contemporaries' fascination with the writer as a woman did not result in a corresponding fascination with

---

7. The critical reaction is surveyed in my book, *Amalia Kahana-Carmon: Monograph*, 1986 (Hebrew). In the winter of 1994, Kahana-Carmon was awarded the Bialik Prize, Israel's most prestigious award.

8. As mainstream Hebrew fiction writers turned increasingly to stories of Israel, Devorah Baron continued to explore the diaspora life she had known as a child. Unlike most men writing during the first half of the century, she avoids surrealistic effects, interior monologue, and overt symbolism. Furthermore, she eschews the collective historical perspective of Zionist-socialism which many Hebrew literary critics of her day considered indispensable for serious fiction.

the vision expressed in her works. Male authors expected that the female author would stay modestly to one side, not challenging the world view created by men. Indeed, as Kahana-Carmon argues in her essays, the literary establishment defined the female writer as a support to the male writer, much as the wife was defined as a support to her husband. The woman writer was to describe reality from the feminine angle, accepting women's limited place and her marginality. Attempting to change the accepted, male-centered world view by means of her work was the unpardonable sin of the woman creator.

Thus, from the start, women's fiction was considered peripheral to the nascent Hebrew literary enterprise. Literary authority was the exclusive domain of the Jewish male. In this domain the spiritual world view of the entire Israeli public was created, but that world view did not incorporate Jewish female vision. Permission to enter Hebrew literary territory was conditional on a woman's willingness to describe the world, and especially herself, in terms of men.

The trap into which the woman writer fell was a double trap. First, her work was judged to be of limited and secondary importance, and she as a writer had to accept this as a proper judgment. In other words, she herself had to assign her work a secondary role. Second, the male literary establishment required the woman creator to write as a woman, but she herself was absolutely forbidden to define womanhood. That is, the woman writer was required to create heroines and write in a feminine way, but this femininity was defined according to men's terms.

Amalia Kahana-Carmon—Creation of the Alternative Model

Amalia Kahana-Carmon's development as a writer differed greatly from that of her predecessor, Devorah Baron. Devorah Baron began writing as a girl of fifteen, when she lacked self-confidence as an artist and her education was incomplete. She was often willing to revise her work based upon comments from her editors, whose encouragement she needed. Furthermore, Baron wrote in the "new process" style common in the late nineteenth century,[9] and only after

9. The new process style flourished from 1891 to 1894 and was notable for its melodramatic plot structure, pathos, emotionalism, sentimentality, its simple sentence structure, and its clear, unadorned writing style.

many years did she adopt an idiosyncratic personal style. Amalia Kahana-Carmon, in contrast, began writing and publishing in her late twenties—after she had fought as a signaler in the War of Independence, attended college, traveled to London, worked, and married. As she was beginning her professional career, she was also caring for her three young children. Furthermore, in her first four years as a professional writer, Kahana-Carmon and her family moved, as a result of her husband's career, from England to Switzerland to Germany and back to Israel.

The early stories of Kahana-Carmon hence reflect a mature, unique voice, and her originality is immediately evident. Moreover, she fought for strict control of the content and the form of her work. She was unwilling to revise based on recommendations by editors. Her aggressive refusal to write according to others' directions was indeed one factor in the long delay between the publication of her first short stories and the publication of her first book, and also resulted in a lengthy legal struggle.

Kahana-Carmon, however, succeeded in defining a new model of Hebrew women's fiction. Though her independence prevented her from gaining quick acceptance, she ultimately gained a more central position within the Hebrew literary world than was achieved by Devorah Baron. Kahana-Carmon's first stories appeared almost unchanged in *Under One Roof* (1966). The novel *And A Moon In The Valley Of Ayalon* (1971) was remarkable for formal innovation, as were the two collections *Magnetic Fields* (1977) and *Up In Montifer* (1984). The novel *With Her On Her Way Home* (1991) was also notable for its artistic daring, and was a testament to the author's independence and self-confidence.

Kahana-Carmon, again unlike Devorah Baron, benefited from the prior literary achievements of women writing in Hebrew. In addition, she benefited from the work of European women writers who had preceded her. Possibly her long stay in Great Britain afforded her knowledge of women's rich achievements in English fiction, and a number of critics have pointed to the similarities between the works of Kahana-Carmon and Virginia Woolf.

Like Woolf, Amalia Kahana-Carmon made a conscious decision

"to be a woman writer."[10] She was not forced to deny her physicality or her femininity, as was Devorah Baron; instead she increasingly emphasized the feminine as her work developed.

In the eighties, Kahana-Carmon published five essays on female writers in Hebrew, and protested the neglect of women's work. This neglect occurs, she argued, because women's experience is seen as marginal. In a 1988 article she stated, "The problems in the world of women, as they know them, do not always and do not everywhere overlap with the problems in the world of men, as they know them. In wide areas of the very same reality, a woman finds herself experiencing the events according to a code, and/or from a point of view, and/or according to a list of priorities, that are not identical to a man's." Therefore, the female writer who remains the most faithful to her experience and is the least willing to imitate male experience is the writer who is most neglected.

Kahana-Carmon stated that the neglect of women writers parallels the position of women in Judaism. Just as a woman is not allowed to serve as the public's representative in the synagogue, she is not allowed to represent the Jewish nation in her work, "because Hebrew literature, even if it is secular, is seen both by author and readers as the national synagogue of the spirit." Women have a secondary role in both synagogue and literature, because their experiences are defined as personal and private. "The [male] person from Israel," wrote Kahana-Carmon in 1989, "cannot identify with the collective 'I' which the female writer uses. Her 'I' cannot express him." Therefore, the more the woman writer's work is endowed with "vision" or "momentum" or "imagination"—the more it is considered "peripheral" or "abnormal." Her work is seen as "lacking seriousness"; it is "the fruit of weak logic ... capricious, self-obsessed, hysterical." Kahana-Carmon concluded that the woman writer in Hebrew can choose between "rape within the framework of marriage"—that is, accept being forced into the male mold—and the status of a "rebellious woman"—that is, she can remain true to her values. The woman writer is always "the other," and the most that her work can aspire to is being the "undermining presence" within literature while express-

10. Amalia Kahana-Carmon, "To Be A Woman Writer," *Yediot Aharonot*, April 13, 1984 (Hebrew).

ing "the truth of desire." Neither by accepting nor by rebelling does the woman writer have the opportunity to be the central artist of her generation.[11]

Kahana-Carmon refuses to accept the status of "the other" or, in her words, the status of one who "happens to sit in the women's section of that synagogue of the spirit which is called Hebrew fiction.... All authors strive, and are convinced, that their words carry universal, objective truths."

In her famous story "N'ima Sassoon Writes Poetry" (1963), Amalia Kahana-Carmon portrays the artist as a young woman. The work was perhaps influenced by Leah Goldberg's novel, *And It Is The Light* (1946). The two plots are similar: a young woman is in love with an older man, who responds to her somewhat, but finally cuts off their relationship. The failure of her first love leads the heroine to self knowledge and she dedicates herself to creative work.

N'ima Sassoon is aware of being a creative artist at a very young age, and sees in this a religious destiny: "But I, please God, when I grow up, will find out how to say this miracle, all the miracles, in writing. I have to. Otherwise, my life is no life." In relations with her beloved teacher she strives to understand "the secret that makes the faint-hearted heroic." N'ima comes to understand this secret when the teacher refuses her love; rejection thus brings her a powerful insight and a rare inner strength. The secret is the religious-like legality that exists in our world and the ability of humans to willingly obey the demands of the world's legal system. N'ima dedicates herself to artistic destiny, so that she finds meaning in life through writing instead of through love.

Subverting the Romantic Myth

The romantic myth is one of the most efficient means of making women accept their low social status. At the center of the myth is a

---

11. Amalia Kahana-Carmon is herself in this position. Although she is considered to be *one of* Israel's major writers, neither the Israeli literary world nor the international critical community considers her to be Israel's central artist. Furthermore, though she has been the recipient of Israel's most significant literary awards, she is relatively little known among American Jewry—unlike her contemporaries Amos Oz, A. B. Yehoshua, or Nathan Shaham.

young, beautiful woman. At her service is a dedicated and enraptured knight who is willing to sacrifice his life for her. As it turns out, the knight is required to perform only one act of bravery, in which he saves the heroine from a grave difficulty. The heroine, of course, falls in love with her savior and marries him, and they both live happily ever after. The romantic myth is, in effect, a story of courtship, a story that has no connection with the rest of the heroine's life. The story instead focuses on the one period when a woman has power over a man. During this period, she can respond to her knight's love or reject it, and in this she causes him happiness or misery. Immediately after she responds to the knight's love, the heroine will, of course, lose the power which the courtship period had granted her, but the romantic myth deliberately refrains from describing her life following courtship.

Women readers are captivated by the romantic myth because it conceals the painful reality of unequal power that characterizes their lives. Shulamith Firestone explains that the societal role of the romantic myth is to distract women's minds from their second-class status.[12] She argues that romance is a cultural tool in the hands of male authority, a tool that is used to prevent women from understanding their true social status. And as patriarchy's direct control over women diminishes (through legal reform of property rights, voting rights, etc., and other societal changes such as women's educational advancement), the power of the romantic myth within popular culture increases.

One of the central tasks of women's fiction has been exposing the truth behind the romantic myth. At times women authors have refused to focus on romance, and at times they have re-examined the courtship story in order to reveal the truths that have been concealed. One effective way to debunk the romantic myth is through reconnecting the courtship period to the rest of the heroine's life. By restoring continuity, the artificial isolation of the courtship episode—which results in its idealization—is undone. Furthermore, by reconnecting courtship to the rest of a woman's life (usually to her childhood and

---

12. Shulamith Firestone, *The Dialectic of Sex: The Case for Feminist Revolution* (New York: Bantam, 1971, rev. ed.).

adolescence, occasionally to her subsequent married life), the author challenges the conception that all of a woman's early life prepares her for the courtship and wedding, and that all of her later life is eternal happiness.

From Passivity to Activism

Devorah Baron refuses to fuel the romantic myth, and chooses in nearly all of her stories to describe young girls or married women. She hardly ever depicts a young woman in love, and the fate of those few who do fall in love is bitter and unhappy. Baron's rejection of the romantic myth accounts for the repudiation of romantic motifs within her work; instead she uses naturalistic descriptions of desire or of barren conjugal life.

The Zionist movement, which proclaimed the cause of women's emancipation, caused intriguing changes for Jewish women. Eastern European women, who had been passive and accepting, as in Devorah Baron's "Excision" (1943), are the same Jewish women who made *aliyah* to Israel, became activists, and worked for women's equality.

The struggle by women of the first *aliyah* (1880 to 1904) to gain the right to vote is depicted in Hannah Trager's story. The young women succeed in mobilizing their male friends and their mothers, and together they triumph over conservative, sexist opposition to change.

Eastern European women strongly influenced their Middle Eastern sisters, as Nehama Pukhachevsky illustrates in "Aphia's Plight" (1925). Aphia learns to read and write with the assistance of her Ashkenazic employer, and, absorbing European values, she refuses to let her husband beat her and runs away from him.

In these two early stories about women pioneers in the land of Israel, power clearly lies in male hands, but women recognize their rights as human beings and demand changes in both their personal and family lives and their political and communal lives.

Like Devorah Baron, these women writing in Hebrew in the early years of the century avoid the romantic myth. They forsake the courtship idyll and instead document the everyday difficulties of the women who are realizing the Zionist vision. For many early Hebrew women authors, their "feminist" protest is transferred onto a heroine who is outside the writer's own economic class or ethnic group. Nehama Pukhachevsky chooses a Yemenite woman, as does Hanna Bolotin in "The Mother and Daughter" (1911). Both authors examine a community that differs greatly from the writers' own Ashkenazic community in its attitudes and its treatment of women, and they thereby avoid direct criticism of the Zionist pioneers. Elaine Showalter shows how British women authors of the nineteenth-century, through identification with poor and dispossessed women, thereby indirectly protest against the existing social order—whose victims are women.[13] A similar identification with the neglected Jewish woman—and a similar protest—occurs in Devorah Baron's work and in the work of women writers of the first *aliyah*.

A radical departure from stereotypical Eastern European womanhood and from the stereotypical courtship episode is presented by Esther Ra'ab in "Wedding" (1934). One young woman from the village takes upon herself the job of savior. With the inspiration of the biblical leaders Deborah and Judith, Ziva rides out to appeal to the British army. At the hour of her mission's fulfillment, she is wounded. Nonetheless, she is the model for the Israeli warrior heroine, ready to sacrifice her life for her homeland.

Fantasy and Delusion—Substitutes for Creation and Authority

That the romantic myth is a delusion which makes women miserable is the subject of Elisheva's stories. In these stories, and in the novel *Alleyways* (1929), the writer presents heroines who fall in love with love, women who are willing to give all for love, as literature has taught them. One of them confesses, "With my love I fell in love and no more." The protagonist of *Alleyways*, Liudmila, falls in love with the poet Galwitz, just as Nina in Chekhov's "The Seagull" falls in love with the writer Trigorin. Liudmila knows Chekhov's play well, yet she is unable to stop herself from falling into Nina's trap.

Elisheva also attacks the romantic myth in "The Truth" (1928). The protagonist is a young woman, unattractive and lonely, who enthusiastically watches plays and movies. Under the influence of

13. Elaine Showalter, *A Literature of Their Own: British Women Novelists From Brontë to Lessing* (New Jersey: Princeton University Press, 1977).

these creations, she writes in her diary of her imagined loves. The ironic title sharpens the point that these romantic interludes are purely fantasy—indeed they are lies. Elisheva emphasizes the character's desperate need to give her life the only meaning that matters—romantic meaning. In effect, patriarchal society does not offer women any source of satisfaction except romantic love—or, more accurately, the delusion of romantic love. In "The Truth" Elisheva presents the delusion as a means by which women escape from the emptiness and disappointment of their lives. The writer also makes clear how all the arts serve the existing patriarchal order, disguising emotional manipulation within poetic truth.

Elisheva creates the image of a woman fleeing to a world of written fantasy rather than the image of a woman as a creative author and authoritative creator. The protagonist of "The Truth" (1924) writes only for herself. In her imagination, she gives form and life to men whom, in reality, she only sees from afar. After her death, when her friends discover the notebook containing her collection of stories, they believe that her inventions were actual occurrences, and the women are jealous of her beautiful and meaningful life. The story concludes with exposure of the delusion: "So all the words of the old book were a fabrication.... The words were a poor absurd figment, her friends envied her in vain, for her life was as deprived, boring, and uneventful as were all their lives in the long lonely evenings." The principal character is shown to be a liar, but the beauty of her writing leads readers to believe that she could have been an author of fiction if support had been given to women in her day.

Elisheva as author distances herself from her creation, arousing the reader's pity. In contrast, Haya Ester identifies with the principal character in "Liar" (1983). Sheindel, who is also a potential writer, does not produce works of fiction because her ultra-Orthodox community condemns secular literature (and views writing religious literature as the province solely of men). Sheindel's marvelous stories, which capture the hearts of children, are the cause of her nickname: the liar. The narrator describes Sheindel's almost hypnotic influence: "Her lies were colorful. Her thoughts sinuous. She would let things slip which we never even saw. We were taken in by her. We got ourselves mixed up in her lies. We saw." Perhaps it is possible to see in Haya Ester, the writer, the twin of Sheindel, the liar, the story inventor, who creates beauty in words.

The Hidden Story—Daughters and Mothers

One of the hidden stories in a patriarchal culture is the complex relationship between mothers and daughters. In Western culture motherhood is primarily viewed as the relationship between a son and his mother; the most notable example is the Christian relationship of the Madonna and child. The story of a woman and her mother has only recently begun to be explored in women's literature. Adrienne Rich states that a rupture between mother and daughter is not accorded the same tragic dimensions as a rupture between mother and son (as in *Hamlet* and *Oedipus Rex*) or as a rupture between father and daughter (as in *King Lear*).[14] Neither love between mother and daughter nor division between mother and daughter are recognized and validated in Western literature. Though the daughter's loss of her mother and the mother's loss of her daughter are the essence of human tragedy, patriarchal society effectively hides that tragedy from view.

In ancient Greece, however, the rupture between mother and daughter was recognized and respected. The myth of the mother, Demeter, searching for her lost daughter, Persephone,[15] was the basis for the ritual mysteries at Eleusis, a key element of ancient Greek religious life. Phyllis Chesler postulates that subsequent Western civilization, by denying the Demeter-Persephone myth, relegated the mother-daughter relationship to the margins of cultural consciousness.[16] Because women share no cultural myth in which they act together independently of men, Chesler states, women are not allowed to "become heroines" of their own stories, and hence are

14. Adrienne Rich, *Of Woman Born: Motherhood as Experience and Institution* (New York: Norton, 1976).

15. Persephone is taken by Hades, the god of the underworld, to his home, and Demeter, the harvest goddess, mourns and searches for her daughter. While Demeter mourns, the land can produce no harvest. Demeter finds Persephone and brings her back up to the earth, but each year Persephone must descend to the underworld for six months. During those months, Demeter laments the absence of her child. The earth is cold and no crops grow.

16. Phyllis Chesler, *Woman and Madness* (Garden City, NY: Doubleday, 1972).

sentenced to helplessness, passivity, naiveté, and weakness. Mothers then transmit these qualities to their daughters.

This accounts for the ambivalent relationships between daughters and mothers. The daughter feels fury because the mother has neglected her in favor of nurturing the father and the sons, and also because the mother is not capable of providing her with strength. Adrienne Rich asserts that a daughter may remain angry with her mother all of her life because of the mother's passive acceptance of "whatever happens."[17] The daughter thereby degrades the mother by placing her in the role of accepting victim, and she also distorts her own soul as she follows her mother in a search for clues to the meaning of womanhood. Rich argues that the self-hate and the low expectations of the mother are the ropes that bind the soul of the daughter.

Since the daughter can draw no strength from the mother, she turns to the father. This causes a rupture between mother and daughter, as they compete for the father. This competition, however, is denied by both mother and daughter, because it is taboo. The competition is made clear, though, in symbolic sources such as fairy tales, where the mother is often transformed into an evil stepmother. In "Snow White" the battle between the Queen and Snow White is conducted by means of a magic mirror, which tells the Queen of her unsurpassed beauty. According to Gilbert and Gubar, the mirror speaks with the voice of patriarchy, determining the status of women according to their external attractions. With beauty as women's only basis for attaining power, competition and bitter jealousy are inevitable. All women are forced to compete with one another, and harmony is impossible. Even within the family, women are sentenced to solitude and struggle.

Release from the bonds of sexism through creation of mother-daughter unity is the story described by Savyon Liebrecht in "Apples From The Desert" (1986). The mother, who comes to identify with the daughter, is willing to oppose her husband so that the daughter can achieve happiness—and the mother thus achieves her own independence from male tyranny. The story centers on a confrontation between a traditional woman—Victoria Abravanel, from the Ortho-

17. Adrienne Rich, *Of Woman Born.*

dox neighborhood Sha'arei Hesed in Jerusalem—and her daughter Rivka—who lives with a man without the legitimacy of marriage. The confrontation leads the mother to decide that her daughter's fate will differ from her own, and this marks a turning point in Victoria's life. For the first time, she is willing to undermine the authority of the father and the tradition. Victoria protects her daughter's right to a life of love, a life which she herself has not had. The feminine covenant between mother and daughter does indeed overcome the patriarchal order. Rivka will not be, like her mother, a victim of matchmaking without love. The daughter's independent deed, leaving the parental home to live together with a man who loves her, is an important step on the way to realizing her freedom, a step which wins the support and admiration of the mother. Because of the daughter, the mother is also liberated.

Prostitution as Metaphor

In "White Lines" (1985), Dorit Peleg presents the romantic myth as the means by which a woman can survive in a man's world. Women's economic dependence on men causes love to be a product that is sold for money. Only men can truly enjoy the emotional benefits of love, while women must stage the love experience in order to win financial benefits. In order to maintain the distorted relationship, the woman strives to bring enjoyment—both emotional and sexual—to her partner and she denies her own needs. The man then believes that he is loved, desired, and wanted.

The narrator of "White Lines" finances herself through prostitution, but she sells much more than her body. She sells the magic of love. The narrator states: "I sell a dream. I deal in an illusion of tenderness. A delusion of intimacy." In order to succeed, she must orchestrate every proceeding with great care, and forgo all spontaneous reactions. The narrator does not allow herself to feel, to love, or to desire, because her body and her feelings are controlled by her intellect, which dictates the behavior that will result in satisfaction of the emotional and physical needs of the man who is her target. Therefore, the narrator is completely estranged from herself, and acts with alarming, mechanical efficiency.

The prostitute, who has rescued herself from the gutter, prefers the independence that her occupation affords to the dependence of married women on their husbands. In her eyes, she sells, cleverly and at a high price, what other women give away in exchange for the delusion of love. And as a result of her clear-sighted understanding of male-female relations, she wins privacy, a comfortable existence, and control. The prostitute thus holds a mirror to the exchange that takes place between respectable women and men within our society. Furthermore, the polarity between respectable women and prostitutes hides from the former the price they must pay for their respectability.

Although the narrator feels that she exercises control over her life, she herself is subject to the tyranny of a sexist society in which all women must compete for men's support. Her hatred of other women reveals her subjugation. She hates all younger women, because they are destined to replace her, and she feels disgusted by all older and less beautiful women, because she knows that she will suffer their fate. Because she hates women and experiences only alienation in her relations with men, she remains totally alone in her room and her existence remains totally sterile. In other words, she achieves absolute control of her life because she forfeits it. The heroine is willing to exist in comfortable surroundings while living an empty life, because she seeks to escape from the weakness and helplessness that characterized her earlier life. She sticks to the rules that she has created, because she fears the chaotic reality of her past days, which she recalls with panic.

In the world depicted by Dorit Peleg, men are all-powerful. Women, because they are economically and socially dependent on men, are unable to love. The wonderful loss of control that occurs when one loves is, according to the protagonist, the exclusive privilege of the powerful; the powerless cannot permit themselves any such indulgence. "His job is to lose control. Mine is to keep it," the narrator says. Therefore women must divide themselves into a control center, on which their ability to survive depends, and into a body and soul which are subject to the control center and respond to its dictates absolutely. A woman who is carried away by her desires and feelings endangers her existence.

New Challenges in the State of Israel

The stories written after statehood describe female assertiveness in different and unexplored areas: The 18-year-old soldier in Dahlia Ravikovitch's "A Slight Delay" resolutely opposes sexual harassment by her superior officer, and she finds the inner resources to survive and come to terms with her experience.

The protagonist of Savyon Liebrecht's "A Room on the Roof" is a young mother. She demonstrates an impressive independence when she takes upon herself—in opposition to the wishes of her husband and in his absence—the responsibility for building a room of her own, because supervising the Arab construction workers is indeed a dangerous task. Yet the young Jewish mother succeeds, and even reaches moments of closeness and identification with one of the workers. Though these moments do not ultimately lead the protagonist to a deeper understanding or to change, Liebrecht seems to say that in the assertiveness that leads to her identification with the Palestinian Arab man, the young mother has become worthy of commendation.

Assertiveness is also apparent in Shulamith Hareven's "Loneliness," in which the sexual attraction that a mature woman feels for a teenage girl causes a lasting upheaval in her world. Sexual attraction outside the cultural norm characterizes "Shrinking" by Ruth Almog as well. Here a mature woman re-establishes a connection with a man who had been her student many years earlier, when she had just begun her teaching career. Although she ultimately recoils from sexual contact with the younger man, the possibility for fulfillment of their relationship testifies to the breakdown of the accepted societal phenomenon of "marrying up."

The stories that conclude the anthology describe four foci of pain within the Israeli community: the memory of the Holocaust in Michal Govrin's "La Promenade, Triptych," the unending fear of terrorism in Savyon Liebrecht's "A Room on the Roof," enduring social inequity in Orly Castel-Bloom's "Ummi Fi Shurl," and bereavement following war in Yehudit Hendel's "Apples In Honey." Great strength is demanded of the Jewish women who must live within this pain. Ultimately, Israeli women's fiction reveals the country's deep longing for peace—to heal the wounds of the past and to create a better future.

Excision

Dvorah Baron

Of all those who appeared before my father, the rabbi, for litigation, the ones who seemed to me most discriminated against were the women who were about to be driven from their husbands' home.

Certainly there were also others robbed of justice: workers who were exploited by their employers, or merchants who had been cheated, except that for these others, matters could be rectified.

The claims were presented and the witnesses testified, and he who was found guilty was convicted. Justice was on the side of the oppressed.

Dvorah Baron was born in Russia in December 1887. Her father, the Rabbi of a small town, taught her all the subjects studied by boys, including the Talmud itself. Their home, in the center of town, housed the Synagogue, the elementary school, and the religious court. From early morning onward, it was besieged by people seeking Rabbi Baron's advice. Dvorah Baron began writing at an extremely young age, and her work was first published in 1903. She was also active in Zionist circles, and in 1911 settled in Neve-Tzedek, near Tel Aviv. She married Yosef Aharonovitz (1877-1937), the labor leader and editor of *Hapoel Hatzair*. In 1915 they were exiled to Egypt, and were unable to return home until 1919. Her works, relying on an extremely supple and precise Hebrew, received great critical acclaim, and Baron was the first recipient of the Bialik prize in 1934. From 1936 until her death in 1956, she suffered from a serious illness which kept her bedridden.

Whereas these women—"divorced in heart" as they were referred to—the judgment against them was harsh.

"When a man takes a woman," it says, and if she doesn't find favor in his eyes, he will write her a "writ of divorce."

For really, what other remedy is there for lovelessness?

It is a malignant disease. Whoever contracts it will never be healed.

For five or ten years the woman sat at home, caring for his well-being; she washed, knitted and mended. She removed all obstacles and ironed out all difficulties with devotion.

Next to buildings in the midst of construction, she gathered wood for heating; from the parks she collected remnants of manure for the two vegetable patches in her yard in which she grew beans, carrots, and beets, and from this she skillfully prepared vegetable soups and relishes. She created something from nothing.

And when the man came home, he sat down to a set table, cut the bread with his strong hands, gulped the soup she served him and through the steam of the hot food, his glance lit upon her, flashing an expression of satisfaction or gratitude, and that was her reward.

And then one day, it happened, everything was undermined. Perhaps the influence of his family who voiced their hatred of the woman or perhaps he found "one more beautiful than she" and he had a change of heart. And without that spice which transforms bitter to sweet, everything became insipid and tasteless.

Suddenly the bread was burnt, or not sufficiently baked, and the meal was spoiled and smelled badly—and a quarrel flared. In the beginning, it was contained, so they would not be disgraced in front of strangers, and later when bitterness had accumulated in their hearts, it erupted in thunder and fury like those heavy clouds, discharged from their electricity, with everything stormy and churning.

If children were present, they protected themselves like chicks in the moment of disaster, when their nest is about to be destroyed. They were full of compassion for their mother and frightened of their father's rage.

He, crazed by anger, thinking that in this way he would hurt her, sometimes attacked them, hitting them relentlessly.

One of the neighbors intervened and took them into his house, and there they sat, abandoned, like objects without an owner, until night fell, for only then did they find the courage to return home. They searched in the dark to find their beds and in mute fear, crawled under their covers, and then the mother regained her dignity and realized that this was impossible, this had to be stopped. And then came the day when she went out to the town hall.

How could she walk this painful path, at the end of which she would be cut off from her home, her life?

The shopkeeper, near the alley by the town hall, stood at his store entrance to stare at her, and from the top of the bakery, in the alley, a woman, a housewife, descended, and greeted her.

They did not have a close relationship, but now she gave her the same look, which only a victim of fate would sense, a touching of raw wounds.

The clerk in the courthouse, who was an acquaintance of hers, chose to ignore her. He was now "at work," and the building itself, when she entered it, seemed like a bridge, with no handrails, a dizzying journey into the horrors of the abyss:

The scribe's instruments on the table, the open and sharpened penknife sparkling in their midst, the judges' chamber, which in her imagination looked like the heavenly court she would have to report to in the future when her time came, and the icy stare which came from the corner in which he sat, fortified by his family—who were like a wall around him.

They—if previously there was animosity between the woman and them—could now not hide their satisfaction. The man was the link that had been detached from their chain, and lo and behold he had returned to be reattached and reunited with them.

Already in the early morning, they had placed a bottle of water in his pocket so that he could wash his hands immediately after giving the *get*[1] and thus "be the first to have good luck"; afterwards one of them disappeared and returned with whiskey and cake, and from behind the wooden partition, he came to request a tray and glasses.

My mother, so courteous and so genial, didn't give it. "It's

1. The Jewish divorce writ.

difficult to reach the dishes," she said, and when the arrangements prior to the writing of the *get* were completed, she brought the woman next to her.

A meadow was visible through the window and from the stool upon which she was seated, she could, in the summer, see its green grass, stretching across the great expanse with a tranquility inconsistent with the struggles and hesitations of a person's heart:

The calm shallow water next to the edge of the gardens, with the heavenly radiance reflected in it, and the solitary linden tree in their midst, should have aroused feelings of encouragement in her heart, since surely, more than once, gales of storms had washed over the lonely tree, and nevertheless it remained standing securely in place.

My mother, on seeing the pensive look she wore, got up and left.

When a person is alone with his inner thoughts, it is sacred—she thought—and no stranger should approach.

But at last, it ceased, the silence, there behind the wall, and the final hour arrived, laden with responsibility and the gravity of judgment.

The words, written in Assyrian script[2] were carefully articulated, the witnesses arose to certify their signatures, and the man, in the presence of a *minyan*[3] handed to his wife her writ of divorce, informing her explicitly that from this moment she was divorced from him. Then the circle around her opened and she was pushed out of it, cut off; she momentarily wavered to and fro, and then she left.

My mother—if it was already night time—put the lantern on the windowsill, but the path of light which extended outward was empty. She was already totally engulfed by the darkness.

And afterwards also there was a continuation.

Some women, either out of feelings of compassion, or because they were dissatisfied with their own lack of domestic harmony, decided to do something for her betterment. They bought sewing goods or food products for her and she would sell them, but she still did not regain her strength.

---

2. The same script used in the Torah.
3. Jewish quorum of ten men, necessary to recite certain public prayers.

She was too weak to support a household whose central pillar had been removed, and everything seemed like one great vacuum:

Near the dining room table on the Sabbath and holidays, near a child's sickbed, and on the bench outside where they'd sat outside in the evening breeze.

And there were dreams, sparks of light reflecting the past:

His warm glance through the window when she returned in the morning from the market, a shared bathing of a child in the warm steam near the bathtub, shoulder to shoulder, and his genuine concern at the sound of her sigh, or cry of pain.

With these residual images in her mind's eye, she stood by her goods the next day and bargained with the customers, while her glance followed and grasped every wisp of smoke which rose from the chimney in his house—in every possible shadow she imagined that she saw his likeness.

And at times, in some nearby alley, she saw him bend and embrace their children, united with her in this moment in a shared love.

—And behold everything was not over, she stood, her whole being throbbing. Why was it so? Why had all this occurred?

But it also happened that one day, there chanced across her path, among the passersby in the street, a little child who looked exactly like him, and like her son who was walking next to her, and the child was told:

"Look, this is your brother. Please come and kiss him."

—And then the ground collapsed beneath her.

There was another type of woman condemned to divorce—women who had stayed with their husbands for ten years and had not given birth, women whose skin had never been scarred from carrying a baby.

Of these divorcees, I remember Zelta, the woman peddler from the valley, a brave woman, always kindhearted.

She had married someone from her neighborhood, a certain Isser Bar, an unemployed bookbinder.

For years she had waited for him—they said—and finally her heart's desire was fulfilled. And from then on she was invested with the spirit that had inspired Jacob when his time came to roll the heavy stone away from the well.

With such ease she carried her two baskets overflowing with fruit and vegetables.

On the banks of the river she washed, between purchase and sale, other people's laundry, and at night at the baker, she kneaded the dough of the rye bread. She received, in addition to the copper pennies, a little bread baked from the leftover dough, which she ate later with her Isser Bar (outdoors in the summer under the pear tree). She sliced and gave him his portion, slice after slice, and the aroma of love came from there, mixed with the smell of the food that she'd made in the night hours in the baker's oven.

The people of the neighborhood, while passing by, would give a benevolent look, similar to the way they looked at a blossoming tree or a sun-and-dew-drenched garden.

But meanwhile the years passed, and the woman who was barren didn't know that their time had come, their limit had been reached.

She was weak in body and several years older than the man, and his family saw that one of the branches of their tree of life was withering.

When the designated year, the tenth year, arrived, his relatives from the village of Kaminka came and took him back with them, and she in her innocence, was happy. "He'll breathe some fresh air," she said.

And for every Sabbath, she sent him the braided *hallot* which he loved and also—to increase his appetite—herring, which he couldn't get in Kaminka.

The day he was supposed to return, she chanced upon some cherries, and with eyes sparkling with the same joyous glow that shone on the dewy fruit, she carried them home.

"I'll fry them for my Isser Bar," she said, "he loves cherry marmalade."

And later on while she was frying them, standing glowing next to the stove, she was surprised to see her two brothers-in-law from Kaminka enter, with the harsh expression on their faces of those coming to execute the court decree, and Isser Bar himself, walking behind them, with a sputtering and flickering look, like a flame doused by a cold wind.

I saw the woman the day of the *get* as she was about to enter the courtroom.

The scribe, in front of the reception table, began at that very moment to rub his knife with a rag, and then she made the movement of an ox who has been brought to the slaughterhouse and smells the scent of blood.

"No, no," she said.

And my mother, who stood at the entrance of the room, took one step backward and quickly averted her face.

A young girl who was the sister of fertile women with many sons had already been prepared for the man, and he quickly married her. And not a year had passed and she sat on the ledge near their house—the daughter of Yonah the carpenter was from our street—with a large baby at her breast.

Remembered for a long time afterwards was the confusion in the synagogue on the Sabbath she came to prayers for the first time after the birth. She was wearing a new dress that she had sewn by herself and that really drew the women's attention, because she was a seamstress who knew the big city fashions, and suddenly a strange cough came from the corner where the woman peddler sat, and then the sobbing burst forth—a moaning that comes from the depths, warding off all words of solace and comfort, and raising doubt in the hearts of the listeners as to whether everything in this world is conducted fairly.

Later, solicitous gestures were still made. She was offered a stall at the front of the market, and the baker from her neighborhood asked her to be the regular assistant in his house, but since she didn't respond, they left her alone, the way they leave a house on fire alone when it is not dangerous to others—and she faded and flickered until she finally was extinguished.

It was a summer day, and from the carpenter's shop came the sounds of sawing, filing, and singing, and then one of the valley people entered and the noise stopped. The funeral passed through the alley, a barren funeral, without the mourners' eulogies or cries.

The people, those who were busy with work, came and stood in their doorways, and the others went and walked until the turn in the road, and then that same silence returned, through which the whispers of the heart buzzed like the words in a telegraph wire.

And finally the woman peddler's neighbor, Esther the pretzel maker, turning toward the carpenter's workshop, or was it the town hall, asked, "Why didn't they kill her, that woman, then, at the time, immediately? What was the purpose of prolonging the agonies of this death?"

Tears fell from her eyes. "If you cut off the head," she said furiously, "then at least cut it off entirely, all at once."

c.1943

Translated by Felice Kahn Zisken

Questions for Discussion

1. The story, written in 1943, explores the world Dvorah Baron knew as a young girl. Consider how the pastoral images of Eastern European landscape and the characters' rustic occupations contrast with the emotional devastation the women undergo. What effect is Baron creating?
2. The Hebrew title of this short story, *Kritut*, is the word for divorce, but also has the meanings: excision, cutting off, spiritual severing, amputation. How do these meanings deepen your understanding of the story?
3. Consider the different reactions of the townspeople: the shopkeeper, the clerk in the courthouse, the women who "decided to do something for her betterment," the narrator's mother, the baker who tried to help the childless woman. Examine your personal reaction toward another woman's divorce. Which of these characters do you most resemble?
4. Compare these *shtetl* divorces to divorce today. Have we "progressed"? Consider Jewish religious divorce law and the work of many Jewish women's groups on behalf of *agunot*. What are the issues today? Do they differ from the issues addressed by Baron? How?

5. How does Dvorah Baron's indictment of Jewish religious law and its consequences fit into the Israeli concept of "negation of the diaspora," with its repudiation of *shtetl* life and *shtetl* mentality, its rejection of the past? (Note that Dvorah Baron at times writes positively of upholding Jewish religious law, as in her story "Family."[4]) How do American Jewish attitudes toward the past differ? Why?

Program Suggestions

1. Organize a panel discussion on divorce within the Jewish community. Include at least one speaker who is knowledgeable about current divorce practice in Israel and its impact on women. Other speakers might include someone knowledgeable about the work of ICAR (pronounced ee-car), the International Coalition for *Agunah* Rights, to discuss abuses of Jewish divorce law, a family therapist, a rabbi, a divorced woman, and/or a child of divorced parents.
2. Compare Dvorah Baron's indictment of *halakhah* to American Jewish authors' attitudes toward Judaism. For example, in the 1923 American short story "The Lord Giveth" by Anzia Yezierska,[5] religion, though spiritually ennobling, is useless in the pragmatic business of day-to-day life. Invite a professor of Hebrew literature or Jewish studies to offer a wider perspective on Israeli and American attitudes toward religion as reflected in literature.

---

4. Dvorah Baron, "Family" in *The Thorny Path*, translated by Joseph Schachter (Jerusalem: Institute for the Translation of Hebrew Literature and Israel Universities Press, 1969), pages 1–37.
5. Anzia Yezierska, "The Lord Giveth" in *How I Found America: Collected Stories of Anzia Yezierska* (New York: Persea Books, 1991), pages 233–244.

The Truth

Elisheva

He used to perform at one of the theaters, the Opera House to be exact, in a large city. Every night he appeared on stage magnificently attired as a prince of days gone by, a cavalryman, or legendary poet. The stagelight projected bluish theatrical moonbeams over him. His clear metallic voice rose, merged with the glow of stars that magically appeared through the curtained ceiling and with the redolence of the vernal linden leaves emanating from the painted bushes on the stage curtains, which slowly swayed right and left. The plaintive sound of violins together with all the other instruments of the orchestra rose and swelled into a crescendo like a mighty wave, compressing the heart to the point of pain, then ebbed like the sea at low tide. The lights came on again, and the theater resounded with shouts from thousands of voices and thunderous applause.... Thus it was evening after evening.

Elisheva is the pen name of Elizaveta Zhirkova, 1888-1949, a non-Jewish Russian poet who became deeply attracted to the movement for Jewish national renaissance at the turn of the century. She studied Hebrew, which she regarded as the "language of the heart of lights and shadows," and went on to publish Hebrew poems, stories, and novels, as well as literary criticism. She converted to Judaism, and in 1925 she and her husband, Simeon Bikhowsky, settled in Palestine, where she was referred to as "Ruth from the banks of the Volga."

She was a tall, thin, young woman. Her chestnut hair, worn in a long thick braid, was coarse, dry, and lackluster. A sickly rash covered her wrinkled skin. Her beautiful deep-set velvet eyes, gray eyes, in bluish circles, glowed soft and warm. Pale thin lips hid her strong sparkling white teeth. No one ever saw those lustrous gray eyes for she hardly ever looked a person directly in the eye; no one ever saw her pearly white teeth because she hardly ever laughed.

In the late hours of the night she crossed the streets of the city alone, without fear or hesitation. The night strollers, not finding her alluring, paid no attention to her. Every single evening she sat in the uppermost gallery of the theater, opera glasses pressed tightly against her beautiful nearsighted eyes. Transported by the music, her bosom heaved, avidly responding to the wonderful atmosphere suffused with the fragrance and gaiety of spring. Her heart rose and fell with every step of the legendary hero, bathed in the pale blue moonbeams and enveloped by enchanting sounds. Her heart rose and fell with every rise and fall of his clear triumphant voice against the background of those melodious sounds. When the curtain fell the electric light hurt and blinded her eyes, the storm of applause deafened her. Spellbound, she sat breathing heavily, her lips slightly parted—hiding an elusive smile seen by none.

Then the first miracle occurred. Behind the mask of a legendary hero, magnificently attired, materialized a man of about forty. He had an upright bearing, walked with deliberate movements. His slightly graying hair was close cropped. His eyes were gray, and their cold distant gleam reflected the metallic quality of his voice. She was in love with this man. For years she whispered his name before falling asleep, recalled it in her random prayers, and on waking in the morning. At midnight, as she walked the great distance from the Opera House alone, the passersby did not touch her. Sweetly intoxicated, she spun her dreams of love. In the morning she searched through the newspaper under "Theater News," and when she came across his name in print, her lips trembled and heart contracted with delight.

She inquired and found out where he lived. In a noisy street in the center of town stood a large house, painted brown, almost black. Behind it, in the middle of a courtyard, was a small two-story house painted a cheery white. The telephone wires extending to its first window were taut like the fibers of her heart. She stood in the noisy street peering through the low dark gate; the house with its white walls and clear windows beckoned invitingly.

✦

On a gray dull winter morning, seated beside the window, she wrote him a letter. The snow in the small courtyard grew light through the double-glazed window panes. She wrote on white paper, tiny wide-spaced letters, in slanting lines sloping downward. This was her one and only letter, a jumble of truth and fiction. Words of love and longing, appreciation and devotion, seared those white pages. The pure white snow lying beyond the window cast a pale, soothing, cool light in the room.

The second miracle. He came to her. She would never know whether he answered her letter. From time to time he strolled with her in the city streets in the evening twilight. Long walks and lengthy conversation, silences and complete understanding. She told him about her childhood and adolescence filled with pain and loneliness, of her great and bittersweet love. He told her about his tranquil life, his wife and beloved children. With simple candor he revealed his many modest thoughts. Offstage not the slightest trace remained of the triumphant, magnificently clad cavalryman; simply a man of forty, tall, with a cold look, who escorted her the length of the city streets. In the snow beneath their feet, blue sparks glistened by the light of the lamps. In spring evenings a light warm mist would descend over the city, covering the domed tops of monasteries and churches. They crossed the huge city square diagonally on a narrow asphalt pathway. Boys selling flowers came running toward them, entreating them to buy whatever they had in their hands. A light drizzle fell, the pathway shone wet and black in the lamplight, raindrops quivered on the large petals of the lovely roses that he bought for her from the flower sellers. Their fragrance was that of warm, humid, springtime evenings, a city fragrance.

Many pages in the bulging blackbound notebook, her diary, were filled with happy memories and joyous dreams evocative of the fragrance of city roses. This was the song of her only secret love, a song of joy, the Song of Songs.

Suddenly he disappeared. He ceased performing at the theater. She no longer came across his name in the newspapers. He had entered her life like a vision in a dream and vanished like a phantom. The large brown house stood in its place and greeted her with dark, menacing looks, and the little house beckoned her with its white walls, the telephone wires—like the fibers of her unrequited love—extending toward it. The fragrance of roses lingered between the pages of the bulging notebook, with its slanting lines sloping downward.

✦

For half a year the snow lay piled up in the streets of the remote village. All the houses had three windows and far too long fences. At the onset of evening a large lamp was lit above the entrance of the only movie house there, and sparks glistened on the surface of the snow. The sharp, biting north wind blew, the lamp swayed to and fro, the shimmering movement of the sparks on the snow blinded her eyes, stirring memories and robbing her of peace of mind.

Shadows moved on the white screen. At the end of a long hall with green curtains and ugly statues above the openings, were many people. People from the silent enchanted world, they appeared in an instant out of the void and in an instant they disappeared into the void. Thousands of eyes were fixed, drinking in the gaiety of a make-believe life, eagerly following the movements of the actors. Thousands of ears strained to catch the magical words uttered by them. A world of artifice, full of movement and silence, sprang to life nightly on the white screen, and held the hearts of the audience in thrall.

The names of "the hero" and "the heroine" were printed in large black letters on notices stuck to the walls of houses, and the sharp north wind ruffled the notices unmercifully. People sat in the movie house closely packed together, with bated breath, their own life suspended, vicariously living the lives of the hero and heroine—gray shadows moving on the screen.

Someone in the crowd sat on one of the benches closest to the screen, because she was nearsighted. Thousands of miles away people in city streets and salons moved about, walked and talked, loved, envied, and hated. Their shadows appeared in front of her evening after evening, repeating their constant movements and mouthing their silent utterances. Imprisoned in this silent world was a powerful magic.

The one—first to love, become jealous, hate, kneel before the "heroine," kiss her on the lips, fire his pistol, or play the violin—was tall, with deliberate movements of one accustomed to the stage. His face was pleasant, his laughter hearty. That was how the other one had laughed; suddenly his face radiated and brightened everything around him. He was completely gray, for he emanated from the world of gray shadows. His close-cropped hair curled slightly, and there was a hard, cold, steely glint in his eyes.

Were he to die, his moving silent shadow would endure forever in the realm of shadows: he would forever tread lightly, gracefully, like people trained to walk on stage; he would forever laugh his youthful laugh. Here there was neither finality or death.

From the dilapidated piano came tasteless tunes, and on the screen hundreds of wax candles burned in the salons of the palace and hundreds of people twirled in a simple dance. These were royal salons of past generations, a kingdom of laughter and beauty and pleasant flirtations—at Versailles or Trianon. The young queen of the ball was magnificent, and her young lover sat at the piano and spun a delicate network of sounds for her, vibrating, like a host of white butterflies, like rose petals in the evening breeze. The wonderful spectacle, "Roses of Love," was shown in the movie house for ten consecutive performances.

✦

Then came the miracle—greater by far was the enchantment of the stormy, snowy nights in the village than the glittering nights in the city. Into her life entered one of erect stature, with cold sparkling eyes and a metallic ring to his voice. As the long winter twilight fell, he used to come to her humble home, where piles of snow came halfway up the windows. He sat at her old, dilapidated piano, and played for her melodies of bygone days, airy and evocative of rose petals dancing in spring gardens beneath moonbeams reaching from sky to earth. He was a student at the music school, who had only stayed in the dreary village just a short while. He never told her anything about himself, and asked her nothing about her life. He was several years younger than that other one, but he had the same natural graceful movements, and his gray eyes beamed at her.

At that time, she read in the column "Theater News" that the movie hero died of a brief illness while still in the prime of his life, as a result of an unsuccessful operation. His silent immortal shadow continued to live on in the world of enchanting shadows. But that wonderful spectacle, "Roses of Love," was never shown again in the village.

The young man, a student at the school of music, kept coming to her little home, in the twilight, when the snow in her garden turned blue and a dim light came into the room through the windows; then he went away, disappeared, without a parting word.

To the black bulging notebook, her diary, were added a few more pages of loving memories and happiness, poems of gratitude and love. A fragrance of withered rose petals, roses of Trianon from former years, emanated from the pages. A scent reminiscent of incense, of shrouds.

✦

There was a poet in the king's domain, a cold proud Northern district. His poetry seemed sculpted from the whiteness of its rocks, and woven from the mists of its white nights. Tens of thousands throughout the country were drawn to him and absorbed the venom of his cold brilliant words. Young girls full of charm and desire, radiating *joie de vivre* all around, crowded together at the foot of the stage. He read his poems at the farewell gathering given him in this town, to which he had been invited, before returning north. It was a May evening, crisp air streamed through the open windows along with the rustling sounds of fresh leaves and the twittering of small birds settling down for the night. The poet read in a clear loud voice, standing erect on the stage, hands in his pockets. It seemed as if he were completely unaware of the large animated crowd at his feet. He stood tall and proud, aloof, calm, an immortal upon earth.

The aging school mistress stood close to the stage, her heart fluttering, never taking her eyes off the tall man with chestnut hair turning slightly gray. His god-like face was honest and plain, calm and trusting, with a weary smile hidden at the corners of his lips. His well-formulated, haughty words fell upon the hushed audience. It was incredible how the words, printed black upon white in tens of thousands of books and absorbed by thousands throughout the land, now became the vernacular of plain trusting folk. They also seemed to be directed to her as the words of one friend to another.

It was also amazing that from her earliest youth she had ardently loved this aging man with deep eyes—whose color she could not discern—with the long delicate fingers and weary smile. On that evening she saw him for the first and last time—and her heart pounded and melted within.

The miracle—small this time, very small—while standing at the entrance of the hall, she got to shake the delicate hand of the poet as he came down from the stage and went into the adjacent room, as the young amorous girls crowded around. She heard a few words addressed to her in the clear voice that came from the depth of his being. She felt his calm, high-minded look resting on her, but even then she was unable to discern the color of his eyes, because she didn't look directly at his face. It was a quiet, warm May evening. The street lamps had just been lit as she stepped out into the wide streets, cautiously guarding the overflowing joy in her heart, as if carrying a glassful of vintage wine.

Another single page, the best of all, was added to her diary, its edges worn with age. The words were succinct and clipped, with a long black line drawn beneath them.

✦

Upon the death of the supervisor of the orphanage—this aging woman, with a sickly rash on her cheeks and a hoarse voice—her few friends came and put her room in order. They gave her clothing and simple possessions to the house servants; they divided her few books among themselves. They turned over to the new supervisor her account books and notebooks, itemizing different receipts and records. Then there remained a bulging notebook bound in black, with writing on both sides of its faded pages.

They read the notebook.

They read and marvelled.

How interesting, how beautiful the tranquil, lonely life of their friend had been! How she went strolling with a famous actor time after time in the spring evenings in the wonderful city a few miles away from here. The young man with the gray dreamy eyes used to keep her company evening after evening in the dreariness of the little village. He brought her into the world of his ethereal dreams, surpassing the spirit of the times, with dreams reminiscent of fragrant withered Trianon roses. Although they read these pages and nodded their heads, they did not understand them fully. Who was this departed person "whose gray shadow remained eternally amidst the many gray shadows, living their lives without finality"? Yet what touched their hearts the most was the last page with its few words, profound and sublimely joyous. They certainly never knew or heard directly from her that she had been privileged to see the hero of the times, the great poet, face to face, to express her adulation in her own modest way. He in turn replied with a word of thanks and shook her hand.

Every unmarried woman getting on in years and in loneliness, every married woman weary of life—deeply immersed in this beautiful and sublime world of memories—acutely envied her friend. They read and marvelled, and deep in their hearts bowed down to her. At the same time they hated her because she did not share her considerable joy with them, for the joy preserved in the treasure trove of her soul was great and boundless indeed.

✦

No. None of this really happened. Although the actor did acknowledge her letter: he sent a picture postcard with a few lines of casual acknowledgment. The hero of the movies died a timely death, and only for a short spell were his light movements and hearty laugh remembered in the imaginary world. New movies appeared and gained acclaim, replacing those famous in his time. No one ever came to her small three-windowed house, and not a single footprint was ever seen on the pure white snow in her garden. The poet got off the stage and entered the adjacent room, without paying any attention to the young ladies crowding around him. Nor was she the one who presented him with a bouquet of lilacs, rather it was a young French woman with a loud voice and a flower-trimmed hat. The poet took the bouquet of flowers from her hand, embarrassed, his weary glance turned inward, busy with his own thoughts; he was oblivious to all that was going on around him.

So all the words of the old book were a fabrication, all those ardent lines hurriedly penned, always sloping downward. The words were a poor absurd figment, her friends envied her in vain, for her life was as deprived, boring, and uneventful as were all their lives in the long lonely evenings. When the heart constricted in the pain of desolation and in the awareness of privation, she sat down at the table and opened her bulging notebook, her faithful companion from her earliest school days. On its white pages in hurriedly written wide-spaced letters, she embroidered a tapestry of idle tales, product of a sickly imagination.

True, there was the merest scent of roses—as well as something suggestive of shrouds—that emanated from between the pages of the notebook as the teachers of the almshouse read it.

c.1924

Translated by Sonia F. Grober and Ida (Ayala) Myers

Questions for Discussion

1. How does "The Truth" use a stereotypical portrayal of an unmarried woman—frustrated and unfulfilled—to make its points? Does this short story perpetuate the stereotype of the spinster? Does it alter that stereotype in any way?
2. What is the author's attitude toward the central character—pity, admiration, scorn, affection? How is the reader to interpret the central character's hero worship, her crushes?
3. Why does Elisheva focus solely on romance and on love, ignoring all other dimensions of the central character's life?
4. How does the Eastern European setting work together with the short story's plot?
5. How does the use of language work together with the plot? Compare Elisheva's style of writing to Dvorah Baron's, for

example. What effect does each author produce in the reader, and how does this influence the reader's understanding of the story?

6. What is Elisheva saying about women's writing? About fiction in general?

Program Suggestion

In Woody Allen's movie *The Purple Rose of Cairo*, the central character falls in love with a movie idol who steps off the screen and enters her life. Arrange for your study group members to watch the videotape, and compare the movie to the story by Elisheva.

Wedding

Esther Ra'ab

A kneading trough with dough. Bread of the earth—blood.

Pink fragrant mouths of babes bending left and right, hungry for bread, for nourishment, for a breast abounding with milk.

Ziva's hands kneaded the dough—tomorrow's bread, the dough of her life was in her long brown hands, it shrank, stretched, squeaked, and became smooth as silk: the flour was made of barley and sorghum—makeshifts. Inferior material became real bread that wouldn't disappoint those who ate it, a yellow-golden orange, baked by Ziva's clever hands.

The dance of bombs overhead was repeated every night. The babies, weeping and wailing, were carried warm from their beds to the cellar. As a cat carries her kittens, Ziva snatched them under her arms

---

Esther Ra'ab (1894-1981) is known primarily as an Israeli nature poet. She was born in Petah Tikvah, the daughter of one of its founders. She joined kibbutz Deganyah in her youth, and after her marriage in 1921 lived for five years in Egypt and Paris. When she returned to Palestine, her Tel Aviv home became a salon for writers and artists. Her earliest poems were published in the twenties, and her first anthology appeared in 1930. She produced two more volumes of poetry, while also writing short stories and essays. She was buried in Petah Tikvah.

and carried them to the shelter, to the cave protected from the bombs all barking around. "*Gott mayn Gott!*"—women huddled up and girls blinking from sleepiness, from the dread of last night's uninvited "concert," children drowsing in the candlelight; the women forgot to be "ladies," and Hannah-Trayne and a fine lady crouch side by side like sisters on the floor of the cellar and bemoan these hard times: everything is topsy-turvy; the splendid orange, true gold, fruit of long years of toil and cultivation, is fed to the cows, whose udders are shriveling more every day from lack of straw and fodder. For how will fodder get to the surrounded village? And every seed, every piece of straw is burned by the army camped all around; sorghum, chicken feed—fed to human beings; the lighting, a sooty oil lamp, makes your eyes water. The sacks of good wheat from the Galilee have run out because the Galilee is cut off from us: two kilometers on this side—the Turks; two kilometers on that side—the English; south and north of the village. And the two camps fight, and over our weary heads, over our hungry bodies—that devil dance of the bombs.

The vineyards not tended or pruned spread out like a stage ready only for battle, some of the vines uprooted and destroyed for more than a year now. The trenches devoured the green body like boils, and every night, the closest field turns into an eerie distance, cloaked in veils of death. Bullets whistle at night among the branches of the eucalyptus trees, and bombs shred the bellies of the hills that used to lie here like cows giving the good milk of peace, and the wood sorrel covering them is trampled like living flesh by the soldiers' feet. A whisper and rustle in the olive trees, and in the vineyards the groans of the wounded Turks and the panther tread of the reconnaissance unit. English patrols or a Turkish patrol?—Who would have known it, in the thicket of bushes and fences, as dark night leaps out, weaving its plots all around? The ears are taut, the nose gropes for smells and follows them like a dog: gunpowder, death, dew-drenched earth—they became a marvelous potion bubbling in Ziva's veins.

The modest hills now turned into a mighty front. Armies were moved, pushed back, giant cannons plowed the fallow earth with their wheels. The village became a joke between those strong forces. If it falls into the hands of the Turks who hated us even before the English came—they'll make an end of us. They know we welcomed the English patrols into the village, that they broke bread at our tables, and parted from us as friends.

Forces of life and death traveled like broad rivers into Ziva's soul. It was a great junction in those days. The blood rejoiced in her veins like wine, wanted to burst from her fingertips, and lifted her above herself, as a wave of warm air lifts a feather. An idea was taking shape in her blood so urgently that the mind couldn't get control of it: she had to get to the English camp tonight—no matter what! She, Ziva, would do that. She is master of herself and her brown, pent-up body—even if she exploded like shrapnel into thousands of slivers. Not Deborah, not Judith—she, Ziva! A sister and mother to lion cubs, to half-starved children. To brothers eaten away by lice and sickness in the Turkish armies. The Turks are plotting a slaughter, the officers' mustaches are bristling with ominous rage, their faces have changed overnight. They're plotting. They'll slaughter us. Like this ... some of them draw their hand over their throat in a clear demonstration, like this.... They'll do to us what they did to the Armenians. Their soldiers are submissive and calm, but the officers—there's an evil, secret spark in their eyes. Ziva revealed her "plan" to her boyfriend Amram who was leaning against the fence whacking his yellow boot with his whip.

"And your father, Zivkah, and the village and the council? That's some responsibility!"

"Amram, the Turks are planning a slaughter. The English are on our side. We have to bring them here—no matter what!"

"Zivkah, you're crazy!"

Ziva began humming: "Go get me a mate." That song inflamed Amram: "Get me a mate," and here was her mate, standing right in front of her—while she sends her eyes off to the distance....

"Let's go for a ride, Amram!" Ziva clicked her white teeth like a Yemenite.

Amram stuck his short legs in the sand, and stood sturdy and stubborn; but his eyes, round as black olives, began to sparkle and move and dissolved in the phosphorescent flickering that danced in a hushed rhythm in Ziva's green eyes.

"Be ready, I'll call you," Ziva tossed out casually, and tapped his cheek to relieve the tension.

Amram's face smiled.

Squeak squeak.... How the saddle squeaks, Ziva. Amram's eyes are round and sparkling like polished jet buttons. The horses' hooves are wrapped in cotton wadding, and the cotton wadding of the night is in the wings of the riders. The sands are dim like velvet carpets. The wrapped hooves of the horses sink without an echo; as in water they float beside the fences. An acacia tendril whipped Ziva's face and a tremor went down her back.

"Amram, give me your hand. Isn't this a dream?"

"Dream? God, you're a fool. I'm not dreaming at all. When are we getting married, Ziva?"

"Tomorrow!" Ziva tries to joke.

Amram's face turns yellow.

Ziva glances over at him and her face grows serious.

"We'll get married if we come back alive, when the English enter the village," she whispers as if to herself. "When the village celebrates, when they come out of the cellar. When we can ride to the Yarkon River...."

The straps of the saddles squeaked thinly. The pistols were taken out of the holsters.

"We have to get out under the fences to the sand, Ziva!"

"Yes, Amram."

"Will you really marry me?"

"Yes."

The sounds of two armies camped in the distance reached the ears of the riders, as from under a layer of water. They came out step by step to the sands.

The sand turned white in the starlight as in the light of a concealed moon. The horses, one after another, continued on the beaten path that went obliquely toward a stand of eucalyptus trees. Beyond the stand, in the almond groves, the English were camped. Freedom was camped, Europe was camped, and beyond the Yarkon—heavy Turks plodding on like restrained panthers, waiting for a sign.

B-r-r-r!—A shot whistled by very close.

"Get down!" Ziva ordered, her head light as a feather. She had eyes and ears down to the tips of her toes. The two of them jumped off the horses and lay next to one another. Amram was warm and trembling. The horses' feet almost touched their faces, and a smell of the stable rose from their hooves. The horses turned around and pricked up their ears.

"Hell! From the stand. An English patrol," mumbled Ziva. "They're far away.... They won't hear if we call, but they'll send their bullets to us, dammit!"

B-r-r-r.... B-r-r-r—the shots came one after another, and together.

"Amram, Amram!"

A stream of blood burst from Ziva's arm and covered Amram's face—

1934

Translated by Barbara Harshav

Questions for Discussion

1. Esther Ra'ab, writing in 1934, paints a portrait of feminine bravery during war. However, most of today's Israeli women writers portray war only indirectly. Savyon Liebrecht and Ruth Almog offer typical explanations for women's avoidance of war as a literary theme. Liebrecht, in a 1989 interview, states that in the past, "the central Israeli experience was war, and women were excluded from that."[1] And Almog, at a 1988 conference, states, "I as a woman do not go to war. I as a woman have no direct experience of war. But even more, I as a woman have no way of knowing anything real or firsthand about war.... My

---

1. "Savyon Liebrecht: 'Writing is a Need'" *Lilith*, vol. 14, no. 3, Summer 1989, page 16.

experience of war comes from the newspapers, from television, not from my senses, not from touch or sound or sight—which are the real tools of the writer."[2] Why is war an acceptable topic for Esther Ra'ab—writing before the establishment of the state of Israel—but is off-limits for most Israeli women writers today?

2. Discuss Ziva's character. In what ways does she embody both heroism and femininity? Show how Ra'ab uses a poetic and heightened language to reveal and enhance the portrayal of character.
3. Can we, as American Jewish readers, relate to Ziva? Is her exhilaration during a time of danger in any way meaningful to today's woman?
4. Although the precise events of the story's ending are uncertain, the outcome is clearly tragic. Are readers more likely to assume that tragedy will result from female rather than male bravery? (Consider the true story of Hannah Senesh, murdered during World War II, who is today a symbol of the brave Jewish girl.) Is Ra'ab in some way punishing Ziva for foolhardy—though heroic—actions? Or, are women writers more likely to foresee a tragic outcome where male writers are more likely to foresee glory?

Program Suggestions

1. Organize a program on Jewish women fighters and warriors. Use the biblical figures of Judith and Deborah to introduce the theme, then present stories of the twentieth century. Many published accounts are now available about Jewish women who fought in World War II, serving as couriers for the underground, saboteurs, and resistance fighters. Stories of Jewish women fighters in Palestine during World War I and the War of

---

2. Ruth Almog, "Polemos and Polemics" in *The Writer in the Jewish Community: An Israeli-North American Dialogue*, Richard Siegel and Tamar Sofer, eds. (New Jersey: Fairleigh Dickinson University Press/London and Toronto: Associated University Presses, 1993), page 89.

Independence have been published as well, and stories of army nurses can also be found in print. If possible, invite a guest speaker.

2. The first poems of Esther Ra'ab were published in the twenties, and she continued writing until the seventies. Invite a professor of Hebrew or a Judaic literary scholar to read several poems in Hebrew and in English translation and to discuss them, along with the story "Wedding," with the members of your study group. For a stimulating program, (1) read and discuss one or two representative poems by Esther Ra'ab, (2) contrast them with one or two poems by Dahlia Ravikovitch, one of modern Israel's most renowned poets, and (3) compare the two prose works, "Wedding" and "A Slight Delay."

Aphia's Plight

Nehama Pukhachevsky

Aphia was very angry. She was working in the home of an Ashkenazic family, and they had insulted Musa. He had come into the kitchen to ask her for the key, with his face covered in soot, and when the men of the household saw him, they burst out laughing. Aphia was agitated. She was busy drying the plates she had washed. Her heart began pounding, and her hands shook so much that she broke a plate, which smashed into bits. She burst out crying and took no notice of the broken pieces. How cruel of them to demean her husband in front of her.

Afterwards, she went back to work, but inwardly she was still seething. "What was so terrible when a person came home after a hard

---

Nehama Pukhachevsky (1869-1934) was born in Eastern Europe, and joined Hovevei Zion at age 17. She came to the land of Israel together with her husband in the "first *aliyah*" period (1882-1903). Michael Zalman Pukhachevsky had been encouraged by Baron Edmond de Rothschild to come to Palestine as an agricultural expert, and the couple founded a farm at Rishon le-Zion. Nehama Pukhachevsky wrote stories and essays (under the pen name Nefesh, "soul"), and was active in public life. She was one of the founders of the Women's Organization for the Rights of Women, and in Rishon le-Zion she succeeded in getting women elected to the local council. She also established a court of family law at her home.

day's work with machines and had a face that looked like a blackened pot? After he had washed he would look just as nice as any of them! Was it right to make a laughing stock of him? Wasn't her Musa far more learned and far more devout than the head of the family? The head of the family didn't even come within a hair's breadth of her scholar. They should treat a pious person who studied Torah with respect!"

She was filled with bitterness. True, they were needy, and as a special favor Aphia and Musa were allowed to live in one of the sheds in the yard. Did any of them care if Aphia and Musa's self-esteem was trampled into the dust? Oh no! She must decide once and for all to leave this place. She could no longer bear such misery!

Then she remembered little Aliza and her heart contracted with pain. Could she leave her? Her thoughts turned to the lovely bedroom where her darling lay asleep in her white cot. Soon she would wake and call in her sweet voice, "Lafia, Lafia!" Her mother would come to lift her out of the cot, but the child would refuse to go to her. She only wanted Aphia!

They would call Aphia. The child's face would beam. She would stretch out her hands, cling to Aphia, and stroke her neck. Oh merciful God! Surely this was a reward for her grief and suffering.

Lately Musa had been reminding her of the fate awaiting her. "A man is forbidden to live without offspring!" he would say. He could no longer bear to remain childless, and with the help of HaShem[1] he would take himself another girl! Heaven forbid that he should take a second wife, a rival to her.

Aphia would wipe tear after tear away with the edge of her thick sleeve and try to comfort herself. Surely he did not mean to do this. He only spoke such nonsense to hurt her when he was angry! He was resentful when she took "her" little girl out for too long a walk. Once when she came home late, he muttered angrily the whole evening: She was hardly ever at home, she took liberties, and on and on. She tried to laugh it off, but he scolded her: Does she not see the Temple was destroyed yet her "mouth is filled with laughter!"[2] Often he

1. HaShem literally means "The Name," and is used to refer to God.
2. Psalms 126:2.

would sigh and grumble: "There is no king in Israel and each man does as he pleases!"[3]

But a change of mood came over him when she returned early from work, baked pita for him, had a pot of hot coffee ready, and his mug to hand. Immediately he was soothed. He bathed himself with enjoyment, changed his clothes, prepared a pipe with a tall bowl and long stem, took a book, and sat contentedly for a long time on the straw cushion, placed for him outside near the tree with the thick trunk.

When he had finished studying, he put his pipe down, sipped his coffee and glanced at Aphia while she attended to the cooking in the shed. She told him about the latest goings on in her mistress's house, and he enjoyed the way her eyes flashed when she was animated. All the while she worked, he gazed at her firm body with delight! Aphia was indeed "fairest among women."[4] Surely Divine intervention had helped him purchase her. He had paid ten realia, only ten realia—for such a girl! What a fool her first husband had been to divorce her while she was still a child!

Suddenly he asked her:

"Child, do you already know the Aleph Bet that your mistress is teaching you?"

"No, Musa! Our little devil tore it to pieces."

"Very good, may the little one be blessed!" Musa said joyfully. "You don't need to learn it, it's not necessary!"

"Why isn't it necessary?"

"It is expressly written: 'Whosoever teaches his daughter Torah is like one who teaches frivolity.'"[5]

"Frivolity? What is that?" Aphia said inquisitively.

He spoke about it at length, and tried to emphasize that a woman is unworthy of learning Torah, because sin clings to her. In a single hour she is capable of destroying what a man takes a whole day to atone for through prayers and Torah learning.

---

3. Judges 17:6 and Judges 21:25.
4. Song of Songs 1:8.
5. Mishnah, *Sotah* 3:4. The Hebrew word *tiflut*, here translated as "frivolity," is also found in English translations of the Mishnah as "lechery" or "obscenity."

Aphia believed that this was a completely mistaken idea, but she lacked the words to argue back. She just retorted:

"How unfortunate!"

After thinking a while she asked:

"If this is so, how can women give an account before the One of Blessed Name? If we are not taught Torah, and if we don't have time to perform good deeds because of the way we have to work like slaves, how will we be able to stand before Him in the world of truth?"

Musa took pride in his little girl's apt remarks. He stroked her back, and put the pipe into his mouth. They sat beside one another on the straw cushion and began to dip their pita into the bottom of a single tiny bowl which still contained a little hilbeh[6] soup.

Light beams danced among the casuarina shrubs growing next to the fence, and threads of gold and emerald gleamed among the branches. Beyond the vineyards, the sun began to sink into the dunes, its glowing arc brushing up against them before finally disappearing.

And from the other side, past the fields, the Judean mountains were covered in purple, blurring their majestic contours. A pink light spread and then faded. A slight breeze blew from the direction of the gate as the couple sat together in complete harmony.

2

One day something occurred that rapidly destroyed their harmony. The neighbor's children, mischievous little devils who were into everything, opened the tiny coop which Musa had built and set the rooster and hen free, after they had been mating for a whole week. The pair hid, and there was no trace of them. The whole morning Aphia searched for them among the bushes and piles of twigs, beneath the vines and acacias. She searched in all the yards, stables, and rubbish dumps of the neighborhood, but she could not find them. Impatiently Aphia waited for Musa to come home from work in the afternoon so that he could help her. When he found out what happened he did not help to search, instead he attacked her in a fit of rage and beat her with his stick.

6. Hilbeh—a vegetable.

She didn't scream. She didn't utter a sound. She just closed the door and the little window, and hid out of sight. Afterwards, when Musa went out, she didn't go back to work at her mistress's house, but sat with both hands on her head and thought. After quite a while she got up, packed her belongings, took the bundle, and stole out of the yard quietly, so that no one would see her go.

When Musa returned in the evening, as usual, he went straight to the coop, then was overcome with amazement and joy: The pair of birds were sitting on their perch. They wanted to jump down and escape when Musa came too near. Musa hurried and closed the door of the coop, and he rolled a huge stone in front of the entrance.

Aphia was not in the shed. He was sure that she was out strolling with "her" child. An hour passed, two hours—yet there was no sign of her. He went up to the employer's house. They did not know anything, and were surprised that Aphia had not returned in the afternoon. They suggested that she might have gone to attend to some matter in the Yemenite quarter. Musa ran there, but didn't find her in the neighborhood. He began to run from house to house, until he discovered that she had been seen walking alone, going toward the town, carrying a bundle on her shoulder.

Musa's heart was filled with bitterness and anger when he returned to his dark room. He lay down on his bed, overcome with remorse the whole night. He kept thinking of different strategies to bring the runaway back. Finally, he decided what to do. He got up at dawn, and after praying, he got his gun, armed himself, put his belongings in a leather pouch, and set off.

He left with a light mist shrouding the area. He passed vineyards and fields of wheat, and when he reached the crossroads, the Judean mountains were bathed in a sea of gold. Musa's face expressed courage and determination as he walked on, erect, armed with a pistol, which he had stuck into a leather belt filled with bullets. As he fearlessly walked on, he thought: What a fool she is, what a fool! Did she really believe that he wanted to kill her? Heaven forbid. Only a few blows on her back with his stick, and nothing more. Did she have to run so far away for such a little thing? In all honesty, one ought to pity the child! She probably thought that their loss was beyond repair. She couldn't have known that the pair would come home to roost.

Now he had really fenced them in well, and "the little devils" would not be able to open the coop at all!

Overcome with pity for the child he had struck, he vowed that in the future he would treat her with compassion and not beat her. It was forbidden to give in to the evil inclination which tempts one to wrongdoing! One really should not beat a child like that! Musa decided that he would buy Aphia a pretty gift in town. When a woman is enraged she needs to be pacified!

His train of thought was interrupted when a large group of Arab workers on their way to work in a Jewish *moshava*[7] came out of an olive grove and streamed toward him. Without attracting their attention he felt for the bullets in the belt beneath his jacket.

"*Markh haba, narkh sahyidh.*" "Bless you, good day," some of the workers greeted him. Absent-mindedly he greeted some of them and half-greeted others. He moved aside a little and began to quicken his pace, because he remembered that last year at this place a person from his hometown who had been walking along, lulled by a sense of security, had been killed. Musa was annoyed with the authorities. How was it that till this day they had not detected the murderers or found any trace of them? In Yemen, the government was far more alert. Immediate searches were instituted, and the murderer had little chance of escaping. And when the authorities could not solve the case, people themselves had a sure way of finding out who the murderer was.

A chill passed through his body when he remembered what happened when he had taken part in a search of this kind. It had been during harvest time there—in Aden. His task was to assist in finding out from the murdered man the name of his killer. The night was dark. He and his friend dug up the grave, took the body out, and carried it to a sloping mountain. They left the dead man there, and sat down one arm's length away from him. Then they held their breath and waited. Musa became confused and saw nothing, but his friend, however, testified that a bird descended from high above, spread its wings over the dead man, and chirped in his ear. Silence reigned all about. Suddenly the voice of the dead man was heard coming out of the

7. *Moshava*—a Jewish settlement, a small village, pioneered in the early nineteenth century.

ground, sounding like a sorcerer. It revealed the whole story to the bird: How the dead man had set off on his way, where he intended going, and who murdered him. Afterwards they brought the body back to its grave and rolled a stone over it, bringing the matter to a close. When the secret was revealed, the murdered man's avengers knew whom to punish.

Pushing these distant and terrible memories away, Musa came back to earth, and with quick steps hurried toward his girl. He marched along the highway, and came across a caravan of camels laden with goods. There were donkeys taking vegetables in boxes, and there were Arab women carrying baskets on their heads, filled with bottles of kutack[8] for sale in the market.

There was bustling movement to and from the town. Here there were orange groves. Between clumps of prickly-pears and acacias, the orange trees with their almost-ripe fruit could be seen. Musa passed alongside an open gate and peered inside. A row of pomegranates led to a lovely residence set far back in the grove. A pair of palm trees towered above the magnificent building. A whiff of sharp aromas floated about, and the sun burned fiercely above the tall green hedges. Musa was bathed in sweat. Suddenly he came upon the town and the market. Here he bought Aphia colorful material for a dress, two pairs of brown stockings, and a measure of black satin to knot around her forehead. In fear and trembling he carried all these purchases to her brother's house. But to his utter astonishment, Aphia was not won over by all his gifts. Her brother was even hostile to him. He demanded ten liras as a fine for the blows that Musa had rained upon his sister!

"Here," the brother claimed, "we have a Sephardic rabbi who defends the honor of women, and does not give permission to beat a wife as is customary in Yemen. Here the laws and customs are different in marital relationships. Aphia will not return if you don't pay the fine!"

All Musa's arguments and excuses were no use. The matter became very complicated, and he saw no way of bringing the rebel

8. Kutack—an Arabic term for a sauce made of sour milk in which bread or other things are dipped.

back home. "The beginning of strife is as when one lets out water,"[9] Musa muttered. He ground his teeth as he ran about, seeking advice among the Yemenites of the town. A wise man who delved in hidden mysteries sent him to seek out a tall man, with a round pitted face, whose name contained the letter "T." He had many kinsmen and friends, he lived on the north side of the town, and his zodiac sign was the sun. From this man, it would be possible to find a remedy that would restore a woman's heart to her husband.

Two weeks of soul searching and anguish passed on both sides, until kind friends healed the breach. Aphia was reconciled and willing to comply, but she did not agree to go home yet. Heeding her friends' advice, she insisted on staying in the town for a month in order to bathe in the sea. "The sea strengthens barren women," the Ashkenazic women would say. They were clever and knew the secrets of childbearing!

Musa returned to the *moshava* alone, and Aphia began going down to the shore to bathe early every evening. She took her clothes off in her corner of the bathers' hut and put a blue tunic on, the only item that remained of all the clothing she had brought from Yemen. She went down the steps, and ran to the water. She went in cautiously, and knelt before a wave. It was very strong and was about to sweep her up. She became frightened and threw herself on the foam-covered sand, and clutched the hand of an elderly woman. The young girls ridiculed her, and wanted to drag her back into the water by force. She fought against them, protecting herself by hurling fistfuls of seaweed, which a raging wave had brought ashore.

After bathing, she dressed. She tied the new satin kerchief tightly above her brow and put a red ribbon above the knot in the middle of her forehead. For a long time she remained seated among a group of maidservants on an outing with their charges. Aphia remembered her Aliza and was overcome with sadness and nostalgia. How good it would be to sit here with her little beauty! To dispel her misery, she bought some sunflower seeds from an Arab vendor, which she shared with her companions. She sat cracking them between her teeth, as she sent her burning gaze toward the silver surface of the sea.

---

9. Proverbs 17:14.

There was a slight storm. The waves were gray, dark. Here, near the shoreline, they broke furiously into a white foam. The west was covered in gray clouds, parting occasionally to show the blue sky. Suddenly a ball of fire appeared among the clouds, and lit up the surface of the sea. Long shining rays streamed from the ball. They passed above the clouds until they reached a patch of pure, clear, cloudless sky.

The sun dipped into the horizon, sank slowly, and disappeared. Only a single faint reddish streak lingered among the clouds. In a short while it was gone. All the golden clouds vanished. The clouds on the horizon remained dark and desolate like orphans.

The month spent bathing passed quickly, and Aphia got ready to return to the *moshava*. She had many fine things to take back with her: a lovely burnished copper pot with a tight-fitting, shiny lid; a tin bowl with a polished finish for kneading bread; two glazed earthenware plates decorated with roses; and two spoons that gleamed like pure silver. Armed with all these treasures, Aphia did not go home on foot, but traveled in a horse-drawn cart. How proud she felt sitting in it as she drove back home.

When she came to her shed, she was overcome with grief, for immediately she learned that her job was no longer available. An Arab girl had been employed in her place. The lady of the house was satisfied with the new maid, and would not dismiss her. The loss of her job went together with the loss of her home. Musa had already received notice to vacate the shed, but he had asked for permission to remain there until Aphia returned. So things had gone from bad to worse. Aphia wept the whole night, and Musa was unable to console her.

3

It was the end of summer and very hot during the day. A cool breeze blew only at night. The cellar, where Aphia had lived these last two months, was stifling hot. She was unable to sleep at night, and she felt very, very bad. Sometimes she jumped up and fled outside at midnight to retch. Musa heard, got up, and came to her assistance. Wrapped in a light blanket she sat next to one of the casuarina bushes and attempted to breathe. Musa sank down beside her. She leaned her head against his shoulder. Her black curly hair, which she didn't reveal during the day, was uncovered. Her eyes were fixed sadly at a distant point.

"Little girl, why are you always so sad? If it's because you miss your little girl, Aliza, know that such longings are forbidden! They are like idolatrous acts!"

Musa stroked her with hands that were hard and black.

This time she no longer held back. With a pounding heart, she revealed her secret to him: They would no longer be childless. He jumped up and stared at her in amazement: "Child, what are you saying, child! Has HaShem really had mercy? And I did not know. The One of Blessed Name has not given me an understanding in things like this!"

Musa did not know how to treat the supple body that lay wrapped against his chest. He wanted to lift her in his hands and fly with her like a soaring bird, but he remained seated with his precious burden. His heart and lips whispered a prayer. He bent toward her, but her face was clouded with sorrow.

"Child, why is your heart so mournful?"

"Bad dreams frighten me, and my heart does not cease prophesying the evil awaiting me. A day will come when you will take a second wife!"

"Child, Heaven forbid. Oh child! How can this enter your mind now, when the Holy One, Blessed be He, has seen our suffering and sent us a blessing?"

She threw the blanket off suddenly, fixed a pair of burning eyes on Musa, and murmured hastily:

"Not now, but later on, when a disaster befalls me. Either I'll become ill, or the child will die!"

"Heaven forbid, Heaven forbid!" Musa whispered sadly.

And she continued to speak in a trembling voice:

"But get it into your head, Musa, that if you take a second wife over me, then let these trees reaching to that pile of stones bear witness that I shall definitely choke her! I shall choke my rival to death!"

Many weary days and nights faced Aphia. She was unable to work any longer, because it was too difficult for her to bend. She had no desire to eat. She could not hold any food down; everything made her nauseous. She longed for the thin wafer-cakes made of cornmeal and baked in oil that they had eaten in Aden for the Sabbath. Here there were no proper ovens for baking them. Musa looked for different kinds of material to build an oven. He did not rest until he had made one similar to the ovens used in Aden, and then for one Sabbath, Aphia baked the bread she craved. But the bread harmed her. She ate to satiety and then became ill.

From month to month she grew sadder. When Musa rebuked her, in his customary fashion, for sinning against the One of Holy Name, she replied: "Do not think, Heaven forbid, that I have not received His gift lovingly. But what can I do when Satan provokes me and sends me illness, suffering, and fear?"

"What kind of fear? Child, what are you frightened of?"

"I fear that death will accompany birth! Every time I feel the baby kicking inside me, it seems that a small devil is bound up there together with him, and when the day arrives, the hand of the devil will prevail over the hand of the human!"

Musa spat angrily, rebuked and reproached her.

At night, she lay awake listening to the rumblings in her stomach. Something underneath her heart pressed and troubled her. She thought it was the devil. This was her calamity, her evil fortune, pressing in fits and starts under her heart. Overcome by terrible fatigue, she wanted to cry and call for help, but she pitied Musa and suppressed her cries. She took a glass of cold water and tried to fall asleep.

After the second watch, she fell asleep for a short while. She awoke as she found herself being caressed.

"I don't want to, I don't want to," Aphia whispered, holding back her pain. But Musa was unaware of her pain and could not feel her torment. In a shuddering passion he quenched his deep thirst.

From time to time, Aphia tried to earn a little money. She would go out to work, but most of the time she came back annoyed. Why did they leave Yemen, she complained. Why did they leave her father's house in Aden? There, they were lords, they had houses and lands. They were among the wealthy members of the clan. Here they had become slaves! They were burdened with hard physical labor, and they were mocked as well, looked down upon in utter scorn!

She found a little household needing help, and she tried to make a contract for a month, but fled when a young man came in and asked:

"Is this your maidservant, madam?"

Immediately she left. She could not tolerate the insolent tone. She returned to her cellar, weeping all the while. "Maidservant! maidservant!" The word was like a sword ripping her heart. She wept bitterly and questioned: "Is this the land of Israel, where we came to be redeemed?"

Musa tried to persuade her to accept suffering with love. The Messiah would not come unless the whole generation was worthy. Sufferings come to atone for sin.

When she felt better, she wondered whether she would give birth to a son or daughter. Contrary to expectation, she wanted a daughter. If she were not as beautiful as Aliza, she wanted her to be like Tirzah daughter of Abigail! In her mind's eye she already saw how she would raise her daughter until she came of age. She would not sell her for money the way the Yemenites did. She would allow her to choose the man she loved. How wonderful this Ashkenazic custom was! How foolish of the Yemenites to scorn the practice!

One Friday evening, when it was dark, she felt such acute pain that she was unable to move.

All that Friday night, the night of the Sabbath, the Yemenite women came and tried to help. She had difficulties in labor, and they attempted all sorts of charms and kabbalist incantations, importuning the unborn child to come into the light of the world. But Satan prevented him, and he refused to come forth. Aphia's strength waned. She ceased shouting, and only moaned quietly. She raised her fingers toward heaven, touching the tip of her nose and her lips, and whispered:

"Oh my God, oh my God, oh my God!"

One woman sat at the foot of the bed and prayed:

"HaShem, open the gates of mercy, open!"

At the onset of night, Aphia had called Musa. She had begged him to call her former mistress, Aliza's mother. He refused. It was the Sabbath, and the Ashkenazic woman would not be bound by the strictures of the holy day. When dawn broke, he could no longer withstand Aphia's pleas, and against his will he went to fetch her.

The mistress dressed hurriedly and sent Musa to call the midwife. He again refused:

"It's not necessary, it's not necessary! Today is the Sabbath. There is no need for alarm, deliverance will soon come. The One of Holy Name will have mercy! He has three keys: of rain, of resurrecting the dead, and of bestowing life!"[10]

The mistress fetched the midwife herself, and they both arrived together. When Aphia saw them, she burst out crying bitterly, grasped their hands and kissed them: In a heartbreaking voice she begged them:

"Give me a little potion, let me die. I have no life left in me, none!"

In the room, a woman stood and shouted:

"Oh Father, oh my God! Compassionate and Merciful, have mercy upon her! Oh Father in Heaven, have mercy upon her. You Who sit on the throne of mercy, have pity upon her! *Allah Karim*,[11] open the gates of mercy!"

The midwife drove the keening women out, demanded utensils, prepared boiling water, and set to work.

All the while, Aphia continued pleading in a whisper:

"Oh death, let me die! A little potion, only a little potion—HaShem will forgive you!"

The midwife gave Musa a note and asked him to bring the doctor. Once again Musa refused:

"I do not want any angels of destruction! Today it is the Sabbath! This is not a case of saving a life! What can a doctor do!"

When the mistress brought the doctor, Musa fled from the house like one demented.

The doctor put on a white apron and came to Aphia. She caught his hand and begged him:

"A little potion, Sir! A little potion! I have no life left!"

"Aphia, we will give you a potion, a life-giving potion to ease your pain!" He stroked her thin hand and comforted her.

---

10. Talmud, *Ta'anith* 2a.

11. *Allah Karim*—Arabic for Almighty God.

A nurse was brought to assist, the instruments were plunged into the flames, they got a table, and set to work.

The child was brought forth still-born.

4

Six months later Aphia recovered from the illness she contracted after the birth. But now her prospects were sad indeed. Musa would not face the death of the boy. He blamed Aphia because she had listened to the Ashkenazim, and he refused to forgive them for desecrating the Holy Name and desecrating the Sabbath on the day of the birth. Finally he went off and became engaged to another girl, a cousin who had just come from Yemen, and made arrangements to marry her.

Heaven and earth wept for Aphia in her plight. Whenever people rebuked Musa for the great injustice he was about to perpetrate against her, he replied with a sigh: "A man's steps are decided by HaShem, and what does a person know about his own way?"[12]

1925

Translated by Sonia F. Grober[13] and Claudia Chernov

---

12. Proverbs 20:24.

13. Translator's note: Although the characters in "Aphia's Plight" are fictional, they are based on two real people, Adiah and Juku, who lived in the basement of Nehama Pukhachevsky's home. Juku was a genuine scholar, whom the author consulted on all questions about Jewish subjects. Adiah was a child-bride, considerably younger than Juku, and she suffered many miscarriages before Nehama Pukhachevsky secured the services of Dr. Sadowski, a famous gynecologist of the day. He was able to help Adiah, and she gave birth to a boy named Joseph. Ruth Arbel, Nehama Pukhachevsky's granddaughter, who kindly granted Hadassah permission to reprint "Aphia's Plight," reported in 1993 that Adiah and Juku were now dead, and Joseph was about seventy years old.

Sonia Grober acknowledges that a generous grant from the HSRC in 1985 enabled her to attend Dr. Lily Rattok's course on women's literature, where she first became acquainted with "Aphia's Plight." Sonia Grober also thanks Mrs. Jean Baharav for her generous help.

Questions for Discussion

1. Why does Nehama Pukhachevsky, herself Ashkenazic, choose to write about Sephardim?
2. Musa frequently quotes from the Bible and Talmud. What is the author saying about religion?
3. Consider the clash of cultures as the midwife and doctor meet the keening Yemenite women in Aphia's room. Here, the forces of "modern science" completely override the forces of "traditional culture." Could this clash have been handled differently? Today, the interplay between modern and traditional cultures is a fertile subject for study. Consider the early 20th century clash between the Eastern European Jews who came to the United States and the American educational, medical, and scientific reformers (many of whom were descendants of Central European Jews) who tried to help the immigrants. Consider also how culture clashes are handled at present, for example the "absorption" of Ethiopian Jews into Israeli society.
4. Aphia adopts many Ashkenazic values, particularly concerning the status of women. Yet in the end these values betray her. Nonetheless, Nehama Pukhachevsky refuses to endorse Yemenite values. Is any answer to be found?
5. What is the symbolism of the pair of birds who escape from the hen coop but are then found on their perch and shut in? Why—beyond adding color—does the author introduce Musa's story of the dead man?
6. How do you react to Aphia's forebodings about the birth? She herself believes that Satan is provoking her—and ultimately her fears are realized. Is Aphia prescient or is she unluckily superstitious? Both?
7. Today's psychologically-minded readers might interpret Aphia's sadness and anxiety during pregnancy as common emotional reactions. How might Aphia be comforted during the pregnancy? (Musa's advice that she accept suffering was extremely unhelpful!) How might Aphia be comforted after the stillbirth?
8. Compare Nehama Pukhachevsky's depiction of pregnancy, labor, and delivery to Haya Ester's depiction in "Liar."

Program Suggestion

The tragedy of "Aphia's Plight" can be said to begin with Musa beating his wife. Though the Jewish community once denied the prevalence of violence against women, the past twenty years have brought significant change, and we as Jews have begun to come to terms with domestic abuse. The Jewish community has also begun to acknowledge alcohol and substance abuse, which are likely to be correlated with battery of women. A program might involve a discussion with (1) a social worker or other professional from a local shelter for battered women, (2) a speaker on substance abuse among Jews today, and (3) a rabbi or Judaic scholar with expertise on wife abuse in Jewish history and culture. A program might also involve concrete assistance to battered women. The program organizers should research shelters in their area and determine what type of help is sought, or they might choose to assist a women's shelter in Israel.

Votes for Women

Hannah Trager

One Sabbath afternoon all we young people assembled in the house of a favorite young married couple to discuss affairs from our own point of view, which, naturally enough, was not always approved of by our elders. After a while we got on to the question of the "emancipation of women," which was already in the air. Now we girls had talked it over already among ourselves, but today the young men were present too, and they declared that in principle it was all very well, indeed quite right, that women should have their say in communal matters, but they would have to be prepared for having a vote by quite a different system of education. This was always a sore point,

---

Hannah Trager was born in London in 1870, but spent most of her childhood in Palestine. Her father was one of the first to build a home in Mea She'arim—the second Jewish neighborhood outside the walls of the old city of Jerusalem. The family was also among the first to build on the land that would become Petah Tikvah. Though Hannah Trager returned to London for schooling, and later married and raised a family there, at the end of the twenties she returned permanently to the land of Israel. She died in 1943. She described her early experiences in several books for youngsters, her best known being *Stories of Child Life in a Jewish Colony in Palestine* (1920). "Votes for Women," set in 1911, is one chapter in *Pioneers in Palestine: Stories of One of the First Settlers in Petach Tikvah.*

because most of the young men had studied and passed their High School or University examinations, but several of the girls had also attended a high school in Russia, but had been shut out from the Universities by the Russian "percentage" and had managed, often at great sacrifice on their own and their parents' part, to go to Switzerland, Paris, or Berlin, and complete their studies there. Others had come with their families to Palestine, leaving an uncompleted school course behind them, and these were the most persistent of all in the matter of the vote, because they were suffering, so they felt, from a double injustice: they might not have a vote because they had not obtained a degree, and this degree they had been prevented from obtaining. "Well," said one of the young fellows pulling a paper out of his pocket, "you girls will like this," and he read aloud an article on the women of America, telling how they were not only insisting on their "rights" but were in a fair way to obtain them sooner or later.

"Then why is it," exclaimed a girl when he had finished, "that American women go forward and we Jewish women stick in one place?

"Look at the old days when the daughters of Zelophehad stood up for themselves and claimed their inheritance. Look at Deborah, without whom the leader of the Israelites refused to go out to battle. Look at Judith, look at the many Jewish women of biblical times who had as much wisdom and courage as the men. Tell me, is it right that we should be treated as if we were only fit to agree to anything that is decided by the men?"

"And now," broke in another girl "is the time for us colony women to take a stand for our fair share in communal matters. Here we are, helping to build up a new commonwealth in a country where we are all really free to do as we like. Are we going to build on a basis of equality or not? Have not we women taken our part in the founding of this colony as fully as the men have? Did not our mothers suffer and struggle as well as our fathers? Have we girls ever refused to help in any kind of work, indoors or out? Have we not weeded in the vineyards in the burning sun, and made the hay, and milked the cows? Have we not done our best in times of sickness and trouble? Are you afraid that we shall fail you in the future? Let us go forward together, not struggling against one another, and if our parents see that you young men are for us, they will begin to look at the whole question with different eyes."

"They are quite right," said one young man after the other, more astonished at this eloquence on a girl's part than they quite liked to confess, while we girls glowed with satisfaction, but at the same time thought it wiser not to say too much just then. One of them, however, remarked,

"We shall count on your help at the next *vaad*[1] meeting, when we are going to bring the question of our vote forward," said the first girl.

"Good," said the young men, "we are on your side and will do what we can."

The next thing for the girls was to talk their mothers over, and persuade them into taking up with the idea of "women's rights." Most of the mothers thought it new-fangled nonsense, and told the girls, that once they were married, they would have quite enough to do without interfering in the management of the colony. The girls, however, explained to them that nothing stood still, that new times were coming when it would be up to the women to see their own daughters treated as they should be, and two or three girls even spoke to their fathers who said neither yes nor no, but discussed it with their wives in their daughters' absence and found them already taking the girls' view.

When the day for the *vaad* came round, everyone went who could, even some young wives with babies in their arms, some to speak for or against, and some to see the fun.

The question was brought up at the end of the meeting, and laid before the Elders of the Colony. They were very angry, and when the young men kept their word and stood up for women having a voice in affairs, it made matters no better.

"What next will you be introducing from America?" they asked. "Strikes, perhaps. We do not want such things in a Jewish Colony in the Holy Land."

"What we want in our colonies," returned the young men, "is the old Jewish spirit of liberty and justice, and not the narrow spirit of bigotry and the oppression of the weaker, from which we ourselves have suffered so much and which we have learned to detest. Go back

---

1. *Vaad*—committee.

to the history of the days of old, and see what the Jewish woman could do when she was given the chance. And what about our women in times of persecution, in the days of the Romans? In the days of the Crusades? Were they behind the men in courage, in intelligence, in devotion? Were they spared by the Inquisition? And now that we are not in the Middle Ages, are we to be narrower and more prejudiced than our forefathers were in the days of old?"

"Let us hear what the older women have to say, if you will not listen to us young folk," said one.

Then some of the mothers spoke, and a few were antipathetic, declaring that their daughters were quite independent enough as it was, thinking themselves superior to their own mothers, but most were sympathetic and said that although they themselves had no wish to interfere in communal affairs, they wanted their children and grandchildren to "come into their own," and to be like Miriam, Deborah, Hulda, and the five daughters of Zelophehad, of whom they had lately heard so much.

At last the elders said they would think it over, and it should be brought up for fresh discussion on some future occasion. But the girls had foreseen the probability of this (having learned by former experiences of the kind) and demanded a decision in their favor there and then. And they had their way.

There was great clapping of hands and the young folk left the hall singing, so that even the elders smiled grimly into their beards.

1923

Questions for Discussion

1. Hannah Trager here lays one foundation stone of the edifice that later generations will call the myth of Israeli women's equality. What are some of the features of this myth? How has the myth worked for and against Israeli women?
2. The young women search for role models within Jewish sources, and they find the daughters of Zelophehad (Numbers 27:1–11, 36:1–12), Hulda (2 Kings 22:14–20 and 2 Chronicles 34:22–28),

Deborah (Judges 4 and 5), Miriam (Numbers 12:1–15, 20:1, 26:59, Exodus 2:1–2, 15:20–21, Deuteronomy 24:9, Micah 6:4, 1 Chronicles 5:29), and Judith (the apocryphal Book of Judith). Read the selections describing these women. Are they useful as role models for women seeking the right to vote? How? The feminist project of reclaiming women in Judaism continues today. How do our choices differ from those of our foremothers who sought the vote? How are our choices similar?

3. How are we, who have benefited from earlier generations' fight to win the vote, to react to the mothers "who were antipathetic, declaring that their daughters were quite independent enough"? How are we to react to the mothers who "had no wish to interfere in communal affairs"? How are we to react to women today who reject feminism?

N'ima Sassoon Writes Poems

Amalia Kahana-Carmon

Do tears know who sheds them?
And hearts know who tills them?
They are tilled by light entering the turf
And the turf does not know what's within.
—"Lament" by Yehuda Halevi, 1075–1142

Our teacher, Mr. Havdala, said, among other things: "Our pupil N'ima Sassoon has given us great pleasure with her splendid poem, 'Dear Teacher,' which is at the top of the latest issue of our wall-newspaper."

Amalia Kahana-Carmon was born in Kibbutz Ein Harod in 1930. She was raised in Tel Aviv, and she studied philology and library science at the Hebrew University of Jerusalem. She has lived in England and Switzerland, and for many years has resided in Tel Aviv. In 1966 her first collection of stories, *Under One Roof*, was published to great critical acclaim. She has since published four novels, as well as novellas, short stories, and critical essays. Her work has received many of Israel's major awards. She is a three-time recipient of the Prime Minister's Prize for Literature, and in 1994 she was awarded the Bialik Prize.

Now, our whole school, the Tent of Sarah School for Orthodox Girls, would read the poem.

We went up to our classrooms in pairs. I passed teacher Ezekiel, who was standing with the headmistress. I did not know what they were discussing. I could hear him saying in his unique voice, a voice that was full of pith though it was broken, like Louis Armstrong's, "There's nothing to it," and her replying, "Let's see you do it, then," while he answered, "What do you want me to do? Leap about on one leg?" and she replied, "Look who's talking!" And as I hear him being spoken to like that, I feel torn.

Teacher Ezekiel is our form teacher. We have learned that a man should not be joyful among those who are weeping, or weep among those who are rejoicing, nor should he keep awake among those who are sleeping or sleep among those who are awake, etc. Yet teacher Ezekiel sits all day at his desk on the little platform in front of the blackboard, and never raises his eyes from his worksheets, his books, and his registers. Mid-morning break. How was it, for an instant, a dream come true—by chance, was it, or was it absent-mindedness—that he noticed me again for a moment, that the green eyes rested on me. And I could not contain myself. I approached. The sun was beaming through the window, and I was wearing a new summer frock which I thought was full of promise. Teacher Ezekiel was now sitting motionless. As though he was trying to turn his annoyance into good humor. And, I told myself, as though he was braced to receive a blow, and I realized again that all was lost. I walked right past him, at full tilt. I tumbled the stones of the blue plums into the wastepaper basket, as teacher Ezekiel, over there at his post, unwrapped a sandwich and began eating. Reflected in him, sitting there, I see the most handsomely dressed young man of his day, languid, a ballet prince, with the profile of Ivor Novello. And then I understand, no, neither is it like that; but that you are a hard man with an extraordinary gentleness. And I am a silly girl. Sick all year. With a kind of blind determination I have brought on myself, let us say, a certain type of cold. A cold with a high fever. And I don't want to be cured. And I no longer have the power to decide. And I am not happy any more. Not happy. Or sensible any more. Not sensible. And because of you, twice a day, I take the wrong bus.

On two occasions there was no vacant seat, except the one beside him. I sat down beside him.

At the first stop he got up. He offered his seat to a woman, who was not young, yet the wrinkled skin on her sun-tanned chest and arms was quite attractive. She sat down, opened her bag and took out a packet of cigarettes. She struck a match, like a man. One of those feeble matches that snap when you strike them, shoot off at all angles, and drop back to burn a hole in your trousers. But since then, whenever I catch sight of her, I don't take my eyes off her, so as to relive the scene once more:

I turned my head toward him. Teacher Ezekiel is standing clutching the leather loop hanging from the bar above. Other people can see a dark moon of a face; green eyes shine clearly out of the face. And none of these people could imagine what strength this young man has stored up in him. But he is like a boxing champion who wouldn't hurt a fly.

"I'll hold your briefcase for you," I tried to stammer out.

Teacher Ezekiel put his briefcase down on the floor between his shoes, stood over me, and the air between us quivered.

And there was another time. By then he would no longer talk to me.

In front of us sat Mr. Havdala, the teacher whom the girls called Mr. Abdullah behind his back. I see him in my mind's eye shaped in the image of Hillel the sage, a pastor of Israel. Next to Mr. Havdala, a man was sitting upright, looking as though he was asleep, reading a newspaper propped up in front of him. Mr. Havdala, fussily self-important, turned to me and kept up a conversation the whole way:

"You're lucky to have curly hair," he said, "you don't need to comb it."

And then: "What do you do when you get home?"

"Nothing. Read."

"Read. What do you read?"

"Nothing. Daddy's books."

"How's your Daddy been doing lately?"

"Nothing. He's ill."

"So what will happen?"

"Nothing. We're selling the business."

"And what are your plans, little lady?"

"I shall study."

Throughout this conversation teacher Ezekiel was looking out of the window. When we came to his stop, I took a chance. I got up and left the bus.

Teacher Ezekiel stayed in his seat and did not get off.

As I stood on the pavement I could see Mr. Havdala, and as he yawned his face looked as it must have done when he was a baby. The man asleep was still sleeping seated. But teacher Ezekiel was no longer looking outward.

Having gone past his proper stop, he must now really be going home. I tried unsuccessfully to cheer myself up. And I reflected: he will get home. He will put on comfortable clothes. His slippers. His wife will be in her chair by the window. Sometimes when I pass by there I see her. She is older than he is. She's got a dog. She is tiny and fragile, with a mouth drawn in pink, only her throat reveals age, and she sits viewing the street. She takes up half the window, a curtain fills the rest. It is elaborately patterned, and if you look at it closely, you can make out among the netting and webbing the shapes of birds in flight like bats, or birds of paradise at rest. And below their flat is a workshop that specializes in embroidery, drawn-work, and plissé. I saw her once coming out of a shoe shop. On her breast she was wearing a locket with a photograph set in it. Was it teacher Ezekiel's photo? A photo of the dog? Now she will probably get up from her chair, and go to put on her locket for teacher Ezekiel. Only the curtain will be left.

Yet, I, however, am still here. The mirror sky is shimmering over the city like a sheet of water. It is brighter now than at any time of day. Zion Square looks as though it is resting on the bed of a calm, translucent sea. Civilians, soldiers. Through this hour made his by the poet Lebensohn the neon-signs fire their cheerful flashes of light: Have you managed to get home all right, teacher Ezekiel? You deserved to break a leg on the way, teacher Ezekiel. And there are the alternating hues of the traffic lights. Even on the flanks of passing vehicles there are multi-colored lights gleaming like precious stones. It's uncanny, how such brisk movement is possible underwater. Only I, with the weight of that transparent sea in my breast, am choking.

"Are you tired, N'ima Sassoon?" he once said to me. "So many mistakes in one math problem." "July. Called after Julius Caesar." There was all the explicitness in the world, in his wonderful, broken voice, and in his look. Together with the pleading, the hopelessness. Which is also a token. But I no longer knew if even that still existed. Now, that was all I asked to know.

Women were driving their cars, women who had beautiful jaws, arched necks. They all had a hard kind of charm, selfish and sharply whetted. A big embassy car, driven by a uniformed chauffeur, went past, with only a child in it. And the lights in the square, up Ben Yehuda Street, and along Jaffa Road, like those of great cities and seaports that never existed, shining seven times more brightly in this twilight hour, in electric splendor, an alien scarlet of wanton jubilation and thriving prosperity smelted into a red river, in untempered orange of sulfur and gold ore, in untempered green, in pellucid sapphire which shone like the terrible ice, in blue and in deep purple, constantly proclaimed the power of red, green and blue worlds, to which one need only find the path. And perhaps none of it is serious. Perhaps it is just meant to enhance the brief life-span of the pearly evening. It is, the evening, like a transparent leaf, etched with thin tracings of colored veins, the first to fall in the autumn, flitting about like a butterfly a long while. An evening which will never be matched in clarity or purity. Or in its quintessential anguish. And there is this vicious circle: I performed an act, offered a gift. And the gift was declined. Why does he never reprove me for my impertinence? Perhaps he has not yet found the words. Perhaps there is some natural reticence: after all, who is one to tell others what to do. Perhaps he lacks the nerve, hopes it will all sort itself out. Perhaps he hasn't the heart to do this to me. Perhaps he is thinking of himself, and is afraid to lose me. But in my heart I knew it was none of these things. It was simply this: there are those who, without meaning to be, are a torch to show others the way.

After that evening he was careful not to sit near me. Or ask me questions. Or look at me. What else had he left to deny me, I asked myself.

And it is already the end of the school year. The last few days.

Days like weak winter flies, that you could touch even while they are flying around. There is the usual commotion and din of the girls. Desk lids are slammed shut noisily. Benches are dragged along. Yet the air is filled with a slow poison, as though the walls have been smeared with arsenic. The accustomed drabness has some new element in it. Like acrid ammoniac fumes dispersing. Something is draining away. And the girls, who look suddenly overgrown in their blue, childish pinafore uniforms, write keepsakes in each other's albums, prepare in groups for the finals hanging over us, get together on Friday nights at this or that one's home, and then go out together, arms linked, dreaming aloud their visions of what is to come.

None of this has anything to do with me. I take no chances. All my evenings I reserve for teacher Ezekiel, sitting at the iron table on our back verandah. At night the blades of the eucalyptus look like tin leaves. In the dry exhalation of the pine tree leaning over from our neighbors' yard, there is some vague, scented guaranty, cool and quickening like the taste of licorice. Beyond the fence is a stony, rocky slope. The nights are lukewarm. In the housing estate on the shoulder of the hill across the wadi, dogs are barking. Its lights are like holes punched out so that you can peer at the fire under the earth's thin rind. Teacher Ezekiel does not come. He never comes. I draw closer to the fence. Some other teacher Ezekiel begins ascending into the space that is between the heavens and the earth. He gazes everywhere, cloaked in a blazing garment. And every night, as I read out the terrible letters inscribed on the crown on his forehead, my heart fails within me, as I know the moment has come, and I can hardly keep from falling into a swoon. Teacher Ezekiel vanishes behind the curtain of the sky. He has reached the place where glory is the bread of the dead. And grief is their water. Streams of suffering, that bear affliction and sorrow like myriad huge leaves in their currents, form their boundaries. All this, I, N'ima Sassoon, have written in the exercise book of my poems, from which I submitted the poem called "Dear Teacher" to the wall-newspaper of our school.

Yet all day, blear-eyed, it seems, I keep muttering to myself. All day I am in his presence, at a distance. It is a teacher Ezekiel of flesh and blood. As though in a dream, he comes in, sits down, gets up at the bell, leaves, comes back with the bell, sits down again. Moving with the conviction of a sleepwalker, with the astonishing trust of a piece of seaweed flung around by the flow. I for a long time now have been unaware of what is happening to me. Teacher Ezekiel comes toward me. He stops at my desk:

"N'ima Sassoon, the bell has gone. Lessons are over," he says, about to leave.

"Teacher Ezekiel," I cry out to him, abasing myself for the millionth time, though the first in weeks. "I wanted to tell you. Something odd happened to me yesterday."

One elbow is resting on the windowsill, and his other arm hugs its opposite shoulder. Teacher Ezekiel stands still, as though he is observing the window frame, or the exposed electric wiring, or the distempered walls. Or is it the hills, the misty eventide hills, like traces of tidemarks, layer upon layer and against the sky, while a distant road winds and rises in the mist as into a future.

But Alfandary, the school janitor, comes in to ask for keys. Teacher Ezekiel does not linger to hear what happened to me yesterday.

Teacher Ezekiel does not turn back to me. Over there by his desk he squats. His pale-blue shirt is taut on his back, his belt almost snapping, as he slips a wedge of folded wastepaper under one of the legs of the desk, to stop it wobbling. And for some reason, seeing him so young, so well-knit, that which I have discovered in him flashes out and pierces me afresh. The wild cub fastened to my heart for many days now, whose claws are in my flesh, frets to rub, and strains at its ropes.

Last try. I went and stood beside him.

Teacher Ezekiel continues staring complacently at his desk's firmness. Fly, O bird, away to your mountains. But instead: "Yesterday I was walking down the street," I say, with lips that seem to be groping, to the back of the neck of the man pretending to be occupied with some meaningless task.

Teacher Ezekiel rests his hand on the flap of his desk, and straightens himself, non-committally.

But illusion has a sham-sweet taste:

"I was wandering along the street," I continued, and having had no sign of encouragement I wasn't sure how to, "and there was a woman there, all untidy. Her head had recently been shaved, and the hair was just starting to grow again, her clothes were all in tatters, and her lips were very swollen. She was trying to strike up a conversation with two small children, who looked as though they were terrified of her. 'I'm mad,' she said to them, like in confidence. 'And she's mad, too.' She pointed at me, and I was amazed. I asked myself how she could have known. But in fact, I was asking you. Because I had this urgent feeling, the sense that this was in direct line with something that turned topsy-turvy," that how is it that I am here, for you to notice me, and you don't, I wished to say but didn't, "or did I make it all up."

"Make it up, make what up, little girl?"

"You ask make what up. That shows it is all made up." My spirits drooped.

And so the school year might have ended: teacher Ezekiel clutching at the sides of his desk, his face the face of an enemy, "I asked what you made up to avoid the question. You didn't make it up," he says, and I stare at him thunderstruck.

From that day onward teacher Ezekiel has behaved as though my place in class were empty. It would never have occurred to me, not even in a dream, to tell him about my poem "Dear Teacher." But it has happened, like this. It is during a lesson and I am sitting listlessly, on my own in my place at the back of the class. "Rabbi Sa'adya Gaon was a very strong-headed man, which did not make for an easy life," teacher Ezekiel was declaring. Idly, I try to sketch his features: the ears that seem attached not quite in place, the lovely green eyes, clear, with a darker rim around the iris. I try to capture them and fail. I give up in despair. But to leave no room for doubt, I have written at the top of the page "Teacher Ezekiel," unaware that the lesson has ended and that teacher Ezekiel has approached and is standing over me.

"N'ima Sassoon, the bell has gone. Lessons are over."

He had not spoken to me for many days, and now he was speaking softly, leaning on the back of my chair, and on my desk, inclining forward a little, to look at my exercise book. Hurriedly, I covered up my sketch, my handiwork, with both hands. But teacher Ezekiel straightened up, reached out for the exercise book and my hands fell away. Then, all shattered—and only because I felt all shattered—without knowing why or wherefore, I said:

"I submitted a poem to the school paper."

Teacher Ezekiel, still examining the sketch, asked preoccupied: "Was it accepted?"

"Mr. Havdala liked it. The headmistress, too, stopped me and praised it. But, Teacher, the credit should not go to me. I had a very special subject. I called the poem 'Dear Teacher.'"

At once teacher Ezekiel dropped my exercise book. He went back to his desk and gathered up his worksheets, his books and his registers, without lifting his head.

I followed him.

"And if you care to read the poem, you will see you are wrong about me," I whispered.

I do not now whether it was my whispering which moved him. I do not know, indeed, what he meant when he answered: "Maybe it's you who are wrong."

"I wish it were," I whispered, as he picked up his briefcase and fled.

A raised threshold, extended arches, each with the verse "For thy Law is my delight" in iron open-work, over an elongated Star of David, rivets in the shape of large-petalled flowers, fluted rods, and a kind of butcher's hook shaped like a clenched fist, as a knocker: the massive gate of our school. One of the doors in the gate, incredibly, is fitted with a smaller door, that has a peephole. Like a toy broody hen, with a broody hen inside it, and, inside that an egg. We were standing, both of us, the next day, which was a Friday, at the bus stop by the gate. Teacher Ezekiel could not have known. As I watched him going out, striding, as he did, rather like a sailor, I summoned up my courage and went out in step with him. Now teacher Ezekiel had assumed the impatient look of someone waiting for the bus to arrive, and was lightly tapping his briefcase against his knees. But it looked as though a shadow was hovering round the edges of his mouth. He must have caught it from me. I was possessed, and my heart was pounding so much:

"Teacher," I said, "ever since yesterday I have talked nothing but rubbish to you, and I can only regret it. But now I would like to ask you a question. Just one. And you will tell me the truth, won't you?"

And I let cross my lips the notion over which in class, and in my bed at night, I have been eating my heart out: teacher Ezekiel is no longer concerned about me, he is concerned with Bathsheba. He always treats her so well. (The idea! Bathsheba is as black as the devil. And it wasn't Bathsheba that I wanted to talk about.)

Teacher Ezekiel looked quite taken aback.

"A new caper. Bathsheba Hayun is it? Why Bathsheba Hayun, of all people? What a surprise. As if things aren't complicated enough without that. No one gets special treatment. Neither Bathsheba Hayun, nor anyone else. Get this clear: there's no special treatment for anyone."

"Why Bathsheba Hayun. I must be having hallucinations now. It must be my imagination," I sighed, and teacher Ezekiel gave me a brisk look. But I added, "I've got another recurring hallucination. Generally, I know you're like everyone else, but sometimes—and this is the hallucination—I think you are different. Apart. Singled out. One more question. Please, just one. Tell me, teacher Ezekiel, are you really singled out?"

The last girls to leave were passing us. "Yesterday I went to the pictures. All of a sudden, a tiger. It sees Jane. Jane starts saying 'The Lord-is-my-shepherd-I-shall-not-want. He-maketh-me-to-lie-down-in-green-pastures. He-leadeth-me-beside-the-still-waters....' Then suddenly: Tarzan. Leaps from the treetop on to the tiger's back. Strangles it. Jane puts her hand on the dead tiger and says, 'This fur coat.' Tarzan says, 'Coat. What-that?' Jane says, 'Never mind. A barbarian trimming.' Tarzan says...."

As usual, teacher Ezekiel takes his time before answering.

"I don't think I'm singled out. But everyone is unique to himself. So I probably don't qualify as a witness."

What was the spell cast over us that moment? Like the innocent moon, waxing and rising. Generosity and goodwill surround us shield-like. The heart rests from its battering. What was devoured is made whole. And for a moment it is as though I too come near the secret which makes the faint-hearted heroic.

A street urchin blowing pan-pipes made of slate went past, stuffed the instrument in his pocket, and bent to pick up a cigarette end from the gutter. He stuck it in his mouth with a very grown-up air. In the distance we could see the bus approaching, lurching from side to side. And I said:

"Teacher, special treatment or not, for me you will always be, how shall I put it, one, unique, and I am so happy that I am lucky enough to know that someone like you exists. I don't know how to say it in words. So I tried to express it in writing."

Till that moment I did not know whether I dared show him my exercise book of poems which I had brought for him. Now I propped my satchel against one of the doors in our school-gate, against the identical copies of a rabbinic proclamation, laid out in thickly clustered lines of print, like samples of type-face, all ranges, all sizes. A manifesto denouncing some disgraceful conduct, terrible enough, it says, to make ears ring at the sound of it. And a condemnation: "Their house is rich and nothing lacks / But mice will dance upon their backs." I tried to unfasten the catch but could not manage it. I felt ashamed that he might notice my fingers trembling. Teacher Ezekiel smiled a little smile, and assuming I meant to take out my purse, rested his briefcase between his shoes, and opened my satchel for me. A joint enterprise. Like two people with a common purpose. But I took out the exercise book, and proffered it to him without looking at his face.

A father, on his way home, got off the bus, and halted: his small offspring was running to greet him, baring his chest that was spotted and scrawled over with a ball-point pen, exclaiming proudly, "Look, tattoo!" I left teacher Ezekiel, and started making my way home on foot. The toddlers had moved on to the pavement out of the way of the bus, abandoning their dust castles that had matchbox balconies and date-stones instead of flags, and approaches made out of wooden splinters laid out crookedly. One infant in a wooden crate was making believe he was a motor car, and his lips were working at the speed of electric fan blades. A schoolboy was bowling a hoop along, running after it. A young bride, in thick stockings, sleeves down to her elbows, her hair tied up in a kerchief, passed by, carrying a basket on her arm. Her face was freckled, and like milk. There was a light shining in her eyes. A little girl was carrying a broad tray on her head, with two Sabbath loaves and assorted pieces of dough on it, toward the bakery. She was taking a short-cut across an empty building site, that had only some derelict foundations on it, a signpost that a Talmudical College was shortly to be erected there, and piles of rubbish. A newspaper was fastened to the side of a kiosk by a thumb tack, and a man drinking orange juice was standing reading it. Above the newspaper was pinned an announcement telling of a most sorrowfully arousing oration to be delivered at eight o'clock, European time, by an exalted member of the rabbinical court, at a memorial service for a distinguished rabbi who had been killed in a road accident. There was a sign saying, "Ice Cream—Family Size—To Take Away." And on the marble counter, a picture of a red watermelon cut in half. Beside it, like a reflection, a real red watermelon, halved. Behind my back I could hear: "I met him in the street. He said, 'What's this, going about now without a hat?' So I answered, 'Just show me where in the Bible it says you must keep your head covered.' 'Heretic!' he screamed." In a backyard children were jeering, "Run-away-cowardy-cow," and a tearful babyish voice cried, "I'm not a cow."

A delicatessen with cuts of cured beef, minced meat, potato-salad, and borscht in tureens, in the sloping refrigerator in the shop window. A small sign with an arrow, pointing to the public baths. A large sign with an arrow, pointing to the charitable institution of Rabbi Meir the Miracle-Worker. A fruit and vegetable store. Crates outside. Spinach leaves. The aroma of over-ripe bananas with a hint of vanilla in it. The aroma of ripe melon and guava, like sweat. A dumpy woman, holding a brown paper bag with pears in it, and counting her money as though she were telling slanders. Then suddenly workmen pounding at the pavement with pneumatic drills. Their muscles jerking, as though in the throes of seizures. And suddenly they break off. Men shouldering a load that is visibly dear to them: An Ark of the Covenant. "And I'll tell you this: the boundary line between the tribe of Benjamin and the tribe of Judah must have run along Jaffa Road," asserts one first lieutenant to another first lieutenant, "that is to say along King David Street, past Rosh Rehavia and the Bezalel buildings, Mazkeret Moshe, Mahane Yehuda market, and Jaffa Road as far as Mei Naphtoah. Romema was the highest point. The Tenth Roman Legion, 'Arteniz,' was stationed where the National Assembly Hall is now." Through a barred window can be seen a mysterious hall, looking most fitting for an orthodox Burial Society. There is a black varnished grandfather clock in there, with Hebrew letters instead of numbers, and a copper pendulum.

A labyrinth of human nesting places. On lower, middle and upper levels. With countless partitions, and outside stairways, as steep as ladders. A burnished frying-pan rests on a window sill. Hard, green tomatoes are ranged on a window sill. A starched curtain is fastened with a light blue ribbon. In the darkness of a corridor gleams the red eye of an electric boiler. An upper beam of a door with a plant pot hanging from it in a cascade of violet-colored leaves. On a sofa by a wall, a woman is lying, with medicine jars and a glass and spoon on the radio beside her. One door of the wardrobe is not shut properly, and the girl at the table doing her homework is tucking her hair behind her ear. On a bench in front of a doorway a big girl is feeding a baby, who is darting out his lips like a baby bird. And now there is the Yemenite synagogue in a cellar: carpets striped in many colors, benches, cushions, and an old man snoozing, with a scrap of paper sticking to his cracked lip, while under the pierced beaten tin chandelier a small boy is waiting with infinite patience.

And I reflected: pick any street. Add some indefinable quality to it. Is it only by the power of sight—the vision of aspiration in eyeless things, humble things, struggling to be realized? I shall atone for them. And I reflected: an enchanting life. All in all, a mountain. Swarming with people, coming in and out like ants, making their living in the bowels of the earth. But each one of them knows: Jerusalem, that art builded as a city that is compact together—and it is Jerusalem where I am. How singular, how wondrous, how privileged. To be so close to the central pivot of things. What a rare privilege, indeed. Everyone senses the miracle in his heart. But I, please God, when I grow up, will find out how to say this miracle, all the miracles, in writing. I have to. Otherwise, my life is no life.

On Sunday I set out early for school.

Coming through the wide, vaulted entrance hall, with its marble plaque in everlasting memory of the charity of the virtuous Mistress Estella Assa blessed shall she be above women in the tents who laid the foundations of and established this house as a sacred memorial to her righteous mother Mistress Sarah who perished in the earthquake at Kirkagac near the town of Izmir, there was teacher Ezekiel at the other end of the corridor coming through a side door.

Seeing me, he veered into a small side corridor, and did not appear till the bell. Perhaps he had something to attend to there.

Lessons were over. Each girl had up-ended her chair on her desk. Everyone had gone.

"Teacher, about the poems. Forgive me, I did not know. This morning you seemed shocked, so to speak."

Teacher Ezekiel turned to look at me, and stayed silent. And as if he had counted to ten, replied, like an actor who had rehearsed his part:

"Your poems. I started to read them. I must have read about two pages and then I fell asleep."

I am not here, I told myself. I am on the distant road that winds up to the hills. A pool of stagnant water, like a gray lake, the color of olive leaves. Rocks at the roadside. Clefts in a tree trunk. Olive trees. The meager strips of land at the base of the hill are narrow furrows of plowed, curving lines. Low fences of heaped-up stones. Heavy clusters of dark grapes swelling in the lap of the outspread, emerald leaves, clinging to the wire. A mulberry tree. Dark cypresses. And it is already autumn. The air is laden, glittering. There is a mercury sheen on everything. On the skyline there is a row of aged pines, disheveled, drooping. Their foliage touches the sky. In the valleys the numbers of the turned-over fields increase. I shall not see the standing corn. For I shall not pass this way again. I shall no longer see Jerusalem. The road winds up and up. Now there is a gray sky, with torn strips of red and very dark gray in it. I am carried, as on an escalator, toward a city. At the end of the street the sun was setting. People were hurrying toward it. People were coming away from it. As though they were coming away from a fire. I who am being swept along at the edge of the pavement, have my hands over my breast, like someone who has lost her child. Gradually, the sky grew all lit up, spilling over the earth its blood-like radiance. The radiance of the End of Days. Its thick glow lasting for a long time. Only the needling rows of the street lamps, spaced out at neat intervals, like a coiling serpent of light, pierced and wounded the russet glow. Until nothing remained except the cloud stallions, galloping on two legs, across the orange horizon. Now people's faces are draped with knotted cloths to cover the eyes that saw. Then there are no more people. Only the stallions of darkness, stallions of the valley of the shadow, stallions of great gloom, stallions of hail, stallions of iron, stallions of mist. The road ran through winter, emerged and reached the bridges. It is noon. And flames are rising and leaping between each bridge and bridge, with great smoke and swirling of cinder dust. My hands are over my eyes.

By chance, was it, or was it absent-mindedness. Teacher Ezekiel is sitting there eating his sandwich. Since morning, some of his hair has shifted to the wrong side, and he looks as though he's playing one of the earlier pioneers of the American West. And in this novelty is an unlooked-for freshness, piquant charm. The handsome cheekbones, the chin, look as though they have been newly carved.

Someone comes up to him with her book. She tells him: "Can't get the hang of this." He takes out his pencil. Points to an earlier passage. "And this, you get? Read it. See if you get this." The patience, the impermeable remoteness. A man totally detached, governed only by hidden, unknown summons. How long ago had I once plucked up courage and said to him, blushing and helpless, "Teacher, you should tell your barber from me to make a better job of it next time," and he felt the back of his clipped head awkwardly and gave a little smile. Long, long ago. When he could still say, passing among the desks and catching sight of the towering palace I had drawn in the margin of my exercise book: "In an excellent neighborhood. Comfortable three-roomed flat. Easy terms."

I finished tumbling out the plum stones. I went back to my seat. Through the window came the counting up voices of the little girls, playing with jump ropes. Bathsheba came into the classroom, and began conferring secretly with the other girls. My heart flutters. It's about my poem. The chestnut, apricot, and peach faces are assessing, examining, murderously. Now it occurred to me, even the headmistress had been speaking to me with great compassion, as though I were ill. And this morning, as she stood there with teacher Ezekiel, as I passed by them, she stared at me and at teacher Ezekiel, and again at me and at teacher Ezekiel. Only Mr. Havdala is color-blind. I folded my napkin. "No, the wormwood tree is not a tree with worms," teacher Ezekiel was replying in the even-tempered voice. "It's a kind of bitter herb. Well then, why precisely wormwood? I don't know. He is a writer. He writes what he feels like." And he went on, "We are concerned only with the idea."

In the corridor I passed dear old Mr. Havdala. Mr. Havdala put his hand on my head. "We must, and please God, we will, send the poem to the papers, to the *Blast of the Ram's Horn*," and talking to someone over my shoulder, he said with pride, "The whole staff-room agrees. N'ima Sassoon is going to be a poet." Now I could see who had been coming up behind me. It was teacher Ezekiel. But teacher Ezekiel did not reply, and walked on.

As soon as Mr. Havdala let me go, I hurried after him. "Teacher, I would like to talk to you."

Teacher Ezekiel shook his head, refusing. He strode on, laughed, and said, wildly gesticulating, unusual for him: "What a morning. Like nothing on earth."

"What does it matter, teacher," I pleaded. "Look. Just now when you laughed and talked with your hands, I didn't recognize you. You were like Bathsheba and the rest of the girls. You were like a man who is shown a picture of, let's say, a statue of Venus, and he giggles and points and says, 'Look, Venus isn't wearing anything.' But that doesn't matter, either. And I told you, Mr. Havdala and the headmistress spoke well of the poem. And that doesn't matter either. It was nice to hear. But I only wanted your opinion, because, 'they are tilled by light entering.' Still, I am not asking."

"N'ima Sassoon. A girl who is altogether too clever for me." Now he stopped. Like a man carved out of chalk, like a pillar of salt, with white lips, and the shadow settled round his mouth, he said, "Cleverness is a real virtue. But it's only one of many. And not one of the most important. And another thing, it isn't always easy to tell, even for you, when or why a man laughs. Besides, you keep pressing me to tell you something. You must see that I can't. I can't," and here he rebelled, "and I don't want to."

Hurt and humiliated, my self-respect means nothing to me: "Why?"

"Because it is not done," he concluded. He pursed his lips.

A hard man. With an extraordinary gentleness. A hard man. Even in hell you would not burn.

"Fine," I said. To my own astonishment, I pointed to the staff-room. "You can go. You're free to go."

"I go this way," he said quietly, and pointed angrily in the opposite direction.

I did not stir. Teacher Ezekiel walked away. But then he stopped, turned his head, shot me a ferocious look, and walked on.

"Teacher," I hurried after him, again, "'They are tilled by light entering the turf / And the turf does not know what's within.' Oh, teacher."

I do not know if he heard. Because while I was still speaking, he turned to me:

"Today, it's school. Tomorrow, life. Listen, and bear this in mind. Limits are set. We are not living in the days when there was no king in Israel, and every man did that which was right in his own eyes. A certain N'ima Sassoon, a certain Ezekiel Da Silva. Will they please stick to the rules. That's how it is here. And that's how we want it." And he turned away.

Oh, my heart seethed within me. Oh, I told myself, if he should bring me my exercise book I would tell him, "Do you see that trash can over there—fling it in there." Oh, I wish I had never written the poems, I told myself, and I couldn't hold back my sobs. The title of a play I had once seen advertised on a billboard came back to me, *The Taming of the Shrew*. And the sleeve of a record album in a shop window, a picture of a whip decked with roses. Then, all at once, I was in alarm at a sudden recognition, as though plucked up by my hair and lifted onto another plane, my eyes struck by flashes of light. It has been spoken. The secret that makes the faint-hearted heroic. I already knew it. I have always known it. How could I not have known I knew it.

"And the Lord answered Job from the whirlwind ... where wast thou when I laid the foundations of the earth? declare, if thou hast understanding. Who hath laid the measures thereof, if thou knowest ... for who shut up the sea with doors, when it brake forth ... the cloud the garment thereof, and thick darkness a swaddlingband for it. And brake up for it my decreed place, and set up bars and doors. And said, Hitherto shalt thou come, but no farther: and here shall thy proud waves be stayed.... Where is the way where light dwelleth? and as for darkness, where is the place thereof.... That's how it is here. And that's how we want it." With the terror of soaring, which for an instant was touch and go, the light that had once begun to break forth like the innocent moon, waxing and rising, now became a blinding glare.

Halfway along teacher Ezekiel stopped in his tracks. Swung round. Came back toward me.

What are the strings that keep tugging at us? He walked. I hurried toward him. He walked. Stopped. Walked. I did not stir. Hurried toward him. He stopped. He walked again. I stood still. He walked, then spun round again. Started coming back. What is the flute we dance to? Now he was standing still, not knowing what to say. Nor did I know what to say. I rubbed my eyes with my fist. Teacher Ezekiel looked at my new frock. "You have got thinner, N'ima Sassoon, you've lost weight," he finally let out in a poor voice, making for the staff-room, crestfallen. I stood where I was, and saw him go in and sit down at the big table covered with a velvet cloth. He sat alone, apart, underneath the oil-painted mural, which showed the biblical tree that was pleasant to the sight with a scroll saying "It is a tree of life for them who put their trust in it" drawn like a curling ribbon below its roots. Someone was describing something. Someone said, "Aspera bré." The books are locked up in a bookcase delicately wrought with iron: *The Duties of the Heart, The Book of Principles, The Correction of the Soul, Examination of the Universe.* Does anyone read them? Sitting on his own, teacher Ezekiel was toying aimlessly with the large, square, china ashtray, the one with the crest and inscription "Palace Hotel" stamped on it in blue. He sat like someone on whose head the blow has finally fallen. His hair shifted to the wrong side now had a touch of mockery in it. Alfandary came in, bringing him a demi-tasse of Turkish coffee. Asleep among those who were awake, awake among those who were asleep, teacher Ezekiel worked his lips in Alfandary's direction, and without looking drew the demi-tasse toward him. But his hand did not let go of the ashtray, did not stop. Oh, don't dear teacher, please don't. There is an enormous wall of water suspended before the event, any event. Now suspended, now falling, this way or that. Which way has it fallen? A moment of birth. What has been born? And if all the sky were parchment, the whole world scribes, and all the forests quills, they could not write down all I have learned from my teachers. "Albert," called the headmistress to teacher Albert, though she turned to look at the door. I quickly slipped away to avoid being seen. And the flute is still blowing. The spirit strives to follow, comprehend, the melody. My ring is in your nose, the bit is between your teeth, and still the spirit yearns.

He never gave back my exercise book. I do not know what became of it. Perhaps he burned it.

I bought a new one.

In the evening I draw a chair up to the iron table on the verandah. A most precious moon is traveling across the sky. Jerusalem slumbers. In me alone phantoms perform. Flying, they reel and wheel: image after image rises, and alters without sound, only with movement and gesture. They plead for their lives, for the stress, the dazzle, the glowing halo, the breath of life of the living, bleeding moment. To rescue it. To redeem it. In safe-keeping. Before everything vanishes, departs from the region of light to the region of darkness.

We have learned, over the bed of King David a lyre hung, and when midnight came the north wind blew and caused it to play by itself. And King David rose and immersed himself in the study of the Law till the morning star appeared in the sky.

But I, with a faltering pen, scribble down and stumble and start again:

"Our teacher, Mr. Havdala, said among other things...."

1966

Translated by Arthur Jacobs

Questions for Discussion

1. Amalia Kahana-Carmon sets N'ima Sassoon's story in a religious girls' school. Why? How do the school's moral teachings[1] emerge in N'ima's thoughts? How does the school itself remind N'ima of the behavior that is expected of her?
2. The author uses a richly lyrical prose that interweaves biblical and religious allusions[2] with candid sensuality. Show how the Jewish and the sensual elements work within the story.
3. The images of water and fire here represent the passions that must be dammed or extinguished. Show how these images are used in the story.
4. Read chapter 38 of the Book of Job. How is God's response to Job pertinent to teacher Ezekiel's rebuke ("Listen, and bear this in mind. Limits are set.... That's how it is here.")? How do God's words and teacher Ezekiel's words coalesce in N'ima's thought? Do you find this an appropriate use of the Book of Job?

---

1. The titles of the four books mentioned at the close of the story are particularly suggestive. These books are moral treatises written by four of the great medieval Jewish philosophers. *The Duties of the Heart*, written approximately 1080 CE by Bahya ibn Pakuda of Spain, stresses the Jew's inner ethical obligations. *The Book of Principles*, by Joseph Albo of Castile, completed in 1425 CE, enumerates the articles of Jewish faith. *The Correction of the Soul* was written by Solomon ibn Gabirol of Spain in approximately 1045 CE; the English translation of the title is commonly given as *The Improvement of the Moral Qualities*. *The Examination of the Universe*, written by HaPenini (Jedaiah ben Abraham Bedersi) of Provence in the early fourteenth century CE, uses florid prose and rich imagery to show the benefits of intellectual and religious pursuits. Also suggestive is the reference to Rabbi Sa'adya Gaon, 882-942, head of the *yeshivah* (academy) in Sura, Babylonia. Sa'adya was greatly influenced by contemporary interpretations of Plato and Aristotle, and he was the first to comprehensively describe Jewish thought in rational terms. As "a very strong-headed man" governing one of the foremost Jewish institutions of his day, he became embroiled in extensive debates, so that he did not have "an easy life."
2. Several passages are direct quotations from the Bible: "For thy law is my delight," Psalms 119:77; "The Lord is my shepherd I shall not want. He maketh me to lie down in green pastures. He leadeth me beside the still waters," Psalms 23:1-2; "Jerusalem, that art builded as a city that is compact together," Psalms 122:3; "there was no king in Israel; every man did that which was right in his own eyes," Judges 17:6; 21:25; "The Lord answered Job," etc., Job 38; "a tree of life," Proverbs 3:18.

5. Is N'ima's contact with reality distorted? If so, in what ways? Is she, as she asks, "mad"?
6. N'ima's artistic and psychological maturation bursts forth as the story reaches its end, with "the light that had once begun to break forth like the innocent moon" becoming "a blinding glare." The rejection by teacher Ezekiel leads N'ima not to insanity or to despair but to a knowledge of her worth as an artist, so that in the final paragraphs, she dares to compare herself, albeit humbly, to King David.[3] Show how the author prepares us for this climax.
7. "N'ima Sassoon Writes Poems" is enriched by depictions of the streets and people of Jerusalem. Re-read several of these scenes, and note which details N'ima chooses to record. What thematic and literary significance do these descriptions of Jerusalem have?[4]
8. N'ima Sassoon feels that writing is, for her, like a religious calling: "Everyone senses the miracle [that is Jerusalem] in his heart. But I, please God, when I grow up, will find out how to say this miracle, all the miracles, in writing. I have to. Otherwise, my life is no life." Similar views of the artist are common in modern Western society. What is your own view? Is the artist's need to produce art analogous to a religious calling? If so, how do women's responses to the calling differ from men's?
9. Adolescent girls sometimes feel a painfully intense affection for their teachers. What is your own experience? Have you felt such adoration for a teacher? Have your friends? Your daughter(s)? How would you rate Ezekiel da Silva in handling the situation? What was the outcome in your own case? What behavior is appropriate? Have you ever been in teacher Ezekiel's position yourself? How would you rate your own behavior?

---

3. The story of King David's lyre is told in the Babylonian Talmud, *Berakot* 3b.
4. For instance, in the description of Zion Square at dusk, N'ima imagines that the city is under water, watches the neon signs "fire their cheerful flashes," sees the multi-colored traffic lights, and mentions Micah Joseph Lebensohn, 1828-1852, a Romantic poet, born in Vilna, who wrote on biblical and historical themes, on the longing for Zion, on nature, and on love. Images of fire, water, and light are used symbolically throughout the short story, and the reference to the great Hebrew poet presages N'ima's future artistic realization.

10. "N'ima Sassoon Writes Poems" depicts a universal theme, one which could be read in translation by readers anywhere in the world. Nonetheless, allusions to Jewish literature, culture, and ethical teachings give the story its deepest meaning. Which aspects of the story are universally appealing and which aspects are intrinsically Jewish?

Program Suggestions

1. The staff and students at N'ima Sassoon's school represent the spectrum of Israeli Sephardic society.[5] Invite a scholar of Hebrew literature or of Sephardic culture to discuss the story. How do the characters' names allude to their roles? Does Mr. Havdala in any way differentiate between sacred and profane, or is his name ironic? (The *havdalah* ceremony at the end of Shabbat differentiates between the sacred time of the Sabbath and the profane time of the rest of the week.)
2. Analyze one or two passages from the story in depth, discussing Judaic references as well as allusions to Western literature and contemporary culture. How do the allusions work together with the plain meaning of the text? The excerpt below is given as one example; an in-depth exploration of almost any of the lyrical passages in "N'ima Sassoon Writes Poems" would yield a remarkable web of Jewish and Western sources.

   "Teacher Ezekiel does not come. He never comes. I draw closer to the fence. Some other teacher Ezekiel begins ascending into the space that is between the heavens and the earth. He gazes everywhere, cloaked in a blazing garment. And every night, as I read out the terrible letters inscribed on the crown on his forehead, my heart fails within me, as I know the moment has come, and I can hardly keep from falling into a swoon. Teacher Ezekiel vanishes behind the curtain of the sky. He has reached

---

5. In addition, the lessons and books mentioned in the story frequently allude to the teachings of the great medieval Sephardic rabbis. And the exclamation "Aspera bré," which N'ima overhears near the end of the story, means "Wait!" or "Hold it!" in the Judeo-Spanish language.

the place where glory is the bread of the dead. And grief is their water. Streams of suffering, that bear affliction and sorrow like myriad huge leaves in their currents, form their boundaries."

First, what is the literal meaning of the passage? Does N'ima imagine teacher Ezekiel as the prophet Ezekiel? Is this a vision? A dream? Is N'ima creating a sexual fantasy—as suggested by "the moment has come" and "falling into a swoon"? Second, the excerpt is richly allusive. (A) "The space that is between the heavens and the earth" refers to Ezekiel 8:3. Fire imagery (like the "blazing garment") is prominent in the vision of the prophet Ezekiel (chapters 1 and 8) and in the verses of the Merkabah mystics—a school of Jewish mysticism in the early talmudic period that drew upon the imagery of Ezekiel. For N'ima, Ezekiel is no longer her teacher, but has become "some other" Ezekiel who ascends upward, assuming awesome, near-divine proportions. (B) "Cloaked in a blazing garment" is also somewhat reminiscent of Psalm 104:2, as is "the curtain of the sky." The Psalm extols the natural world as the work of God, which again hints at the mixture of earthiness and spirituality in N'ima's attitude toward teacher Ezekiel. (C) The "terrible letters" refer to the Tetragrammaton (YHWH), the name of God, which is believed to have ultimate power. The crown most likely refers to the High Priest of the Temple. Again, the images are of holiness and power. (D) The blazing cloak also alludes to one of the trials of Hercules, a fiery shirt that Hercules was compelled to wear. The parallel to teacher Ezekiel is clear. (E) The water imagery of the concluding lines is reminiscent of Danté's vision in *The Inferno*. Here the images are of unending grief and sorrow, which form the boundaries that separate N'ima from teacher Ezekiel.

Apples from the Desert

Savyon Liebrecht

All the way from the Orthodox quarter of Sha'arei Hesed in Jerusalem to the great stretch of sand where the driver called out "Neve Midbar" and looked for her in his rear-view mirror, Victoria Abravanel—her heart pounding and her fists clenched—had only one thing on her mind. She took some bread in brown paper and an apple with a rotten core out of her string bag and joined the blessing on the fruit to the prayer for travel, as prescribed. Her eyes were fixed on the yellowing landscape spread out in front of her—and her heart was fixed on her rebellious daughter Rivka who left the Orthodox neighborhood six months ago and went to live on a kibbutz of secular Jews. Now, Victoria had found out from her sister Sara that Rivka was sharing a room with a boy, sleeping in his bed and living as his wife.

Savyon Liebrecht was born in Munich, Germany in 1948, the child of Holocaust survivors, and came to Israel as an infant. She began writing seriously at age 18, while serving in the Israeli army, and later studied philosophy and literature at Tel Aviv University. Her work, however, failed to attract a publisher until, at age 33, she began attending a weekly writing workshop led by Amalia Kahana-Carmon, who gave one of her stories to an editor. Savyon Liebrecht has published three collections of short stories, and has also written scripts for television. She lives in Tel Aviv with her husband and two children.

All through the eight-hour trip, she pondered how she would act when she was face to face with her daughter: maybe she would cajole her as if she weren't angry with her, teach her about a girl's honor in a man's eyes, explain sensitive issues, one woman to another. Or maybe she would start out with cries of despair, shout out the grief, the disgrace that Rivka had brought down on their noble family, shriek like a funeral mourner until the neighbors heard. Or maybe she would perform her mission stealthily, draw her daughter away from there with false news and then put her in her room under lock and key and obliterate all trace of her. Or maybe she would terrify her, tell her about Flora, Yosef Elalouf's daughter, who fell in love with some boy, gave up her virginity for him and he deserted her; so she lost her mind and wandered around the streets, pulling little children by the ear.

On the road from Beersheva, she came up with something new: she would attack the boy with her nails, rip off his skin and poke out his eyes for what he did to this change-of-life daughter of hers. Her daughter would come back to Jerusalem with her. Which was what she promised her sister: "I'll bring her back by the hair."

From her sister Sara, Victoria already knew that her daughter was sixteen when she met him. He was an army officer and was brought in to tell them about military service for Orthodox girls. Later on, there was a fuss about letting people from the army come and poison the girls but the venom had already worked on Rivka. Cunningly, he'd sent her letters, through a friend, even after he went back to his kibbutz. And she, the fool, who was known for neither grace nor beauty—even when she was a baby, people would mistake her for a boy—she fell for it, and when she was eighteen, she picked up and went to him in the desert.

The further Victoria got from Beersheva, the more her heroic spirit deserted her and the pictures in her imagination made her sigh: What if Rivka turned her back on her and threw her out? What if the boy raised his hand to hit her? How would she spend the night if they locked her out, and the bus doesn't leave till tomorrow morning? What if they didn't get her message? She didn't know anything about traveling, hadn't been out of the neighborhood since the barren Shifra Ben-Sasson of Tiberias gave birth four years ago.

But when the driver called out "Neve Midbar" again and found her in his mirror, she got off the bus, pulling her basket behind her. She stood there in the sand, the dry wind struck her throat. How could you leave the pure air and beautiful mountains of Jerusalem—and come here?

By the time she came to a path and found a woman to ask about Rivka, drops of sweat were streaming from her kerchief. Coming toward them, on the opposite path, was a girl also wearing pants whose hair was cut short. "Here's Rivka," said the woman. Just as Victoria was about to say: "That's not the one I meant"—she recognized her daughter and burst into a shout which rang like weeping. The girl put down the laundry basket she was carrying and ran to her, her head thrust forward and her eyes weeping.

"What's this ... what's this...?" Victoria scratched her nose. "Where are your braids? And those pants ... that's how you dress ... oy vey!" Rivka laughed: "I knew that's what you'd say. I wanted to get dressed but I didn't have time. I thought you'd come on the four o'clock bus. When did you leave home? Six? Come on. Enough crying. Here's our room. And here's Dubi."

Stunned by the short hair, the frayed trousers with patches on the back and the shoes spotted with chicken droppings, Victoria found herself squeezed in two big arms, a fair face was close to hers, and a male voice said: "Hello, Mother." Her basket was already in his hand and she—not understanding herself, her hands suddenly light—was drawn after her daughter into a shaded room and seated on a chair. There was a glass of juice in her hand at once; her eyes looked but didn't know what they saw and, later on, she'd remember only the double bed covered with a patchwork quilt and the voice of the giant with golden hair saying "Welcome, Mother." And, as soon as she heard him say "mother" again, very clearly, she swallowed some juice which went down the wrong way and started choking and coughing; the two of them rushed to her and started pounding her on the back like a child.

"Leave me alone," she said weakly and pushed them away. "Let me look at you," she said after a moment. Once again she scolded Rivka: "What is this, those pants? Those are your Sabbath shoes?" Rivka laughed: "I'm working in the chicken coop this week. They brought in new hens. I usually work in the vegetable garden. Just this week in the chicken coop."

Weary from the journey, confused by what she was seeing, shaken by the vicissitudes of the day and straining to repress her rage which was getting away from her in spite of herself, and always remembering her mission, Victoria sat down with her daughter Rivka and talked with her as she had never talked with her children before in her life. She didn't remember what she talked about and she didn't remember when the boy who called her mother left, only her eyes saw and knew: her daughter's face looked good. Not since Rivka was a little girl had she seen her eyes sparkle like that. Even her short hair, Victoria admitted to herself, made her look pretty. Not like when she wore a skirt and stockings, with her broad shoulders, like a man dressed up in women's clothes.

"You don't miss the neighborhood?"

"Sometimes. On holidays. I miss the Shabbat table and the songs and Aunt Sara's laugh. But I like it here. I love working outside with the animals.... You too, I miss you a lot."

"And Papa?" Victoria asked in a whisper into the evening light filtering in.

"Papa doesn't care about anybody. Especially not me. All day long in the store and with his books and prayers. Like I'm not his daughter."

"God forbid! Don't say such a thing," Victoria was scared. Of the truth.

"He wanted to marry me off to Yekutiel's son. Like I was a widow or a cripple."

"They talked. You heard. We don't make forced matches. And anyway, Yekutiel's son is a genius."

"A pale, sick genius, like he sits in a pit all day long. And anyway, I don't love him."

"What do you think? You think love is everything?"

"What do you know about love?"

"What does that mean?" Victoria was offended and sat up straight. "This is how you talk to your mother around here?"

"You didn't love Papa and he didn't love you." Rivka ignored her and went on in the silence that descended: "I, at home ... I wasn't worth much."

"And here?" Victoria asked in a whisper.

"More."

A question began to take shape in Victoria's mind about Dubi, the fair-haired giant but the door opened, a light suddenly came on and he himself said: "Great that you're saving electricity. I brought something to eat. Yogurt and vegetables on a new plastic plate, that's OK, isn't it? Then, Rivka, you should take Mother to Osnat's room. It's empty. She must be tired."

In the room that went out to the darkening fields, Victoria tried to get things straight in her heart. But years of dreariness had dulled her edge and yet she already knew: she wouldn't bring her daughter back to Jerusalem by the hair.

"Why did it take you half a year to come here?" Rivka asked.

"Your Papa didn't want me to come."

"And you, you don't have a will of your own?" And Victoria didn't have an answer.

When Dubi came to take her to the dining hall, she poured all her rage on him and yet she was drawn to him and that only increased her wrath.

"What's this Dubi, what kind of name is that?" Anger pulled words out of her mouth.

"It's Dov, after my mother's father. The Germans killed him in the war."

"That's a good name for a baby, Dov?" She hardened her heart against him.

"I don't mind." He shrugged, and then stopped and said with comic seriousness: "But if you do—I'll change it tomorrow." She strained to keep from laughing.

In the evening, the two of them sat at the table with their eyes on Rivka as if she were all alone in the big hall, walking around with a serving cart, asking people what they wanted.

"You want something else to drink, Mother?" she heard him ask and returned the question angrily:

"You call me mother. What kind of mother am I to you?"

"I'm dying for you to be my mother."

"Really? So, who's stopping you?" she asked and her sister Sara's mischievousness crept into her voice.

"Your daughter."

"How is she stopping you?"

"She doesn't want to be my wife."

"My daughter doesn't want to get married. That's what you're telling me?"

"Exactly."

As she was struggling with what he said, he started telling her about the apple orchard he was growing. An American scientist who grew apples in the Nevada desert sent him special seeds. You plant them in tin cans full of organic fertilizer and they grow into trees as high as a baby with little roots and sometimes they produce fruit in the summer like a tree in the Garden of Eden. Apples love the cold, he explained as their eyes wandered after Rivka, and at night, you have to open the plastic sheets and let the desert cold in. At dawn, you have to close the sheets to preserve the cold air and keep the heat out.

"Really," she muttered, hearing these words now and thinking about what he said before. Meanwhile, somebody came to her and said: "You're Rivka's mother? Congratulations on such a daughter." And suddenly her heart swelled in her.

Then she remembered something that came back to her from long ago and far away. She was fifteen years old. On Saturdays in the synagogue, she used to exchange glances with Moshe Elkayam, the goldsmith's son, and then she would lower her eyes to the floor. In the women's section, she would push up to the wooden lattice to see his hands that worked silver and gold and precious stones. Something arose between them without any words and his sister used to smile at her in the street. But when the matchmaker came to talk to her about Shaul Abravanel, she didn't dare hurt her father who wanted a scholar for a son-in-law.

At night, when Rivka took her back to her room, she said: "You came to take me back to Jerusalem, right?"

Her mother chose not to answer. After a pause, she said apropos of nothing: "Don't do anything dumb."

"I know what I want. Don't worry about me."

Victoria plucked up her courage: "Is it true what he told me, that you don't want to marry him?"

"That's what he told you?"

"Yes or no?"

"Yes."

"Why?"

"I'm not sure yet."

"Where did you learn that?"

"From you."

"How?" Victoria was amazed.

"I don't want to live like you and Papa."

"How?"

"Without love."

"Again love!" She beat her thighs until they trembled. A gesture of rage without rage. They reached the door. Victoria thought a moment about the bed with the patchwork quilt and heard herself asking: "And the *Sh'ma* at bedtime, do you say that?"

"No."

"You don't say the *Sh'ma*?"

"Only sometimes, silently. So even I don't hear it myself," said Rivka, laughed and kissed her mother on the cheek. Then she said: "Don't get scared if you hear jackals. Goodnight." Like a mother soothing her child.

Facing the bare sand dunes stretching soft lines into the frame of her window as into the frame of a picture, Victoria said a fervent prayer, for both of them, her and Rivka. Her heart both heavy and light: "... Let not my thoughts trouble me, nor evil dreams, nor evil fancies, but let my rest be perfect before Thee...."

And at night she dreamed.

In the dream a man approaches white curtains and she sees him from behind. The man moves the curtain aside and the trees of the Garden of Eden are in front of him: the tree of life and the tree of knowledge and beautiful trees in cans of organic fertilizer. The man goes to the apple tree, there is a lot of fruit on it, and the fruit drops off and rolls into his hands and, suddenly, the fruit is small and turns into stones. Victoria sees: handfuls of precious stones and gold and silver in his white fingers. Suddenly, the man turns his face, and it's Moshe

Elkayam, the goldsmith's son and his hair is flaming.

All the way back to Sha'arei Hesed she sat, her eyes still holding onto their rage but her heart soothed, her basket at her feet and, on her lap, a sack of apples hard as stones that Dubi gave her. She remembered her daughter asking: "You see that everything's fine, right?"—her fingers on her mother's cheek; and Dubi's voice saying: "It'll be fine, Mother."

All the way, she pondered what she would tell her husband and her sister. Maybe she would sit them down and tell exactly what happened to her. When the bus passed the junction, she considered it. How could she describe to her sister, who had never known a man, or to her husband, who had never touched her with love—how could she describe the boy's eyes on her daughter's face? When the mountains of Jerusalem appeared in the distance, she knew what she would do.

From her sister, who could read her mind, she wouldn't keep a secret. She'd pull her kerchief aside, put her mouth up to her ear, like when they were children, and whisper, "Sarike, we've spent our lives alone, you without a husband and me with one. My little daughter taught me something. And us, remember how we thought she was a bit backward, God forbid? How I used to cry over her? No beauty, no grace, no intelligence or talent, and as tall as Og, King of Bashan. We wanted to marry her off to Yekutiel and they were doing us a favor, like Abravanel's daughter wasn't good enough for them. Just look at her now." Here she would turn her face to the side and spit spiritedly against the evil eye. "Milk and honey. Smart too. And laughing all the time. Maybe, with God's help, we'll get pleasure from her."

And to her husband, who never read her heart, she would give apples in honey, put both hands on her hips and say: "We don't have to worry about Rivka. It's good for her there, thank God. We'll hear good things from her soon. Now, taste that and tell me: apples that ripen in summer and they put them in organic fertilizer and their roots are small—did you ever hear of such a thing in your life?"

1986

Translated by Barbara Harshav

Questions for Discussion

1. In "Apples from the Desert" a mother learns from her daughter. What have you learned from your daughter(s)? What have you taught your mother?
2. Victoria Abravanel realizes that a secular life suits her youngest child better than a religious life. In American Jewry today, we occasionally read or hear of the opposite: parents whose children find that a more observant way of life brings them satisfaction. Discuss how your own choices about religion have affected your parents, and how your children's choices have affected you. (For thought: Is the very idea of religion's suitability or lack of suitability for a given individual a secular idea? How might this story have differed if Savyon Liebrecht had been a member of Victoria Abravanel's world? Also for thought: Both Victoria and Rivka are influenced by their male partners in their choice between religious and secular. What is your own experience of men's influence on women's choice?)
3. Rivka chooses rural, agricultural labor in contrast to her mother's urban existence. This is a choice made by very few American Jews. What is your own attitude toward agricultural labor? Would you feel differently about your daughter working on the land of Israel or on the land of, say, California?
4. Consider the typically female occupations in which we observe Rivka, carrying laundry and serving food (while Dubi learnedly discusses agricultural techniques). Nonetheless, Rivka is sexually liberated, and she demands the right to think for herself and make her own choices—at least as far as her emotional/sexual/romantic future is concerned. Do these facts represent a contradiction? If so, what can we conclude?

Program Suggestions

1. In this very brief story, Savyon Liebrecht illuminates two of the most important themes of Israeli life—tension between religious and secular, and love for the land. Use either or both topics for a program that will increase participants' knowledge of Israel. The essay "Religious Pluralism in Israel" by Deborah Dash

Moore in the 1992 Hadassah study guide *Israeli and American Jews* presents an excellent overview of the ways in which the Israeli understanding of Judaism differs from the American. Refer as well to Charles S. Liebman and Steven M. Cohen's *Two Worlds of Judaism: The Israeli and American Experiences*. In the *Textures* article "Sacred and Secular in Israel: The Two Nations," Aviezer Ravitzky presents a short essay on the two poles within Israeli society. For a program on the land, background reading should include "Zionism and the Environment," Unit 9 of the Hadassah 1993 study guide *Judaism and Ecology*. Because 5754 (1993-94) was the Year of the Environment in Israel, a number of speakers on this topic should be readily available. Consider inviting a representative of the Society for the Protection of Nature in Israel (SPNI).[1]

2. As Professor Rattok states in the Introduction, the relationship between mothers and daughters has only recently been explored in fiction. Compare the mother-daughter relationship in "Apples from the Desert" to the mothers and daughters in current American Jewish women's fiction. Sylvia Barack Fishman's anthology *Follow My Footprints: Changing Images of Women in American Jewish Fiction*[2] offers selections from Vivian Gornick's *Fierce Attachments*, Anne Richardson Roiphe's *Lovingkindness*, Gloria Goldreich's *Four Days*, and Gloria Kirchheimer's "Food of Love"—all exploring the bonds between mothers and daughters.

---

1. Deborah Dash Moore, "Religious Pluralism in Israel" in *Israeli and American Jews: Understanding and Misunderstanding* (New York: Hadassah, 1992), pages 91-100; Charles S. Liebman and Steven M. Cohen, *Two Worlds of Judaism: The Israeli and American Experiences* (New Haven, CT: Yale University Press, 1990); Aviezer Ravitzky "Sacred and Secular in Israel: The Two Nations," *Textures*, vol. 10, no. 1 (December 1991); Hadassah Jewish Education Department, "Zionism and the Environment" in *Judaism and Ecology* (New York: Hadassah, 1993), pages 120-130. Hadassah National Speakers Bureau as well as your regional Speakers Bureau will be able to assist you in finding speakers on the land of Israel.
2. Sylvia Barack Fishman, *Follow My Footprints: Changing Images of Women in American Jewish Fiction* (Hanover, NH: University Press of New England, 1992).

Liar

Haya Ester

1

Friday night. A concave darkness is transforming itself into a moving gray. Gulping up the last of the light. Silence flows. Far off, in another neighborhood, a baby cries. A woman. She holds out the palm of her hand. Pale. Encircled by a hesitant blue vein. Tries to open a glass door. A faint voice is muffled by the door. Her eyes have a limpid warmth which glazes over with passing thoughts. I'm not mistaken. It's Sheindel. "The Liar," we called her.

Haya Ester (Godlevsky) was born in Jerusalem in 1941, and graduated from the Hebrew University in 1979. Since 1982, her stories and poetry have appeared in leading Israeli publications, including *Mosnaim*, *Davar*, and *Yediot Aharonot*. She has published two collections of short stories, and she is currently preparing her fourth book for publication. Haya Ester is also active as an artist. Her paintings, etchings, collages, and mixed media works have been exhibited in group shows as well as solo exhibitions.

She's come to immerse herself in the *mikveh*.[1] She's washed her hair that day so as to be able to immerse herself that evening. About two weeks after giving birth. She opens the door. Comes in. Waits. Sits on the bench. The room is crumpled. Absorbs muttering.

An expectant air, as if something will burst forth in its wake. The door opposite turns on its hinges. She hates the flaking wall; a pointless hatred. Some of the plaster has fallen from the wall onto the floor. It's hot. Sheindel undoes a plastic button. Her neck is attentive. Her thoughts curl about, toward the warmth of viscous eyes.

Specks flicker in her eyes, like clusters of children. One of them is all alone.

She sits—she's inside a floating blue dress, resting on restless breasts, quivering; descending slowly to the black stockings covering flaking toes.

She looks like she's wearing something else over her dark clothes. Weary colors go astray on the thin black shawl. It's moving, caught transparently about her face. Her fingers caress scraps of air and swoop onto her purse. Carefully. Skilled in writing receipts, wrapping parcels, computing accounts. Her fleshy lips are parted, hinting at a pampered fruit. At the corners, they surrender themselves to a smile. Running after another lie?

Her lies were colorful. Her thoughts sinuous. She would let things slip which we never even saw. We were taken in by her. We got ourselves mixed up in her lies. We saw.

Winter. Rain melted the road all the way to the square.[2] Sheindel

---

1. The *mikveh* is the ritual bath. Orthodox wives immerse themselves each month, seven days after their menstrual period has ended, in order to attain ritual purity and resume sexual relations with their husbands. During menstruation and before immersion in the *mikveh*, husband and wife have no physical contact. Physical contact is also forbidden during and after the bleeding of childbirth. Prior to ritual immersion, one must be clean. Thus, Sheindel has washed her hair.
2. The square refers to Kikar HaShabbat, the main square of Mea She'arim, at the intersection of Malkhei Yisrael, Yehezkel, Yeshayahu and Mea She'arim Streets.

promised us a gentile galleon,[3] setting sail on the open seas. We ran after her. She stopped. We too. A group of children leaning on damp stones, hard, colored with an elderly gray. We glanced up, we saw an enormous ship making its way toward the market. The counters of the stalls were gaping, bare. We forgot the name of the neighborhood. The Warsaw Houses[4] were part of the ongoing lie.

A long time ago. A summer's evening. The darkness cut to a baked brown by an orange lamp. Amid the scent of rolls from the Avihail Bakery appeared the brazen lie. Disturbing. A child was rolling a barrel down the slope. His *yarmulke* blew off.

We said: It's sin.

Sheindel said: The rolling barrel is making a noise; it isn't empty. There's a sin sitting in it.

One Friday night at dusk. Pink clouds set out in a flotilla of lights toward—the Shabbat. In the yard, Fall gave out the scent of lemon rind for the Shabbat cake.

Sheindel sat on the steps. Deep in thought. A little girl. There was movement in her body. She would wander around toward the Street of the Prophets or would climb up on the roof of the Everlasting Life Yeshivah and its soup kitchen. Her face hearkening like a slender flute. There appeared the playful lie. She said: I've heard a melody.

She drew out scraps of paper, smiling with an excess of intuition. She said: "This, is a prayer book."

Once on Shabbat, the smell of a flan with dark brown sugar lingered in the yard. Sheindel sat inside on a baby's cot. It stood

---

3. The gentile galleon alludes to a *midrash* in the Jerusalem Talmud (*Berakot, Ro'eh*, 1). Sailing in a ship full of idol worshippers is one young boy who is Jewish. A terrible storm arises, and the non-Jews all pray to their idols, but the storm still rages. They then ask the boy to entreat the God of Israel to end the storm. The boy prays, and the storm dies down. When the ship reaches the shore, the non-Jews acknowledge that their gods had remained in Babylon or Rome, or if their gods had been on the ship, they were as good as absent. The Jewish boy, however, had his God with him wherever he went. (Citation supplied by Haya Ester.)

4. The Warsaw Houses, *Batei Warsaw*, an Ultra Orthodox row of dwellings to the right of Kikar HaShabbat, were built in 1894.

empty, a rusty white. Waiting for a baby. Frouma's baby.

On its sides shimmered pictures of dancing black figures. Like demons. Sheindel hurled them down the road. Suddenly she sprang up. We after her. We peeked into the room where Frouma was lying on the bed.

We looked—a mass of belly resting at the edge of the corridor. Its slopes rising toward the palm of the pregnant woman's hand. From there outwards. We saw a street spilling itself into the square in a stubborn gray, tense. Sheindel saw the slopes of an enormous belly. The belly of a woman.

We called her: "Liar." When the stone hit Sheindel, she was silenced.

The same Shabbat. A milk container is about to arrive in the square. On the way to the Tnuva Milk Products factory, transporting milk.[5]

Penetration! Desecration of the Shabbat!

Folded-away stones become spectators to what's happening.

You could cut the air, hard. Painted in the gray of dust. From the nearby streets burst faction upon faction of young *yeshivah* students.

The stones have increased. Something has moved in them. Power. The area of dark black grew and grew. The milk container emerged, fumbling toward this enmity. Entered.

Distress.

Around the container, non-religious people. Colorful. Their

5. Until the mid-fifties, there was a Tnuva dairy in Yehezkel Street, just beyond Mea She'arim. Every Shabbat milk trucks would drive through Mea She'arim with the containers from the Shabbat milking, and these trucks became the focus for violent demonstrations of the Ultra-Orthodox population against the secular "invaders." (Jewish religious law forbids all work on Shabbat; driving and delivering containers are classified as work.) The campaign against desecration of the Shabbat continued for about three years, and was ultimately successful. The Tnuva cooperative was compelled to shut down the Yehezkel Street dairy. The demonstrations, led by the charismatic Rav Avraham Blau, both politicized and mobilized the various religious factions in a united stand against secular Jerusalem.

shirts checkered with hatred. A fist for outsiders who're weird, threatening. Violence for the arrogant, with their sweaty black, sort of impenetrable.

The sides of the street are groaning. The container is drowning in the coiled shouts. "*Shabbos*!"

Round, black top hats. Policemen. Batons.

A whirlpool of bitter sweat.

The demonstration swelled. A religious bird of prey. The transgression of Shabbat desecration. A blind hatred. A great clash.

Stones.

The black is fearful, adulterated by the colorful. Windows spew out stones. The square, full to brimming, is swept along, crazed, crushed, stampeded. Heels in it. Someone throws a stone from a window of Frouma's house. The stone has honed in.

Sheindel.

Hit her on the stomach. A painful, gripping pressure. The surroundings grew dark. Shadows extended their arms. She saw the flock of religious black felt hats around on the roofs. And far away on the hills at the fringes of the city.

Distant neighborhoods.

Colors mixed up in her. Her voice faltered. And since then I hadn't seen her.

2

It's her. Here, at the *mikveh*. Still seated. Announcing to the waiting room at large: "I've come to immerse myself, after giving birth." Another woman asks: "How many children have you got?" Sheindel answers: "Five times, and then this one." Way down inside, at the end of the corridor, a room awaits her. Empty. She enters. Plaster flakes have crumbled from the sides of the door frame. A thin film glazes her eyes. She has to lean against something. Takes off her stockings. Discovers the pale soles of her feet. On her little finger, a scab from a slight injury. She scratches it. It bleeds slightly. She was bleeding then too.

Then. Dr. Zacharia threaded his faint blue eyes over the brown of her eyes. He said: "Abortion."

Intense piercing whirled about her, twisting into her stomach. A demanding finger tore into her belly. Deep inside. Inside. Then scrunched itself up. Drained away over the slope of a hill. A solid mass slipped outside. Limbs, strange locust-like shapes, fragments of bleeding pieces. Faintness overcame her.

The concaves of her thighs were sticky with a viscous liquid. The pain a sour frothiness. The remainders. Her stomach was gripped. The doctor's two hands, on her. One stretched across her, the other digging in.

Enough.

She laid aside the thought of it. A crease furrowed around her lips, listening to the weeping of a rusty drainpipe.

The square-faced exterior of Sha'arei Tzedek Hospital wore an indifferent white.

She came to. The women's ward, her female relatives around her. Chatting away. Idle chatter.

Their dresses were wrinkled against her eyes. Like someone who screws up his eyelashes and his strength dims when it grows light. Like that. Five times. She returned to her home. She'd left, almost intentionally, a shawl of hers at the doctor's—quiet but fine and womanly. In his proximity, the shawl had opened slightly like the lips of a woman. He. Wiped his eyes on the sleeve of his white gown. And wrote her name on the white card on his desk.

They had the *mezuzot* checked. Shook out the demons. So the opening on the *mezuzot* might be undamaged and no demon nor harm come near it. They added more names of fertile women to her name.[6] But nothing happened.

And now the birth.

---

6. The custom of adding a name to the name of a sick person, in the hope of vitalizing the sick person with the force from the other name. When a woman is childless, she is given the additional name of a fertile woman, such as the Matriarch Leah, who had several children.

3

Sheindel's eyes rest upon an old bath. Its legs dancing a strange dance. She takes off her clothes. Leans herself against the wall. A sloping, conciliatory shoulder. Toward a transparent ear. The skin behind the ears seems to be listening to the solitary white of her neck.

A naked belly. Soft, distended.

Sheindel lays a warm caressing hand on it. A belly needing to be massaged. Stretch marks on it. One, facing toward the direction of the roof. From there following itself back, inside, like a distorted mouth that went to the navel. As if it was crying. And after it, small tributaries of stretch marks rearing up, others fanning out. A network of such fine lines, flakes dashing all over the place. Scraping. Scratching away at the locked-up womb. Echoing empty.

The slopes of the belly, like silk paper, fragile, transparent. They shout at it: a folded-up purse. A walnut in a cup.

Patches. A crushed belly.

A slight, fluttering ticklishness about her breasts. Her warm breasts are encased in nakedness. Dreaming. The nipples pointing forward. Like a small piccolo. Weaving themselves into a sticky-sweet indistinctness.

Around them a slender halo, caressing. Yearning to be united with a mouth—a baby. They feel as if a warm, tiny fist tightens on them. Sheindel whispers: "Child."

Was there a voice? A cry?

The breasts are getting dark, heavy for her. Stones. Pulling down and down. Getting closer to the water. She sits on one of the steps as if on a birthing stool. Her thighs are getting terribly cold. The edge of the step which descends into the waters of the *mikveh* grates at her thigh. A segment of memory comes to her.

A woman in the water. Her own waters have burst. At the sides of her belly and back a familiar pain, tightening up. It bursts from within to her legs, spreads over her back. A force. Takes a bite. Fire in her belly. Torn. Hanging askew against the wall. A cold desire spins about. Steely fingers are pulling her legs open wide, ploughing into her. Stretched over a grounding of whimpering back. Her end. The end of the world. Wait. Breaths upon breaths expanding wings toward drops of sweat. Inside her, a torn bird. Large. Stretching its wings. Screaming. A scream. Pressure bubbling up. Opening. At once. God Almighty.

Birth.

A stillborn. The umbilical cord wound about it. Strangled. Gone.

Sheindel's legs are trembling. Like a bird whose neck has been wrung. Her breasts heavy. Stones in them. Pulling down, further and further, toward the bottom of the *mikveh*. From the light bulb, a ray of light implores her: "Surely the Holy-One Blessed-be-He is keeping His eye on the newborn babe. And just didn't see fit to let him into the world."

The *mikveh* lady enters. Sheindel breaks off, flustered. She immerses herself in the water. Says: "Who has made me according to His will."[7] Like someone trying to explain the judgment to himself. The *mikveh* lady is astonished: "That's not the blessing."

Sheindel gets dressed. Leaves the *mikveh*. Goes out. Shuts a mottled glass door. With a smile. She grasps its flattened side. Her steps are light. Forward glances. The wind paints gusts of gentleness about her. Footfalls in the air. Rustling, growing fainter; then coming together.

Like the flame of a candle.

Children? Her children?

Does the lamplight paint a transparent lie?

A car approaches. In the synagogue they are welcoming in the

7. This blessing is said as part of a woman's morning devotion. Upon immersion in a *mikveh*, a woman says the following: "Blessed are You, O Lord our God, Ruler of the universe, Who has sanctified us with Your commandments and has commanded us regarding the immersion."

Shabbat. A baby cries in the nearby house.

Sheindel's thoughts curl about her, depicting something inside her; oh, could this be prayer?

1983

Translated by Aloma Halter

Questions for Discussion

1. How would you describe Sheindel's "lies"—as stories, folk tales, fantasies, imaginative inventions? How does Haya Ester show that Sheindel's lies are essentially literary, artistic creations?
2. Why is Sheindel called the liar rather than the storyteller? Does Sheindel's Ultra-Orthodox community ever view the lies in a positive way?
3. What purpose do the lies serve for Sheindel herself? What purpose do they serve for the children to whom she tells them?
4. "Liar" is written in an impressionistic style that breaks all rules of logic and communication, so that readers are unable to construct a narrative meaning. In this style, which was inaugurated in Hebrew by Amalia Kahana-Carmon, the reader is meant to experience the character's reality, to subjectively absorb a specific event from a specific perspective. Does Haya Ester's style serve this purpose for you? Compare Haya Ester to other authors who choose non-linear writing techniques. In what ways is Haya Ester unique?
5. Some literary critics believe that breaking the rules of logic and of narrative composition, as Haya Ester does, is a peculiarly female literary strategy. Women are said to experience reality as an organic whole rather than as components, to synthesize rather than to differentiate, to experience a flow rather than to impose control. To what extent might this be true for the author of "Liar"? To what extent does the style increase your empathy for and understanding of Sheindel?

6. The narrator knew Sheindel as a child and then as a young woman who lost a pregnancy. Afterwards the narrator lost sight of Sheindel for very many years. Yet the narrator speaks from Sheindel's point of view in depicting events and feelings. What is the effect of the narrator's identification with Sheindel? Why does Haya Ester include a narrator who has an actual connection to Sheindel, rather than writing in the first person or writing as an omniscient narrator?
7. Haya Ester fills the stories with aromas, tastes, colors, and sensations. How do these physical images affect you? Are women writers particularly likely to portray images of the physical world? Why or why not?
8. What is Sheindel's role in the fight between the religious and the secular? How does this mirror her role within her community?
9. Discuss the "ongoing lie" of the gentile galleon. In the most literal interpretation, the children, who have never been to the seashore, pretend the tall buildings of Mea She'arim are ocean-going vessels. In a more symbolic interpretation, Sheindel can be compared to the young boy in the *midrash* from the Jerusalem Talmud (refer to footnote 3). In what way is she surrounded by idol worshippers? How does she have God with her everywhere? In what way might she be said to save her community from drowning?
10. Sheindel contemplates her body in a sensual way that is unusual in literary works. She is presented neither as a desirable, attractive woman observed from another's vantage point, nor as an undesirable woman observed by an ironic or reserved narrator or character. Her flaws (flaky skin, prominent veins, etc.) are clearly yet appealingly drawn, and the reader sees Sheindel's body through Sheindel's eyes. Furthermore, Sheindel herself accepts her body and finds it pleasant. Review the images of Sheindel inspecting her body. How do you react to these passages? How do you usually react to images of women's bodies in literature? In paintings or sculpture?
11. The author slightly distorts reality by placing Sheindel alone, dreaming and remembering, on the steps leading down to the

waters of the *mikveh*. In actuality, the *mikveh* lady would be with her or another woman would be waiting to immerse herself. What literary and thematic purposes are served by allowing Sheindel to linger on the steps?

12. Sheindel's six pregnancies have ended tragically, in spontaneous abortions or stillbirths. What do childbirth and the inability to bear children symbolize? How are themes of creation, fulfillment as a woman, etc., related to imaginative creation, storytelling, and lying? During the demonstration, a stone thrown from the window of Frouma's house hits Sheindel on the stomach, and this stone seems to cause the first miscarriage. How does the intolerance of the ultra-Orthodox relate symbolically to the miscarriages and stillbirths? Haya Ester states: "When the stone hit Sheindel, she was silenced." How does Sheindel's silence relate symbolically to the miscarriages and stillbirths?
13. Why does Sheindel leave her shawl at the doctor's? Consider both the doctor wiping his eyes on his sleeve and the sentence "He."
14. What is your attitude toward the women who visit Sheindel in the hospital?
15. Why does Sheindel say the wrong blessing at the *mikveh*? How do you react to Sheindel's resignation and acceptance?
16. The short story ends positively. What consolation does Sheindel find? Purification through the *mikveh* ritual? The hope for actual children? The knowledge that her creations, her lies, result in spiritual children? How could Sheindel's thoughts "depicting something inside her" be prayer?
17. What does "Liar" tell us about the connection between body and soul?

Program Suggestions

1. Storytelling is an art that flourishes in pre-literate societies and among the illiterate members of literate societies. What was the place of storytelling among Jewish societies of the past, and how

were Jewish women particularly active in maintaining oral traditions? Invite a modern storyteller to offer a Jewish historical perspective—and to tell stories!

2. Haya Ester offers poetic depictions of miscarriage and of childbirth. How do you react to literature about these exclusively female events? Do authors limit themselves to a sort of women's ghetto by focusing on topics such as menstruation, childbirth, menopause? Or do those authors expand the possibilities for serious literature? Are written depictions of bodies and their functions inherently distasteful? Are Haya Ester's descriptions distasteful? A program could include readings on women's bodies as portrayed in women's fiction and poetry (perhaps briefly contrasted with their portrayal in men's fiction and poetry) as well as readings from essayists and scholars on cultural attitudes toward women's bodies.

Shrinking

Ruth Almog

"Why you doing that, Miss Avigail?" said Mrs. Rabinowitz.

Avigail—who was hunched over, whispering, "Pssst, pssst," and coaxing Goliath to come and take the chicken leg with the clipped toenails from her hands—stood up and turned around.

The downstairs neighbor stood in the courtyard entrance: a small, heavy woman on high heels, the flabby white skin of her double chin quivering on her neck.

Avigail smiled at her and said, "What do you want, Ida?"

"Ida?" shrieked Mrs. Rabinowitz. "Since when am I Ida to you?"

Avigail smiled and said nothing.

"Stop smiling like that."

"Sorry, Mrs. Rabinowitz," Avigail said calmly.

"A thousand times I tell you to stop with this!" she complained.

"With what?" Avigail asked in surprise.

Ruth Almog was born in 1936 in Petah Tikvah to an Orthodox family, and she attended a teachers' college and the Hebrew University of Jerusalem. She has taught literature and philosophy, and is the author of novels, short stories, and children's books. Since 1967, she has been a regular contributor to the literary section of *Ha'aretz*, Israel's leading daily newspaper. She has won prizes for her children's literature and was also awarded the Brenner Prize for her novel *Roots of Light*.

"With cats! You bring to our courtyard cats from the whole city."

"So what? Why does it bother you?" Avigail asked.

"It brings dirt."

"Nonsense. Cats are very clean animals."

"But, Miss Avigail, it's scary to take out the garbage! When you get there, they jump."

"That's because the neighbors don't bother to close the door. That's not my fault."

"I hate them! I don't want them here!" yelled Mrs. Rabinowitz.

"Ida," Avigail said, "you know there are lots of mice here. Especially you, who live on the ground floor, should be interested in having cats around. Imagine if the mice started coming into your house. Don't you think it's better that the cats eat them?"

Mrs. Rabinowitz looked at her with undisguised hatred and said slowly, "So long as you give them food, they won't eat mice. I'll tell in the municipality that they should put poison here. Also your cats will die."

Avigail was alarmed and said in a whisper, "No, Ida, please don't do that."

"Yes. Tomorrow in the morning I go to the municipality. You know that every night the cats cry and don't let me sleep."

"That's a lie, a crude lie. This is not their mating season. They only cry when they're in heat."

"What is this 'in heat'?" Mrs. Rabinowitz asked irritably.

"In heat, Ida, you don't know what that is? That's when their time comes to couple. Do you know what coupling is? That's making love, Ida. They're crying out of pleasure, from a lot of pleasure."

Mrs. Rabinowitz was totally red. It seemed to Avigail that even her chubby, short arms were blushing. For a moment Avigail thought: She's going to have a heart attack. But Mrs. Rabinowitz pulled herself together and said, "You should be locked up, you crazy nut," and turned to leave.

"Hey, Ida, wait a minute," Avigail called after her. "I want to show you something."

Mrs. Rabinowitz hesitated for a minute, but her curiosity was piqued, and, in tense, agitated anticipation, she turned around and stared at Avigail.

"What do you want?" she asked.

"Look, do you see that beautiful black cat? That is the biggest male in the neighborhood, his name is Goliath. Look at how gorgeous his fur is. In the season of love he chases all his competitors away from the area. Look at that redhead, so sad, always gloomy. His name is Job, and I love him very much. And look at that gray one, a coquette. Look how soft and pampered she is? Don't you think they're sweet? And you want to kill them? Killing is all you have in your head. They don't do any harm, Ida. They're not at all like people."

Avigail, swept up in her emotions, knew she'd lost, because Mrs. Rabinowitz hadn't stayed to hear Avigail's song of praise to the cats. She had left with a demonstrative show of bad manners, her little heavy body wobbling on short legs, her pointed high heels tapping.

How cruel, Avigail thought bitterly. She threw the cats the food scraps she'd wrapped in newspaper and then crumpled the paper into a little ball in her fist and went to throw it in the garbage can. When she reached the gate, she saw Mrs. Rabinowitz waiting for her. The little woman lifted her hand and shook a threatening finger at her, "I'll tell about you to tenants' committee, you hear? You should be locked up in a mental hospital, you crazy nut."

Avigail looked at her and said, "You don't know how to put on rouge, Ida. You've made your whole face red and you've also put on too much powder."

"What?" Mrs. Rabinowitz flinched. "What do you say?"

"I said that you have to learn to put on makeup. Your lipstick is disgusting."

Along the way, Avigail entered a supermarket and bought several items. While waiting on line, she saw a little round container in the shopping cart of the woman ahead of her. She turned to the woman and asked, "What is that? Something new?"

"Yes. It's a cheese delicacy," the woman said.

"Any good?" Avigail asked.

"It's a matter of taste," the woman said.

Avigail asked her to watch her cart and went to get two containers. When she returned, she said to the woman, "I decided to try it," but the woman didn't answer.

From the store, Avigail proceeded to her father's house. She opened the door with her key. From outside she could hear the television. She thought nervously: Why does he play it so loudly? I can't stand the noise.

In the entrance hall, Rex, the shepherd dog, approached her and sniffed her basket.

"This isn't for you," she told him.

From the back of the room, her father's voice called: "Avigail?"

"One minute," she yelled and went into the kitchen to unload the basket. On the marble counter, cups and plates were piled and she thought: What filth. He always leaves me all the work.

She took the food out of the basket and opened the refrigerator. A bad smell flooded the kitchen and she hurried to put the food inside and close the door. Next she washed the dishes, and when she was finished she scrubbed the marble counter with cleanser. The strong smell made her sneeze. She opened the window and gagged. Everything is always closed here, how does he stand it? She looked at the floor and said to herself: I'll wash the floor tomorrow and I'll also defrost the fridge. When she went into the living room her father said to her, "Shhh ... don't bother me."

He sat in an armchair facing the blaring television. Newspapers and magazines were strewn on the rug at his feet. Avigail bent down to pick them up.

"You're bothering me," her father said. Then when she was about to leave the room, he said, without taking his eyes off the screen, "Did you bring *HaOlam Hazeh*[1]?"

"Afterwards, when I go out with Rex," she answered.

"Good, good, be quiet now," he concluded irritably.

Avigail brought the newspapers to the kitchen, folded them carefully and put them in a corner on a tall pile of old newspapers. Afterwards she went into the bathroom and started to clean the sink. The bathroom smelled terribly. The crevices between the cracked ceramic tiles were black. She opened the window and sprayed a bit of lavender spray. But she immediately started to cough and she

1. A newspaper whose name means "this world."

thought: This isn't good for me, and she went out and closed the door behind her.

The dog followed her into the kitchen, wagging his tail and rubbing against her leg.

"You want to go out?" she said to him. She got his leash and collar, tied it around his neck, peeked into the living room and said, "I'm going out with Rex for a while."

"You're always bothering me," her father said, then called after her, "and don't forget to buy *HaOlam Hazeh*."

Rex was old and heavy. He walked haltingly next to her on short, thin legs, his tongue hanging out. Avigail said to him, "You poor thing. Summers are hard for you, aren't they?"

She thought, sadly, that he was old and sick and maybe it would be necessary to kill him so that he wouldn't suffer. On the way she met Mr. Mayer, from her building, who said, "Listen, Mrs. Rabinowitz is complaining about you, about the cats, you know."

"So what do you suggest?" she asked.

"I really don't know," he said uncomfortably. "It doesn't bother me, but one must be considerate of her."

"She's just a pain in the neck," Avigail said rudely. "Tell her to bug off."

Soon this vacation will be over, Avigail thought, and afterwards summer will be over, and then another year and I'll be able to resign. If I don't find a position in another school, I'll quit. The new principal is getting on my nerves. She doesn't know a thing about education. When she thought about it, she felt as if she were choking, and she stopped a minute to catch her breath.

It was very hot and the summer days were unbearably long.

When she got back, she prepared dinner for her father and called him to the kitchen to eat. On the kitchen porch, she put a little dog food in a bowl for Rex.

"Come eat," she yelled, "the flies will come."

Her father came into the kitchen. "I've told you a thousand times not to bother me when I'm watching TV," he complained. Avigail didn't answer. She stood next to the door and observed him as he ate. He chewed loudly, and when he finished, he began to make a series of sucking sounds. Avigail couldn't take it anymore and said, "I'm going. Would you like roast chicken tomorrow?"

"Whatever. It doesn't matter," he said.

"Don't forget to let Rex out before you go to sleep."

"Where are you going?"

"To a movie, in the museum. Want to come?"

"No, I can't stand the air-conditioning."

"Should I stop at the library and exchange your book?"

"I haven't finished it yet, maybe tomorrow."

She went over to him and bent down to kiss him, but his smell repulsed her. As he hadn't even bothered to pick up his head, she immediately straightened up, controlling the nausea which gripped her.

"Don't wear that shirt again," she said. "Tomorrow I'll take it with everything else to the laundry."

"I stink, eh?" he said and in his eyes lurked a glimmer of mischief.

"A little," she said.

"I smell from old age, not from perspiration. Nothing can change that."

"Take a shower," she told him. "And you haven't shaved today. You look totally neglected."

"For whom should I shower and shave? I have no strength."

"You must. You can't go on like this."

"Why? For whom?"

"For me," she said. "Aren't I a person?"

When the lights went on in the little auditorium, Avigail remained in her seat for another few minutes. Then, exhausted, she went up the stairs leading to the entrance hall. Unlike those who lingered in the museum, she went directly to the big stone plaza outside. The bright light which flooded the white plaza during the day was replaced by the pleasant ash color of twilight, and only in the sky was there the usual rosy glow. The heat had abated a bit and a cool breeze blew, mixed with trails of dust. Avigail sat down on the low stone wall on the edge of the plaza. Opposite her a man wearing red pants approached. She heard him speaking. She looked at him for a minute, and then she averted her eyes and stared in the opposite direction. But the man stood in front of her and began reciting verses in Russian. Against her will, she turned to look at him. His arms sliced the air with sharp and aggressive gestures. Maybe he's Pushkin, she thought. There was an aura of anger around the man and she was afraid to breathe.

When he finished, he stood on his tiptoes like a ballet dancer and bowed deeply, accompanying the bow with a sweeping gesture of his hand. When he straightened up, Avigail clapped and called "Bravo!" In her heart, she wondered: What am I doing? Have I gone crazy?

But the man just smiled a childish smile at her and the aura of anger vanished. Light shone in his face. He bowed again, and then he moved on, starting a new recitation in front of two women who were walking toward him from the museum. They turned away and quickly passed him. The man turned around and smashed the air with a clenched fist. The two women came and sat near Avigail on the low stone wall.

"He's crazy," one of them said and the other one said, "Loneliness is what makes them go crazy like that."

Avigail inched over little by little, until she sat next to the two women. She listened to their conversation and said, "An amazing film, isn't it?" One woman nodded her head and the other one, who sat next to her, turned, flashed her a sharp look and immediately turned her back. She said to her friend, "The children's performances were superb."

Avigail said, "Did you notice that there was almost no dialogue in the film? So few words and so much power."

The woman who had turned her back didn't bother to look at her, but the other woman said, "Yes, now that you mention it."

"Japanese cinema is great," Avigail said, "Kurosowa—" but the woman next to her had already gotten up, her friend in tow, and Avigail's words hung in the air. She followed them with her eyes and saw that they had gone to sit somewhere else.

On the nearby library stairs, a gaunt young woman with a strained, depressed face, descended, holding a small dog in her arms. Avigail's face lit up, and she waved and motioned to her to come over. The gaunt woman, wearing a long black dress, came over to Avigail. With a friendly look she said, "Hello. How are you?"

"What a cutie!" Avigail said, "a Yorkshire?"

"Yes," the woman said and patted him, "a sweet and spoiled Yorkshire."

But when Avigail wanted to pat the small puppy with a pink velvet bow-tie pinned to his forehead, the woman backed off and blurted out, "No, no. He bites. He's bad-tempered and a grouch."

"Like Heathcliff," said Avigail. "He was also from Yorkshire. I would like to visit there once, the Brontë family house."

"Yes," said the gaunt woman. "It's really amazing, isn't it? What they were able to produce out of their terrible loneliness, those sisters. When you think about that remote place and how they grew up in the shadow of death, and also take into account the conservative society they lived in, it's definitely astounding."

Avigail gestured toward the dog and asked, "What's his name?"

"Yambus," said the gaunt woman. She then looked around and said, "Perhaps you've seen my husband?"

"No," Avigail said, but exactly at that moment she noticed a tall, heavy man dressed in a white shirt and black tie, coming toward them from the road. "There he is!" she shouted and pointed to him.

The man came over to them, greeted Avigail with a smile and hugged the woman in his arms. The gaunt woman was almost completely enveloped in his embrace. When she extricated herself, the dog stretched his head toward the man and extended his two front paws to touch him.

"Look, look," shrieked Avigail. "How he loves him! You have other dogs, right?"

"Four more," said the man.

The puppy, who was in the woman's arms, wriggled and stretched toward the man, and she handed him over. The man took the puppy lovingly, lifted him up high and kissed him on the mouth.

"Ha, ha," giggled Avigail.

"Come," the man said to the gaunt woman. "I'm parked illegally."

Together the two of them went toward the road, and the man, who was holding the puppy in one arm, put his other arm around the gaunt woman. Her long black dress trailed after her. Avigail watched the two of them lovingly, almost longingly. Like a ball of wool, she said to herself. I must buy him a beautiful blue ribbon, not of velvet but of grosgrain....

A young man walked toward the museum from the road. He passed her, and Avigail looked at him quizzically. She debated as to whether it was in fact him, and she followed him with her eyes. The man approached the cashier and Avigail thought: It's too late. The second performance started a while ago. Then she saw him returning. He walked slowly, and his glance chanced upon her. She said, "Eli?"

"Hello, my teacher," he said surprised.

"Hello, Eli, how are you?" she asked with a trembling heart.

"Thank you, my teacher," he answered. "I almost didn't recognize you."

"My teacher!" Avigail blurted out, pronouncing the words with scorn. "You must be a father to older children by now. What happened? Did you forget my name?"

"Avigail," he said with a trace of shyness.

"So what are you doing?" Avigail asked.

"I'm a lawyer. Until recently, I worked for someone. I've just opened my own office."

"And how is it going?"

"It's going okay. There is actually a lot of work. Even too much work."

"And how many kids do you have?" Avigail asked.

"None, and no wife either. I'm divorced."

"I'm sorry to hear that," Avigail said.

"Can I sit for a bit?" he asked.

"Please, please," Avigail asked excitedly.

When he sat next to her, he looked at her for a minute and then said, "Are you still teaching?"

"Indeed, yes. Is there a choice?"

"Why? Don't you love the profession?"

"I love it. I actually do love it. But it isn't the same. Everything's changed.... Today one only works for the money and the vacations. Not out of love."

"And you're here alone?"

"I was at a movie, an amazing movie. It's worth your while to see it. I think I'll see it again."

"I also wanted to see it, but I came too late."

"So what? Go another time."

"Maybe you'll join me?" he asked.

Now Avigail sensed it coming, like the fragrance of a young spring blossom. Her throat constricted and she began to breathe heavily.

I can control this, she thought, I have to calm myself and it will pass.

The young man pressed, "So what do you say?"

"We'll see. Perhaps next week," she spoke with difficulty.

"Do you remember?" he said. "You liked me then, when I was your student," and when she didn't answer, he demurred, "In any case, I thought so."

Avigail didn't answer. In her imagination she could clearly see that awesome picture. The beautiful Japanese woman stretched nude on the bed in the cabin of the riverboat. How beautiful she was, she thought.

"You know," she said, "it is a movie in which almost nothing happens, but you are not bored for a minute. There is such tension."

"How have you managed on your own for so many years?" he asked. "I find the loneliness very hard to bear."

Avigail looked at his hands resting on his knees. The scars on them had whitened in the dark, and she said, "A minute ago it was still light and now it's already totally dark. Night falls so quickly."

"I got divorced two months ago," he said "and that's not a long time to be alone, is it? But it's very difficult for me."

"There are such beautiful people among the Japanese," Avigail said. "The woman in the film, I can't forget her face."

"I go to a movie almost every night, so as not to stay at home alone. But I hate to go by myself."

"You must see this movie, it's just amazing," she said.

"Promise me that you'll come with me," he said and smiled at her in the darkness.

Avigail got up, "I must go now. It's already late for me."

"But no one is waiting for you at home," he said in a hard voice, "and it's summer vacation now, so you don't have any notebooks to correct."

"I must go to my father. He's waiting for me," she lied.

"Good-bye," he called after her, "and don't forget next week."

When she came to a place in the street where he couldn't see her, she stopped and leaned on a tree. Her whole body shook, and her already overtaxed lungs gasped for air. She heard the sound of heavy steps behind her, and she moved from her spot and began to walk quickly. Her hand searched in her purse until she found the inhaler; she put it in her mouth and inhaled while walking. It afforded her no relief, though, and the whole way she stumbled along, the inhaler attached to her mouth. At the entrance to the courtyard of her house, she stopped for a minute, and then she started climbing the stairs to her rooftop apartment. The higher she climbed, the hotter and more stifling it became, and when she opened the door of her apartment, a fiery blast of air engulfed her. Avigail didn't turn on the light but went right out to the porch and sat there, in her armchair in the dark. Slowly her breathing returned to normal and she relaxed. Then she opened her eyes and looked at the squares of light in the house opposite her. In one light square, she saw people sitting and watching television. On the table was a bowl of purple grapes. In a different square of darkness she could only see a bright, blue, blinking light.

All the heat from the whole day, she thought, is in the house, the roof should be whitewashed.

After a while she went into the room and turned on the air-conditioning. When the room had cooled down somewhat, she closed the doors and the windows, and put a record on the record player. She lay on the sofa and closed her eyes. When the singer sang the lyrics, "Now I understand what you tried to say to me / How you suffered for your sanity ... Vincent / The world was never meant for one as beautiful as you," tears poured from her eyes, and she said to herself: How beautiful, how beautiful.

When the song about Vincent was over, she got up, turned off the record player, put the record in its jacket, and returned it to its place. For a while she continued to sing the song about Vincent to herself, saying the pleasurable but terrible words, which always made her cry. Finally she got up, washed her face, and went out for a walk.

The streets were empty and dark. A soldier passed by and stopped next to a shop window. When she caught up to him, he started to walk next to her. He said something to her. He spoke quietly and she didn't understand. "Get lost," she told him. "You Medusa," he said insolently, almost spitting the word in her face. "Cyclops," she answered and laughed to herself as she thought that there wasn't a night when someone didn't bother her.

When she was back in her apartment she went to the drawer and took out the big album in which she had pasted all her class pictures. Avigail didn't have to look far. It was the first year. Her first year as a teacher, in a suburban area of the city, a neighborhood of little red-roofed houses with well-tended gardens, and on its outskirts, an immigrant neighborhood. She had only stayed a year there. It wasn't for her.

In the little photograph, Eli was all eyes. Surprised black eyes. Avigail thought: What a mistake he made when he said that I liked him. I had to control myself so as not to hug and kiss him. But all that freshness which he once had, it was almost all lost. The delightful smooth and taut skin was now marked by a certain roughness. How beautiful he had been, she thought, the nice black eyes ... and what sweet innocence. Avigail estimated: He is already thirty seven. He looks much younger.

She remembered. The day after Lag B'Omer she had entered the classroom. She immediately noticed that something was wrong. Eli's chair was empty, and the children's faces were solemn and grave. They were unusually quiet, unlike themselves. "Sit down," she said and read off their names. When she got to Eli's name, he was one of the last—Sha'ar, Eli Sha'ar—his neighbor, Irit, the girl at whose home he ate lunch every day, raised her hand. Irit said, "We were sitting around the campfire. Someone said, Let's see who has the guts to jump over the campfire. No one volunteered. Everyone was afraid. Only Eli got up and tried. He didn't succeed, teacher. He jumped right into the fire. He's in the hospital. He's covered with burns."

In the hospital she sat next to him. If she had allowed herself, she would have sat there all night. Without him her class was empty. His bandaged arms were placed on the white sheet, his bandaged chest was exposed. Avigail sat and suppressed her crying.

Eli's father said, "He won't be a violinist anymore. His hands are ruined."

Father Sha'ar's big dream. How had he phrased it when she'd made a home visit? "My Eli will be the second Paganini." And the child played and played, four and five hours a day. Out of love for his father he played. Avigail remembered the composition he had written for Mother's Day. She had kept it in the album in back of the class picture. Now she took it out carefully. "My mother is a doctor. She's a very busy woman. She works hard in the hospital, and she has a lot of rotations. I almost never see her. We have an arrangement with the neighbors, my father pays them money and I eat lunch there. My father also works hard. He only comes toward evening so I do all the shopping. My father leaves me a list every day of what to buy and also money. Father cooks the food for Sabbath. When Mother is not on duty, the three of us eat together. But that seldom happens. Mother's Day is the saddest day of the year for me. I always prepare something for Mother, a little surprise, a drawing or picture, but she is never home to receive it."

Avigail remembered how her heart had broken when she read the composition. She didn't know what grade to give. She didn't know how to explain to him that she couldn't give this composition a grade. Her heart went out to the child. She tried to give him all the love he was lacking, but she knew that it was impossible, that she was just a teacher. That was why she made home visits that year. The Ministry of Education did in fact require the visits, but her colleagues in the teachers' room had teased her. "You're green," they had said.

Even though Avigail made all the visits only in order to get to Eli's house, she had enjoyed them. Home visits changed a lot of things. The eighth grade students to whom she taught science had stopped standing on the hill after class. Before that, they used to ambush her when she'd walk home. They would stand on the red clay wall, yelling vulgar words at her and singing vulgar songs. She never understood why they did this. Wasn't she always in her plain brown army sandals (and still was today), and a simple blue skirt and white blouse (and still was today, most of the time)? Sometimes one of them would even throw stones. The stones never hurt her. She knew that they didn't intend to hit her, but she was afraid. Now when she remembered, she could hear them yelling and singing, "At midnight when the stars are bright, Avigail and Moshe are f---." Moshe was the gym teacher. Avigail had nothing to do with him. She didn't tell the principal. She was ashamed, and was sure that the fault lay with her. She also didn't tell anyone that she was unsuccessful in teaching eighth grade science. When she entered the class, the unruly behavior would begin and she would stand and wait until the students sat in their seats. She never yelled. Sometimes she would say quietly, "We have such an interesting topic today, isn't it a pity to miss the class?" But once someone shouted, "We want an explanation about sex," and afterwards she stopped saying that. Even after they finally sat in their places—the bully of the class would make them be quiet, order them to sit down—they would continue to make noise while she was explaining or drawing on the blackboard. But after she started the home visits, the number of students who gathered on the hill dwindled, until they finally stopped entirely and she breathed easier. Her class also became more disciplined, easier. Eventually there was only one violent child who couldn't control himself. After he burst into the class with a big stick, flailing wildly, she was forced to order his expulsion from school. "He's too dangerous," she said to the principal sadly.

As usual, her father was absorbed in watching television. Avigail entered the kitchen and unpacked the basket silently. The air in the kitchen was foul, heavy. Avigail opened the window and the porch door, and then went and peeked into the living room.

"Why is everything here always closed? One could suffocate here," she said.

"It doesn't bother me," her father said.

Avigail went inside and started lifting the blinds and opening the windows, one after the other, banging them angrily.

"Stop making noise!" her father called, and the dog followed with a sharp bark.

Avigail left the room and returned to the kitchen. She fried an omelet, made a salad, and after cleaning the small kitchen table, she set it.

"Come eat," she yelled.

"Don't bother me now. I'll eat later," her father answered from the room.

Avigail went and stood in the doorway, and said to him, "Flies will come."

"So cover everything," he said irritably.

"This place needs redecorating. It's really depressing here," she said in a coaxing tone.

"After I die," he said.

Avigail cleaned the bathroom and after she'd finished, her hands reeked of the disgusting smell of bleach. She washed them several times with soap, but the smell stubbornly clung to her hands. "I'm going," she called from the entrance. "Don't forget to take Rex out."

In the alley, the stench of summer greeted her. It's from the dead mice, she thought, and quickened her pace. When she reached the main road, the headlights from passing cars glowed in the haze and polluted air, dancing crazily in front of her eyes. While she waited by the crosswalk, the buses blew their poisonous exhaust fumes into her face. Tears choked her, as she thought: Hell, really hell. She decided to go down to the promenade to breathe a little fresh air. She really didn't like the ocean air, but she preferred the quiet, darkness, and light wind to the tumult, stench, and crowding.

Avigail walked toward the ocean. She went there often and would stand facing the ocean for a long time, her elbows on the damp, salty railing as she contemplated the setting sun, the bathers, the pink horizon. Along the way she passed the house of her university friend Rachel, and she decided to visit. She stopped in a nearby store and bought several red sugar-coated chicks and chocolate cats' tongues as well as a bag of mixed toffees. Rachel's children were always happy when she came, and Rachel too greeted her warmly. But this time, for some reason she was tense. "A friend is coming any minute to photograph the children," she told her.

"How nice. Who?"

"Someone by the name of Akhsa, you don't know her. She's studying photography and wants to specialize in children's photography."

"Akhsa?" Avigail said. "I knew an Akhsa in our youth movement."

Akhsa burst into the house like a storm, loaded down with different cameras and out of breath. She unloaded her equipment, and then Rachel introduced them to each other.

Avigail looked at Akhsa with a smile, waved her hand and called gleefully, "Long live progressive socialism!"

"Are you crazy?" asked Rachel.

"Not at all. Akhsa knows exactly what I mean. What? You don't remember me? We were fellow idealists. Mookie was your counselor, right? I don't forget a thing. A photographic memory. You were the most beautiful girl in our youth movement, and you had a gorgeous embroidered Russian blouse. With such an unusual name, no one could ignore you. Do you remember when we went to put up posters? Those were the days! Ideals and struggle and fulfillment. Do you remember that harvest in Tel Yosef? Our hands got all blistered. But you dodged it, you had delicate hands. You went to shepherd the flock on the Gilboa with that handsome kibbutznik. His name was Motke. I don't forget a thing."

Akhsa gave her a cold and impatient stare. "I don't remember. I'm sorry," she said.

"It doesn't matter. Who was I then? A scrawny little girl. But after so many years, it's nice to meet with a sister to the struggle. You were very active then and you continued on. You went to the *Nahal*,[2] right? And when you came back to the city, you continued to work in the commune. Do you remember the play at the Hanukkah party—"

"Enough of this nostalgic drivel," she interrupted. "I've come here to work. I don't have time for this nonsense. It was over a long time ago. I've already forgotten. Life has changed." And to Rachel she said, "Bring the kids, I have no time."

Avigail said, "Okay, okay, but you needn't be so rude. I just thought—"

"It doesn't matter what you thought. I'm in a rush. I told you, I have no time."

Rachel called the children and Akhsa yelled, "Bring toys, spread them on the rug, and play."

The two children dragged the box of toys and emptied its contents on the rug.

One of the boys said, "What do you want us to play?"

---

2. *Nahal*—the Hebrew acronym for Pioneering Combat Unit.

"It doesn't matter," she said, "play and don't pay me any attention."

"And I thought ..." Avigail said, and the unfinished sentence, full of disappointment, hung oppressively in the air. Avigail looked at Rachel, searching her face for some approval, but Rachel avoided her eye.

And again Avigail said, "What can I say? I thought that sisterhood is something that lasts."

"You're disturbing my concentration," Akhsa said. "Move away from there, I don't need you in the frame."

"Why are you so nervous? One might think—"

"Think what you will, I couldn't care less. Just don't bother me. I need to do my work."

"Don't worry," Avigail said, "I'm just leaving."

At the door she said to Rachel," Can you believe it? I would never have expected it."

"I'm sorry," Rachel told her, "We scheduled this job and she's uptight."

"Uptight, really?" Avigail said and she turned and left.

On her way down she remembered that she hadn't given the children the candies she'd bought for them.

Avigail walked to the promenade as usual and leaned on the railing and stared at the ocean. The metal bar was cold and sticky. Across from her stretched an endless amorphous blanket of darkness, and only on the horizon could clear skies be seen.

A man stood next to her, and Avigail said aloud, "For heaven sakes, it's absolutely impossible to be alone for a minute in this damn city!"

The man didn't answer but he also didn't move from his spot.

"Get out of here," she said without turning around, "I want to be alone."

"You're not gonna tell me where to stand. This is not your private property."

"But there's so much room. Why must you stand here?"

"I'll stand wherever I want," he told her.

Let him drop dead, she thought to herself, and she moved away. Avigail walked northward, and when she got to London Square she went up the stairs toward Yarkon Street. On the bench under the street lamp, two men sat embracing each other, and when she passed them, she averted her glance and walked very erect and tense. Now she advanced along Yarkon Street until she reached an elegant new hotel. She hesitated momentarily and then walked by the doorman through the large, heavy glass doors and went inside. Scattered throughout the main lobby were couches upholstered in red velvet, and on the walls were displays of silver and ceramics. It was chilly inside, almost cold. Tourists came and went, and girls in shorts or bathing suits stood in a little group and spoke English loudly. Avigail sat on one of the soft couches, took out cigarettes from her bag and poked around looking for a lighter. Her hand touched the smooth cellophane wrapper of the chocolate cats' tongues, and she was momentarily bitter. She sat for a while and smoked. She saw a waiter pass by holding a tray of drinks and sparkling tall glasses. I'm thirsty, she thought. Just then she heard a man say, "Hey. What are you doing here?" A teacher, a colleague. Avigail smiled at him and said, "Just sitting, escaping from the heat. And you?"

"Looking for relatives," he said, waved, and walked toward an old couple.

Avigail stubbed out her cigarette in the metal ashtray next to the couch, got up and left, again going through the heavy doors. The doorman greeted her with a nod.

And again that terrible heat which was suspended high up in the stairwell and under the roof. Avigail turned on the air-conditioner and stood outside in the dark until the room cooled down. In a square of light opposite her, people sat and watched television. On the table was a large bottle of Coca Cola, glasses, and a bowl of grapes. On the floor below, a blue light blinked in a black square.

Avigail went inside, closed the windows and the doors and put on a record. This time she chose Schubert's Trio Opus 100. She lay on the sofa and listened, waiting for the staccato part she loved. But the telephone suddenly rang.

"You're never home," he said. "I've called many times."

"Who is this?" she asked, not recognizing the voice.

"Eli. Eli Sha'ar. Have you forgotten that you promised to come with me to a movie at the museum?"

"I didn't promise anything," she answered.

"So what do you think?"

"No, I don't feel like it. It's too fresh in my memory."

"So let's see a different movie."

What does he want from me? she thought, and she didn't answer right away.

He said, "I'm dying to go to a movie and I don't feel like going alone."

"No," Avigail said. "I'm busy."

"You're not busy. You're just avoiding me. You're just not interested in my company."

Avigail fell into the trap. "No. Not at all. I'm really busy tonight. How about coming over tomorrow evening for a cup of coffee?"

"What time?"

"Seven thirty?"

"Seven thirty."

When she replaced the receiver, she thought: Why on earth did I invite him? In the meanwhile she'd missed her beloved staccato part. She picked up the needle and turned off the record player. "To hell with it!" she said aloud.

Avigail went to the bathroom and looked in the mirror. Wrinkles, she thought. I'm covered with wrinkles. She took a tweezers out of a small drawer on top of the sink and started to tweeze her eyebrows. The tweezed skin became red and looked infected. Avigail rubbed it with cream. Then she tweezed her mustache. The way I look, she thought, and asked herself once more: Why did I invite him?

Before she went to sleep, she read in bed for a while.

"Come in, come in," she said and gestured with her hands toward the living room.

Eli entered and looked around. "It's nice here." he said. "So many books! You even have a piano. Do you play?"

"Not any more. I used to."

Eli picked up the heavy piano cover and fingered one of the keys.

"My father dreamt that I would be a second Paganini," he said and slid the flattened palm of his hand on the keys, producing a discordant glissando.

"I always thought that you jumped into the campfire on purpose," Avigail said.

"There is something to that," Eli said. "Sometimes I'm sure of it."

"You really didn't want to be a violinist."

"No, it was too difficult. To practice every single day for so many hours and I had so little talent." Avigail was silent and he said, "He died, you know."

"Who?"

"My father, two years ago. Cancer."

"I'm sorry," she said.

Avigail wanted to ask about his mother but she didn't dare.

"Play something for me," he said to her.

"Oh no. Impossible. The piano isn't tuned and there are several broken keys. I haven't played in years."

"Too bad ..." he said.

"Come, let's go into the kitchen. I prepared a light supper for us."

His face lit up and he said, "That's really nice of you."

They ate in silence. But suddenly he said, "My wife never prepared supper for me. Since childhood, I've had to fend for myself. It's nice when someone prepares for you."

He finished and put his knife and fork sideways on the plate.

"It's warm," she said. "Let's go to the other room."

When they were seated, she asked, "Why did you get divorced?"

"It didn't work. I guess I just didn't have a model, you understand."

"No," she said, "I don't understand."

"A model of marriage, I mean. You know, don't you, that my mother left us."

"For good?"

"Yes, in the end, she left for good. She went to America. It wasn't good for her here."

"And you haven't seen her since then?"

"I went several times. But she wasn't enthusiastic. She married there, and she had children with him. I also went once with my wife. I don't know why. It didn't work out. But it's still fresh, and sometimes I miss her. My wife I mean."

"It's sad," she said.

Suddenly he got up and said, "I'm going." He almost ran away. And she thought, I must have disappointed him.

The Schubert was still on the record player. Avigail turned it on and put the needle down carefully. As always she waited for the movement she loved. The section of awesome staccato sounds. The expectation which was translated into music filled her with tense pleasure. She lay down, her arms and legs very taut, and her whole body penetrated by an infinite sweetness which at times was too heavy to contain. At the end came that section, and she cried silently, the locked mass of pain submitting to the music, blending within her. Her whole body ached from the internal collapse which is in the total involvement with pain. Afterwards there was a moment of terrible silence, which was abruptly interrupted by the scratching noise of the needle on the spinning record. The scratching grated on her nerves and her tense body loosened up. Now she could retreat from the pain and press the safety latch—a gun unable to shoot.

She lay there like that for a while, the scratchy needle singeing her empty brain, and afterwards, when she realized that her strength had returned, she got up and turned off the record player. She went out to the dark porch, leaned on the railing, moist from dew, and breathed deeply, but the air was turbid, heavy.

When the phone rang she awoke with a start. She turned on the light and looked at the clock, and saw that it was two in the morning. She picked up the receiver without saying anything. Eli said, "I'm sorry that I rushed off like that. I want to apologize. Let's go to a movie tomorrow."

"You woke me," she said.

"I'm sorry. I couldn't fall asleep. I had to talk to someone."

"It's all right," she said.

"So we'll go."

"I don't know now. Call tomorrow, okay?"

"No. You're never home. I already know. You'll avoid me. Let's set a time now."

"For which showing?"

"The second. I work late."

"Okay. I'll wait downstairs at a quarter to nine."

"Goodnight," she said, and hung up.

For a long time afterwards she lay awake. Before she fell asleep she thought: Tomorrow I'll go to the cosmetician.

The cosmetician poured strips of wax on her legs, also under her arms. The pores of her skin opened in the warm steam of the chamomile essence and a white mask. Afterwards she went to the hairdresser. From the hairdresser she went to a clothing store and bought herself a new, flowery, young-looking dress. But when she stood in the store and looked into the mirror she thought: The dress is beautiful, but I'm not. And when she finally went home to rest a bit, she said to herself: Nothing can help me any more. For a moment she longed to rip her new dress, mess up her hairdo, scratch her hot face. But she immediately got hold of herself: she closed her eyes and listened to her breathing until she regained the composure at which she excelled.

In the evening, when he came toward her—as she stood under the street lamp and allowed herself to feel a little like a high school student—he said, "You look good. You changed your hairstyle. It suits you."

The movie bored her. Despite the air-conditioning she perspired continuously. She was afraid to put her arm on the armrest, and she sat all hunched up. Slowly her lungs constricted, and she began to breathe heavily.

"I must go out," she whispered to him. "I'm choking." And she got up and pushed through the audience, careful not to step on anyone's feet and stumbling in the dark until she was outside. She took out the inhaler from her bag and put it in her mouth.

"Come," Eli said suddenly, "I'll take you to the hospital, to the emergency room."

She hadn't noticed his arrival.

"It isn't necessary," she said. "It'll pass right away."

Eli brought her home in his car, and she got out of the car and said, "I'm sorry. I ruined the evening for you."

He didn't come inside after her. He immediately started the engine and left.

In the kitchen she poured herself a glass of seltzer and swallowed a tranquilizer. She lay down and quickly fell asleep.

As usual, her father was watching television.

"I brought you grilled chicken for the Sabbath," she told him, peeking into the bleak and stuffy living room. As always it smelled of mold.

"Shh, don't bother me," he said.

"What's this? You're learning French?" she asked, surprised.

"Yes, and how. I study all the time. Don't bother me."

Avigail put the chicken in the refrigerator. It reeked, and she thought that she must defrost and clean it, but she had absolutely no desire to do so now.

"If you don't need me, then I'm going," she told her father.

"I don't need you, I don't need you," he grumbled.

Along the way she plucked light purple lantana flowers from one of the hedges. She went up to her friend Stella and presented them to her.

Stella said, "You can never come without bringing something."

Avigail giggled, "I just plucked these from the hedge outside."

Stella put the flowers in a vase and said, "I actually like their pungent odor. But they wilt quickly."

"Perhaps you have an interesting book for me?" Avigail asked.

"No," Stella said. "I have nothing new. Let's go to a café for a while."

"All right," Avigail agreed.

Stella showered and dressed, and when she appeared, Avigail whistled and said, "Some broad!"

"You should take lessons from me," she said.

When they sat in the café, watching the passersby and drinking milkshakes through thick straws, Avram, Rachel's husband, passed by with the children. Avigail called them and gave them the red sugar-coated chicks. Avram said to her, "I heard what happened. I'm sorry I wasn't there. She would have gotten it from me, but good."

"Nonsense," Avigail said. "I've already forgotten."

Stella sat leaning back, her long, tanned feet stretched out in front of her. Avram fixed his eyes on them and said, "I can't stand her, that Akhsa."

"I know. Rachel told me," Avigail said and saw how Avram's eyes wandered over Stella's body. Her blouse was open, showing her cleavage, and through the thin fabric, her nipples were conspicuous.

"Come and visit," Avram said and walked quickly after the two boys who were already further ahead.

"Akhsa, the beauty from the youth movement?"

"She became a photographer in her old age," said Avigail. "She is a year older than I am."

"Stop thinking of yourself as old and then you won't look old," Stella said. "Take it from me."

Avigail looked at her and said, "You've got guts. I'm not like that."

"Then the time has come for you to change."

"Why?" Avigail asked.

"So that you'll catch yourself a guy."

"I'm not interested," Avigail said. "I don't need a guy who will snore at night and stain the pillow case with his oily hair."

"It's your loss," Stella said.

"No," said Avigail aggressively, "it's my gain."

In her heart she thought that two weeks had passed since she'd gone with Eli to that movie and he hadn't called. Somehow she knew that he hadn't forgiven her and that he was just punishing her.

That night—and this time it was three o'clock in the morning—he woke her from sleep.

"Did I wake you?" he said to her.

"What do you think?" she retorted as though angry.

"I can't sleep. I would come to you now but you surely wouldn't receive me at this hour."

"You're not mistaken," she said dryly.

"I'll come tomorrow, okay? In the evening, at eight?"

What does he want from me, she thought. I'll call him tomorrow morning and cancel. I don't want him to come.

Avigail made a real effort this time. She prepared three types of salads and bought Greek olives and pickles and a variety of cheeses in the *shuk*.[3] Eli ate with relish and she was full of joy.

"What a pleasure," he said and she felt so grateful that for a moment she put her hand on his white scarred palm. She immediately withdrew it in confusion.

"Come, let's go somewhere," he suggested. "In the summer I love getting out of town at night."

Avigail was glad. She thought: It's better than sitting and being afraid all the time.

On the highway the car accelerated, and Avigail saw that the speedometer registered ninety kilometers per hour. "Don't drive so fast," she told him.

"Are you afraid?" he asked in a laughing voice, and accelerated even more.

"This is dangerous," she said quietly, but he heard and slowed down.

"I'm an excellent driver, you needn't be afraid," he said.

After a while he went off the main road and drove on a dusty road toward the ocean until they reached a rocky low plateau. "Let's go see the ocean," he said and got out. Avigail went after him, her feet leaden with fear. She couldn't remember ever having been so afraid. She took out the inhaler and put it in her mouth.

"What's the matter?" he asked.

"I have asthma, don't you remember?"

He didn't answer and she said, "Ocean air isn't good for me."

"So why do you live in Tel Aviv?" he asked rudely. "You should have lived in Arad. I'm sure they're lacking teachers there."

"Because of my father," she said, totally tensed up, a wheezing sound in her breathing.

---

3. *Shuk*—market.

Eli said, "Listen."

Avigail didn't answer. She, too, heard the roar of the ocean, but she couldn't enjoy it.

She wanted to return to the car and go home, but she was afraid to insult him and she remained silent.

"How I love the ocean," he said.

A thin sliver of a moon hung in the middle of the darkness, cold and sparkling.

Suddenly he touched her arm and said, "Come, let's go back."

All the way back, she prattled obsessively, talking mostly about politics, infusing protest and bitterness in her attacks on the government, members of Knesset, corruption, theft, and the terrible social situation.

When she finally got home, she closed the door after her and leaned on it, exhausted. She closed her eyes and groaned out loud. I can't anymore, she thought. I don't want to see him anymore.

"Take Rex out," her father said. "And on the way exchange a book for me at the library. Suspense or spy stories, if they have any."

When she returned, she gave Rex dog food in his bowl on the porch. Her father, who was watching television as usual, suddenly called, "Tomorrow the school year starts, doesn't it?"

Avigail said, "Yes. The summer vacation is finally over."

"You should have gone abroad, like I told you; then you wouldn't have been so bored."

"Who said I was bored?"

"Oh, well, never mind," he said. "Are you going already?" and when she nodded her head, he said, "Then I wish you a good year and good luck."

Late at night, when she was sitting and preparing her lesson for the first day of the new year, Eli called.

"I wanted to wish you a successful year of work," he said.

"Thank you," she said, surprised. "Nice that you thought of it."

And then, against her will, she added, "I thought you had forgotten me."

"I was in the reserves. Three weeks," he said, and she noticed something in his tone that made her not believe him. "What are you doing?" he asked.

"Preparing for tomorrow. Lesson plans."

"After so many years you still prepare."

"You'd be surprised," she said.

The next day he called to see how the first day went and he said, "If you invite me for supper, I'll gladly come."

"Please do," she said, and she didn't know whether to rejoice or regret. But when he arrived, she had difficulty containing the happiness which swelled in her.

She told him, "I didn't have a chance to prepare anything. I had a very full day and I'm still not used to it. After school I went to my father and the day passed too quickly. Sit in the living room and watch television, and I'll be in the kitchen. It won't take long."

When they ate, he said, "I don't like eating alone. It is always so pleasant here."

"You need to find a girl and get married," Avigail said to him merrily.

"Perhaps you'll marry me. It'll be nice for us together, I'm sure," he said and smiled.

Avigail said, "Please don't tease me."

"God forbid, I'm serious."

"Nonsense," she said.

"No, no," he said. "You don't understand. I'm totally serious."

"I could be your mother," she said argumentatively.

"So what? If anything, that's a reason for and not a reason against."

"I don't have a sense of humor, Eli, so there's no point in telling me jokes."

"Avigail, I'm totally serious."

Avigail got up, and standing very erect said, "Enough of this." They watched the movie on TV together, and when it was over, Avigail said, "It's late, I have to get up early tomorrow."

She accompanied him to the door, and at the threshold, he said to her, "Thanks for the meal" and leaned over and kissed her on the cheek. She almost closed her eyes to savor the sweetness and calm which touched her, but she caught herself just in time and said to him, "Don't come anymore."

"What?" he asked in confusion.

"Don't come anymore, I said."

"If you can tell me why, I won't come."

"I can't say why. Just like that."

"I'm not willing to accept that as an answer."

"I don't owe you any explanation."

"I think you do. In light of the situation that has developed, I think that you definitely owe me some sort of explanation."

"There is no situation."

"Aren't we friends, Avigail?"

Avigail hesitated. She wanted to say, "Not any more," but she couldn't lie. "You don't have to be so afraid of me," he said and tried to hug her. But Avigail evaded him and said stubbornly, "I'm asking you not to come anymore."

"You don't enjoy my company?" he asked in a hurt tone.

And she hesitated again, and he said, "You can't fool me. I know that you're attracted to me."

"No! That's not so!" she shouted. "Now go and don't come again, do you hear?"

Eli turned and started going down the stairs. Midway he turned and said to her savagely, "I'll continue to come and bother you until you tell me why I can't come."

Avigail didn't answer and closed the door in his face.

The next day, suspecting that he'd come, she sat in a café with Stella. When Stella went home, she walked and walked until her strength gave out.

When he rang the doorbell she didn't open for him. When he phoned she didn't answer and she put down the receiver as soon as she recognized his voice. But one day he waited for her at the gate to her courtyard and when she passed by without stopping, he grabbed her arm and said to her, "What kind of behavior is this?" Avigail said, "You want to know. So I'll tell you. I hate you. I hate you and I don't want to ever see you again."

From the corner of her eye she saw Mrs. Rabinowitz standing on her porch looking at them. He stood and held her arm and looked at her with hard eyes. Avigail couldn't move and she said to him, "Leave me alone, please." But Eli didn't release her arm and he continued to glare at her. Avigail couldn't guess his thoughts and suddenly she felt it coming, like the fragrance of a young spring blossom. Her throat constricted and she began to breathe heavily. Eli noticed and let go of her arm. Now she had to take out the inhaler from the purse and put it in her mouth in front of him. But the attack came, strong and grunting. Her breath had a wheezing sound.

"Take me to the hospital," she said to him and when she collapsed next to him in the car, her head thrown back, her lungs contracted as they'd never been before, Eli said, "Calm down, Avigail. I won't come anymore. If this is what I cause, I won't come anymore. I'm sorry. I didn't read you correctly." And then immediately she felt a little better. Eli noticed that, stopped the car and parked on a street corner. He asked her, "Do you want to go home now?" and when they got back to the house he asked her, "Can I accompany you upstairs to see that everything is all right? I promise you I won't come again. You needn't worry." Avigail whispered. "All right," and when they left the car, she noticed that Mrs. Rabinowitz was standing on her porch and watching them.

Eli went up to Avigail's apartment with her, opened the door for her and asked if she wanted something. She told him where the medication was, and he brought it to her with a glass of water. She drank, swallowed the medicine, and sat in the armchair with her eyes closed.

After a while he asked her, "Do you feel better now?" and Avigail nodded her head, exhausted.

"Before I go I want to tell you something. I understand that I shouldn't come anymore, and I won't come. But I'm sorry about that. And I'm even sorrier that we didn't meet years earlier. Maybe then I could have taught you to love yourself a little more. Now it's too late for that, and it's such a shame. You deserve more. And there's something else I wanted to tell you, something I never told you. The hours you sat next to me in the hospital when I was a child were among the happiest of my life. I never forgot them." And when she didn't respond, he added, "You really gave me a lot of warmth that year."

"But apparently it wasn't enough, because you had to go and jump into the campfire."

"Right, it wasn't enough." He got up and said, "I'm going now, don't get up. I'll manage by myself."

Avigail finished grading the exams and got up from the desk. She took the chicken legs with the clipped toenails out of the refrigerator and wrapped them in newspaper. She stood downstairs in the yard and whispered, "Pssst, pssst" and immediately the cats began to crowd around. Goliath approached her and rubbed against her leg. The touch of his fur on her exposed leg was pleasant and she said to him, "You are so beautiful, Goliath." Avigail bent down and gave him one chicken leg. Goliath grabbed it and ran to a corner to eat quietly. The other cats waited patiently, looking at her with desire. She threw them the scraps from the newspaper and folded the paper between her fingers. Mrs. Rabinowitz stood some distance away and watched her. When Avigail turned toward the garbage cans, she called after her, "The young man doesn't come anymore, eh?" but Avigail didn't wait.

"I'll tell the municipality. I'll tell them to kill all your cats."

When Avigail left the yard, she saw Mrs. Rabinowitz waiting for her. "Tomorrow I go to the municipality," Mrs. Rabinowitz said with a smile.

"Go ahead, Ida, go ahead," Avigail said, and added, "You've smeared rouge on your whole face again."

On the way to her father, she met Rachel and the children.

"You haven't come to visit in a while," Rachel said.

"I'm afraid of your friend Akhsa," Avigail said.

"I'm sorry about what happened," Rachel said.

"Do you want candies?" Avigail asked the children gaily and took the bag of toffees from her purse and offered it to the older one. "Share them," she said.

The children said "thank you," and the older boy tore the plastic bag and took out two toffees.

"There's the trash can," Avigail told them. "Don't toss the

wrappers on the street."

"Come and visit," Rachel said and Avigail answered, "okay" and continued on her way.

When she stood in the darkened door, her father said, "Shhh, don't bother me."

"Now we go down the negative axis," the broadcaster said, and Avigail thought: So now he's studying mathematics.

Avigail washed the dishes which had piled up on the marble counter. From outside came a terribly sad wail. She looked out the window and saw a male cat using his teeth to hold a female cat by the scruff of her neck. On the porch, Rex led out an angry bark and the female cat freed herself and escaped.

Autumn has arrived, Avigail thought, and began to sing to herself quietly: "Now I understand what you tried to say to me ... Vincent / The world was never meant for one as beautiful as you."

1986

Translated by Felice Kahn Zisken

Questions for Discussion

1. What is Ruth Almog's attitude toward Avigail? Is there anything admirable or likable about the character? About any of the characters? How do these people symbolize Israel today?
2. Why does Avigail end the relationship with Eli? Ruth Almog seems to "blame" Avigail's personality for the break-up rather than Eli's actions. Do you agree? Is Avigail afraid of intimacy? (Consider the relationship with her father.) Does she want to remain single? Does the author imply in any way that Avigail's life as a spinster holds some advantage?
3. Avigail's father is particularly unpleasant, and Ruth Almog offers no hints that his character has ever differed substantially. How does his personality affect Avigail's life choices and her own personality? Why does she play the role of her father's

"enabler"? Is this a role which women adopt unthinkingly, or is Avigail unusual in caring for a monstrously selfish father? What is your experience in caring for those who are less than worthy?

4. At their first meeting as adults, Eli responds harshly when Avigail says she must go: "But no one is waiting for you at home." He here initiates a pattern of ignoring or minimizing Avigail's own personal needs. He calls her at two and at three in the morning (though neither one is a college student!), waits weeks between phone calls, probably lies to her about his service in the reserves, and drives extremely fast even after Avigail expresses displeasure. Yet he proposes marriage, is hurt when Avigail rejects his friendship, and seems genuine in his gratitude toward her. Why does he behave with so little consideration? Is he testing her? If so, why?
5. Avigail has strikingly low self-esteem. In the scene with her father, she asks, "Aren't I a person?"—and she implicitly understands that to her father she is not. In what other ways does Ruth Almog illustrate her character's lack of self-worth? In general, do women have lower self-esteem than men?
6. Avigail suffers from asthma and tells Eli that the ocean exacerbates her condition. Yet not only does she often go to the ocean by herself, but she smokes a cigarette in the hotel lobby. What accounts for her self-destructiveness? Discuss your personal experiences with chronic disease. (For instance, why do people with heart disease continue to eat salty or fatty foods?) Also, Avigail's asthma attacks are caused by emotional stress (rather than by, say, viral infections—the more usual precipitating factor). What is the author saying?
7. Avigail's response to Schubert's Trio Opus 100 has sexual overtones. What point is the author making?
8. Analyze any or all of the following recurring motifs: cats, hair removal, Vincent Van Gogh, children and candy.
9. Akhsa, the promising beauty of the progressive socialist youth movement is now working as a children's photographer. Moreover, she treats Avigail contemptuously. Is Ruth Almog symbolizing a failure within secular Israeli society? And if so, which failure—to bring about a Zionist-socialist utopia or to ensure

adequate employment opportunities for women in their late thirties and forties?

10. Lily Rattok in the Introduction suggests that "Shrinking" subverts the model of "marrying up." Should we subvert this model? Discuss the positive and negative aspects of marrying up—for ourselves, our daughters, and our sons.

Program Suggestions

1. Compare Ruth Almog's portrayal of a single woman to Elisheva's. Do American Jews, more than other Americans, see single women as deviant? Do Israelis? Read the articles in the "Single" section of *Jewish Marital Status*, and choose a program based on the many excellent suggestions in *A Companion Guide to the Book Jewish Marital Status*.[4]
2. The portrayal of Eli's mother is unremittingly negative. Both Eli and Avigail view her as the cause of Eli's unhappiness, and the omniscient narrator in no way counters that view. Today large numbers of women work outside the home—and some significant percentage of those women workers are doctors! Nonetheless, even today, enormous hostility exists between women who choose to work at home raising their children and women who choose to work outside the home at various other jobs and careers. Organize a panel discussion with women in your community, and invite speakers to discuss the following issues: society's view of working mothers; society's view of full-time mothers; economic necessity versus the myth of having it all (such as: the mother works to pay for a skiing vacation in the Swiss Alps); the role of fathers; and workplace realities today (maternity leave, flex time, on-site child care—how widespread are they, what are the benefits and costs for employees and employers, how could your company institute them?).

4. Carol Diament, ed., "Unit I. Single" in *Jewish Marital Status: A Hadassah Study* (Northvale, NJ: Jason Aronson, 1989), pages 3-59. Ellen Singer, *A Companion Guide to the Book Jewish Marital Status* (New York: Hadassah, 1989), pages 1-16.

Loneliness

Shulamith Hareven

Mrs. Dolly Jacobus, who in recent years had arrived at a sure and sedate self-love, sat at her desk pondering how to finish a letter. It was a letter to her husband. All morning long she had basked in the fact that he was at an architects' conference in Malta, and that she could write him there, write the word Valletta, which had such a light and chivalrous sound that it made her think of a young, robed knight quickly dismounting and elegantly stripping off his riding gloves:

Shulamith Hareven was born in Warsaw in 1931, and came to Palestine at age 9. She grew up in Jerusalem, where she lives today. She has published thirteen books in Hebrew, including poetry, novels, stories, essays, a children's book, and a thriller (under a pseudonym). Though she speaks several languages, Hareven writes only in Hebrew, "the richest and most precise of languages." She was the first (and for twelve years the only) woman member of the Academy of the Hebrew Language. As a teenager Hareven participated in the Haganah underground. She was a combat medic in the siege of Jerusalem in the War of Independence and an officer in Operations in the Israeli Defense Forces. She reported from the front line in the Yom Kippur War. With the help of Palestinian friends, she spent time in Arab refugee camps at the height of the *intifada*, and her widely-read press column strongly advocates the Peace Camp position. Yet Hareven draws a distinct line between her public activities and her literary work, and she wishes her fiction to be judged for its artistic merit, not for its topical allusions. She is married and has two children and four grandchildren.

Valletta. Not until she had sat down to write did the reality become too much for her: what really did she know about such places, or about the space, proper or outlandish, that Meir Jacobus occupied in them? She could never imagine her husband once she was no longer by his side. Perhaps he had a different existence then, a different face.

Mrs. Dolly Jacobus took her pen and continued to write:

It is ten a.m. now. Lots of light strikes the desk through the branches of the big olive tree. Do you remember how uncertain I was whether you had planned the window correctly? It seemed so high. But I'm glad of it now: there's just the right amount of light at just the right times. It's a lovely house, Meir. When I go to town and come back—and I don't go that often, because it's still been very rainy, and between one rain and the next the whole city is out in the streets trying to catch up on its affairs—it seems to me that someone has been in the house and has managed to slip away while I was still on the stairs. I look in the mirror and try to make out who it was. Perhaps it's a sign that you're thinking of me and the house. If you're planning to bring me a lace scarf from Malta, please bring a golden, white, or ivory one, and, in any event, not black. And since I have no idea how you're managing your time there, let me remind you of the advice that you once gave me: *surtout, pas trop de zèle. Adieu*, my dear friend.

She quickly reread the letter: yes, it would pass muster beneath her husband's finely critical eye. There were no annoying questions in it of the how-are-you? when-are-you-coming back? variety, no burdensome I-miss-you's or it's-so-difficult-without-you's. Meir Jacobus had taught her long ago that an undue concern for the practical arrangements of life was a distinctly plebeian trait. Within a year or two of their marriage she had learned not to ask what would be. What will be, will be, he would quietly answer her. Sometimes, taking pity on her anxiousness, he would add: "In the station that you've reached, Dolly, you can afford to be impractical."

Mrs. Dolly Jacobus took a long envelope, sealed the letter inside it, and addressed it to the hotel in Valletta in a slightly slanting hand. Her handwriting was unusual: the letters were long, tall, personal, somewhat squared at the edges, as though she had practiced developing a private calligraphy of her own. Only her signature was small and crumpled, a shelter within a shelter within a shelter. A graphologist had once frightened her with the opinion that it was a drawing of a fetus in the womb. Four consecutive miscarriages of indeterminable cause had left her without children and with the perpetual irritation of an impatient soul that strives for wholeness and cannot understand why it has not come, what can be taking it so long? Only in recent years had this irritation begun to wane. It was with a measure of optimism that she now looked after her home, her husband, and her many flower pots. She regarded herself in the mirror with a satisfied if slightly critical air. She went to lectures at the university, where she had her favorite professors whom she never missed, and her passing academic friendships with their head-nods across rows of chairs and their between-class banter.

Self-love had descended on her slowly, by degrees; it had grown securely out of that greater, more comprehensive love that she had felt for her beautiful home, her books, her paintings, her expensive shoes that were too elegant to be Israeli, her restaurants, her credit cards (yes, Mrs. Jacobus, of course, Mrs. Jacobus), her view of the walled Old City of Jerusalem on which the windows of her house looked down. Dolly Jacobus considered this view to be a private performance put on in her behalf, which she would watch from her gallery in all its many aspects of time and light. Once a visiting friend from the university had sat at the wide window bathed in Herodean light and asked after a long silence:

"Do you mean to tell me that you can go on looking out on all this every hour of the day without feeling anxious?"

Dolly Jacobus lifted and dropped one shoulder.

"And you can just go on looking down on all this?" the visitor asked again wonderingly. "Just looking down?"

"I must be a butterfly," said Dolly Jacobus. Her face broke into the lopsided grin that helped make her so likable. "But I want you to know," she added, "that being a butterfly is something that I have to work at very hard."

She was too rich for anyone to feel really sorry for her, yet people still said "poor Dolly" when they mentioned her. Nobody knew why. A year before, she had taken up batik and made gifts of her many creations, but the dyeing proved too messy for her and she gave it up in the end. Instead she tried writing haikus. She would in fact have sent her husband a few pithy haikus right now in lieu of a letter, but for her fear that the poems might travel poorly and spoil in the course of their flight over the unnecessarily large ocean that separated her from Meir. All a person really needed in the way of room, she had once thought to herself, was three or four streets around him. Only someone who had never been a refugee could dare dream of oceans and great expanses of space. And twenty-five years ago Dolly Jacobus had been a refugee. To this day she was astonished by such things as central heating which kept on burning warmly, really burning, in a house while the rain remained outside. Truly outside, it wasn't just an optical illusion.

It turned out that she was out of postage stamps, and since she had planned a trip to a delicatessen downtown anyway, she decided to go buy some. Settling into her small car, she reached into the glove compartment and took out a pair of embroidered house shoes in which she preferred to drive. With her feet in the soft slippers, the car itself became a kind of private room. The rear-view mirror showed her a pointed, attractive face with the barest hint of—not that she actually had the beginnings of one, but the skin above her lip was a trifle darker than elsewhere, so that in all her photographs she was obliged to have it lightened—a mustache over her upper lip. Dolly adjusted the mirror and turned the key in the ignition. To her satisfaction, the motor started at once despite the cold weather.

The city sped toward her in a rush of confusion. People had trouble deciding whether to open their umbrellas or close them: those who opened them had them blown inside-out like a funnel by the wind, while those who closed them were liable to be drenched by a sudden gust of rain. Both parties hurried impatiently, lengthening a stride to avoid a puddle or shortening one against a blast of wind. The hair of the women blew wildly; here and there a young girl ran giggling to catch her kerchief that had flown away. Dark patches of rain stained the walls of the houses. Blotchy clouds sped through the sky between the roofs, through which at irregular intervals the sun struggled to appear. Some children were sailing a paper boat in a dirty puddle. A gray truck whose driver seemed lost in thought drove right through it, spraying grimy water mixed with bits of paper in every direction. The city stone seemed dim and weary. The whole street smelled disagreeably of wet dog fur. For a minute Dolly contemplated turning back to shelter within the clean, warm comfort of her house with its central heating that burned, really burned, cheerily all the time. But she had already come too far.

She parked in a lot downtown. Meir Jacobus's office was nearby, on the top floor of one of the new sharp skyscrapers that seemed determined in their hatred of the city to get as high above it as they could. No private individual would ever build such a thing for himself; people did such things in groups to get rich quickly from the city. The contracting firm that built this particular building also employed its guards and maintenance staff, as well as the attendants in the nearby parking lot. Once, while having her car washed, it was whispered by one of them in Mrs. Jacobus's ear that the firm was not on the up-and-up, and even short-changed its employees in their paychecks. For a while she thought of doing something about it; after all, people should have a union that will press their demands. Not that she knew the first thing about it, far from it, but these were matters that everyone read about in the newspaper: workers had unions and even went out on strike. It upset her to see people ill-treated, and she raised the subject one day in Meir's office. It was afternoon and she had come to drive him home. His sister and partner, Bilhah, an architect herself and a triple divorcee with an exaggeratedly svelte body and a passion for jewelry, was there too. Almost apologetically, Dolly Jacobus murmured something about exploitation, about overtime, something about unions. Bilhah glanced up from her drafting paper, her bracelets and bangles coolly silent, and said:

"Really, Dolly, I don't know why on earth you should want to be such a do-gooder."

Dolly didn't want to be a do-gooder. She dropped the subject. Still, something of the good will she felt remained with her, something of that indefinable sympathy that everyone can sense even if no one can put a finger on it, so that the men would smile at her especially and inquire how she was. Sometimes she would put a question to them herself and get an answer. She knew, for instance, that the parking-lot attendant on duty today had recently divorced his wife after no end of tribulations and appearances in court. Now, having parked according to his directions that bore more resemblance to a personal plea, she observed him carefully through the window, then took a little notebook from her bag and wrote down:

"The divorced man: his shirt more pressed than usual (laundries), his shoulders more hunched than usual (restaurants)."

Her notebook and the insight that went into it improved her mood. She considered herself an astute observer. Dolly has a keen eye, she often remarked to herself. She snapped her bag shut as the attendant approached the car window, "Good morning, madame, how are you today, maybe you'd like the car washed?" She flashed the broad smile that she reserved for her faithful followers. "No thank you, the car won't be here long enough, but please don't forget to remind me next time, you know how forgetful I am, really, I don't know what I'd do without you." As she talked, she felt that she was overdoing it, saying and smiling too much. Meir would have gotten the same message across with two words and a short wave of his hand. The attendant too was confused and didn't know whether to stay or leave. Was there something else the lady wished to say to him? Luckily, another car entered the lot at that moment and saved him from his predicament.

Dolly locked the car door and made a mental note to give the man a gift for his politeness on the first available holiday. Indeed, Purim was next week: perhaps some imported deodorant would do. It was a pity how few people in this perspiring land understood the importance of deodorant. Such a gift would be both practical and pleasurable. Yet Dolly Jacobus was far from a brainless woman: what would happen, she asked herself, when the supply of expensive deodorant was used up? The parking-lot attendant had alimony to pay and certainly could not afford such luxuries, while she and Meir could hardly supply him with deodorant forever; a can every holiday, or perhaps even every week, how absurd. In the meantime the sun reappeared and the clouds in Dolly's mind dispersed too. She would give it to him this once and take her chances. What was so wrong with making a man happy just once? Life was all ups and downs anyway.

Having withstood the temptation to succumb this time too to an undue concern for practical arrangements, which was always a source of anxiety, her mood improved even more. Dolly Jacobus was an orderly woman who didn't like to leave problems unsolved, not even the bare thought of one. She smoothed out her dress and walked to the building. A silent elevator took her quickly to the top floor, where her husband's office was.

The door was open. Bilhah was inside by herself, bent over some tracing paper with a compass. She was always bent over something. A low desk lamp cast an intense pool of light on the table, in which Bilhah's rings bubbled as though being brought to a boil.

"Oh, it's you," said Bilhah Jacobus unenthusiastically. Her rings fell silent for a moment, then started to bubble again.

"Are you alone? Where's Esther?"

Esther was the secretary, a tall, ugly, unpleasant, gum-chewing girl who wore a wig made of someone else's hair and had never learned to answer the telephone properly. Moreover, she didn't even need the job, nor did Meir and Bilhah really need a secretary; but her parents, of a prominent Jerusalem family that had two or three different marriage ties with the Jacobuses, had pleaded for her.

"Esther has been working so hard all year long," said Bilhah sarcastically, "that she decided to take a vacation. Now that Meir is away, she thought she had one coming to her."

"Maybe she did."

Bilhah threw her a mocking look that left nothing out or unalluded to, from Esther's glum, gum-chewing slow-wittedness, to the niggardly, have-pity-on-me vibrations that she gave off. Before such realities Dolly Jacobus could not but bow down. In Meir's and Bilhah's tolerance of Esther, it seemed to her, was a certain hypocrisy, a kind of mock stoicism that was too much for her to understand.

"What are you doing now, Bilhah?"

"The same as before Meir took off."

"What's that?"

"Entrances for Zone Three of the Jewish Quarter. Didn't Meir tell you?"

Bilhah knew perfectly well that Meir never told her anything.

"Show me."

But Bilhah placed her hand over the paper.

"There's nothing to see yet. You wouldn't understand it anyway."

Each time Dolly felt all over again how out of place she was in this office, which was Meir's workaday world. Whenever she telephoned and was answered by Esther's wooden voice, her depression was so great that she couldn't remember what she had called to say. More than once she had actually forgotten some urgent matter and hadn't dared call back again. It was like standing by a sea rail and watching things fall from one's hands into the water, irretrievable.

"I'm going to the post office now, Bilhah. Is there anything urgent for Meir?"

"Look on his desk," came the indifferent reply. Bilhah returned to her measurements. Two heavy bracelets jangled on her wrist.

Dolly Jacobus went over to the window, which wasn't a real window but an immovable panel of glass. The sight of the bare, unshaded light bulb burning in the broad daylight of the room made her uneasy. There was something abnormal, something hybrid and unlifelike about it, almost a sin against those natural processes that have their own relaxed flow. This dizzying, too high, too enclosed, eternally air-conditioned room with its hermetically sealed windows and its strong lamplight at eleven o'clock in the morning, when a premature spring wind was whirling outside, disturbed her peace of mind and all but depressed her. She felt the need to get outside into the fresh air and wind, though it flail at her with blown paper and leaves. From time to time an unmistakable gust from the south pierced the galloping whirlpool of air, flaring the nostrils with keen desert desire—a southern breeze such as could only be felt in Jerusalem in autumn and spring. To get away, away, to gallop quickly, to give oneself away.

Nothing of this could be felt in the office. Bilhah Jacobus was confined to her white beam of light, from which she declared:

"There's something there from Grandma Haya that Meir hasn't seen yet. She commands us to close the windows in her dining room that face out on the new housing projects. She says that she can't stand to look at them, that each time she sees how they've ruined her mountain, her blood pressure goes up."

There was always some new story about Grandma Haya that was always being told with the same helpless affection. Grandma Haya was a monument, and monuments are a law unto themselves. She was eighty-nine years old, though she confessed to only eighty-seven, and still cooked all her holiday specialties for her daughters-in-law, who—poor things!—had no strength of their own. One time she paid a royal visit to Dolly's and Meir's house, where she sat for a long time at the broad window that looked down on the Old City from above. Yes, yes, she said. It all belonged to her. She could look out on it all, she who had never been a young starving refugee with a funny family name that had to be changed in a new land. Grandma Haya appraised Dolly sternly and asked if there were roaches in her kitchen. "No, Grandma Haya, there aren't," said Dolly, hiding a smile. Grandma Haya declared firmly:

"I congratulate you."

Meir's and Bilhah's grandmother lived in an old house full of arches with an outdoor toilet that she used day and night, summer and winter, and refused to exchange for a modern, indoor one such as Meir and Bilhah had been begging her to install for years. The rooms of her house were abrasively spotless, cleaner than clean, with their white curtains, whiter tablecloths, and heavy silver candlesticks polished to such a brilliance that they seemed to shine even at night. In his childhood, Meir claimed, he had been afraid to sleep in the same room with the candlesticks because of their light. Each time he awoke, he thought he was seeing a thief's flashlight.

One wall of Grandma Haya's bedroom was covered with a large map of the world in which were stuck little flags. Grandma Haya was a sixth-generation Jerusalemite, she had grandchildren and great-grandchildren all over the globe, and she wanted to know exactly where each one of them was. An orange flag with the name Nurit on it was thrust into London. A bright blue flag that said Elisha and Tali was near Tel Aviv. There was a reddish flag for Yoav somewhere in Sinai. (Not that Yoav ever served in Sinai, but Grandma Haya assumed that if he was in the army, it could only be there.) She had once been in Sinai herself with her departed husband, the doctor, on an expedition of Englishmen, and had ridden sidesaddle as was the custom of ladies in those days. Her memories of the trip—more portraiture, really, than memory—were of ravens, cliffs, and untold dangers. Perhaps vague longings for the place lingered on, for why else would she so staunchly insist that Yoav was there when he wasn't, braving all those dangers, especially when she couldn't even recall very well how he looked?

Grandma Haya was distressed that so few of her flags were in Jerusalem, while in the United States alone there were three, one belonging to Adi, who had been married there in a Catholic church. At first Grandma Haya had wanted to pull that flag out of her map, but at the last minute she relented, so that it remained crookedly in place as though it did not quite belong. Dolly clearly remembered the moment nearly twenty years ago when Grandma Haya had risen from her seat and planted in the heart of Jerusalem a lemon-colored flag that said Meir and Dolly on it. They had already been married two weeks at the time, but to all of them this seemed the real wedding. At last Dolly had come home. The bare, goaty hill outside the window had seemed to her a potential disaster area of which she alone was afraid. Now that her flag stood firmly in Grandma Haya's map, she felt that she too could relax.

Dolly Jacobus stood in her husband's office and pressed her head against the storm-beaten forever-sealed window; Bilhah sat in the strong beam of light silently swearing at some unsuccessful calculation, her jewelry coming slowly to a boil again, and up on her hillside Grandma Haya sat at home, furious at the intruding projects that had put her old age to shame. For once in her life she too had no strength to fight back.

There was a long line of people in the post office. The fan on the ceiling wasn't working. At the head of the line stood a messenger boy from some office with several dozen registered letters. As soon as he finished, two soldiers advanced out of turn and demanded to be served. The post office kept growing more packed; it was as though half the city had decided to crowd into it, each person with many items to mail. The clerk at the window was slow and incompetent, complaints began to be heard. Dolly Jacobus would gladly have left, but she was already nearer to the front of the line than the rear, and to elbow her way back out through the dense crowd seemed harder than waiting her turn. Perspiration formed on her forehead.

Directly in front of her stood a very small teenage girl with the emaciatedly thin, almost monkey-like appearance of a stunted child. Only her chest and her buttocks stuck sharply out like false appendages that didn't quite belong to her. There was something pitifully sharp and shrunken about her, as though privation had caused her to stop growing in the womb; she seemed more a homunculus than an actual person, a snuffed-out, lightless little candle. A strong smell of the cheapest violet-scented perfume came from her body together with an odor of cigarettes and sweat. No doubt the perfume took the place of daily baths, very likely she slept in her clothes. Amid the great press of people, her curly hair was thrust right beneath Mrs. Dolly Jacobus's nose. She wore tiny doll-like blue jeans that were slightly open at the waist and a purple blouse still shiny from some bargain stand. Where the two failed to meet, a strip of naked pathetically lackluster skin was exposed, on which grew a dark tuft of animal-like hair. She looked concentrated, smoky, and bad. Her neck was unwashed.

In the girl's hands, Mrs. Jacobus saw, were two registered letters from the law office of Advocate Yitzhaki on Ben Yehuda Street. Dolly Jacobus and her husband knew Yitzhaki well and had often visited his large home in the German Colony, which somehow made the girl seem less a stranger to her. With her usual avidity to be liked by her inferiors, or perhaps out of a loneliness so habitual that she no longer even sensed that it was there, she smiled encouragingly at the girl. The complaints and congestion had grown worse, if such a thing were imaginable, and Dolly Jacobus sought to free herself of them by moving forward a bit, when she suddenly realized to her astonishment that the dark-skinned waif of a girl not only failed to move too, but deliberately seemed to press backward and turn her head, so that her dark mouth unmistakably delved like an inquisitive kitten's against the soft silk bodice covering Mrs. Dolly Jacobus's right breast. A current of rare flame shot through Dolly's body, and with it, an indistinct fear. She sought to move away once more, which was far from easy in the great throng of people that had long ceased to preserve even the semblance of a line. This time, however, there was no possibility of error: the girl pressed against Dolly Jacobus's stomach again, as though in an open and explicit invitation. She could feel the burning, monkey-like heat of her seemingly chronically feverish body. All of a sudden the girl looked up and regarded Mrs. Dolly Jacobus with a sharp, clairvoyant impudence.

A hot wave, heavy, tropical, and damp passed over Dolly Jacobus. She jerked back her hand so as not to touch the girl's waist and offendedly clamped her mouth shut. Yet she knew, with a weak, sinking feeling, that she could no longer resist the wave of desire rising, illimitably shameless, within her. Not that she was unaware of the element of sadism in this sudden new passion, of her need to trample, to assail. But the girl appeared not to mind, appeared to size up the situation exactly with an omniscience as old as the world. Compared to her, I'm an amateur, Dolly Jacobus thought to herself, a rank amateur. She shut her eyes, conscious that in another moment she would move closer to the knowing little body of her own accord. Just then, however, the post-office manager sent a clerk to open a second window; the line melted away, and the girl stepped forward with her registered letters as though nothing had happened. She mailed them and left the post office without looking at Mrs. Jacobus.

Dolly Jacobus put stamps on the letter to Valletta, which was no longer a knight or even a geographical place but simply a sound. She bought a few extra stamps and dropped the letter in the mailbox, as though glad to be rid of it. When she turned to look for her, the girl had already disappeared among the passersby and been swallowed up by the street. Dolly Jacobus retraced her steps toward the parking lot, entered a dimly lit café on the way, drank something hurriedly, and thought that the storm had subsided. Yet when she turned onto Ben Yehuda Street she felt suddenly so faint, and the slope of the sidewalk seemed so steep, that she feared she would have to negotiate it on all fours. How, she wondered, could everyone else be taking such a precipitous drop in stride? I will never make it to the bottom, she said nearly out loud to herself. Hesitantly she began to walk step-by-step to her car, when she chanced to meet an acquaintance, a tall, merry young student from the university wrapped in a duffle coat against the errant wind, who mercifully accompanied her part of her way. By the time he took his leave with seven-league strides, he left her feeling better, sorry to see him go.

Dolly Jacobus had often wondered about the meaning of home. There were so many homes in the world, so many houses, and out of them all each person had one alone in which he knew where everything was. Of all the hundreds of thousands of homes, she thought, there is one alone to which I have a key and know that in the top drawer of the chest in the bedroom to the left is a tan camel's-hair sweater; of all the impenetrable, anonymous houses there is only one in which I can find right away the set of dishes that Meir brought from Spain. The lighter. The broom. The wash-and-dry sheets. Now, however, as she sat motionless in her car, she was no longer so sure of this nexus of knowledge between her and her house. If she were to return to it at this minute, she felt, the key might not fit the door, so that she would remain trapped outside in impersonal space. And if it did fit, her memories might not. The sweater might not be in its drawer and who knew whether the chest would be there at all; whether a different table would not be standing in place of the one she knew; whether the whole familiar house would not turn out to have been a dream, and the house she returned to a strangely furnished place that she had never arranged. Instead of her rose bushes there might be a strip of concrete on which an electric generator clanked intolerably away. Perhaps a gang of workers. Perhaps the house had been condemned already without her knowing it.

She ran a hand over her forehead to drive the nightmare away. It wasn't the first such ghastly vision she had had in the past two or three weeks. Several times she had dreamed that a stranger, someone she should have known but somehow was unable to recognize, had broken into her house; struggling with the hideous, mocking secret of who he was, she had broken free each time with a choked little cry. When Meir was home, he would wake her. Now she was alone, and it was hard waking by herself in the middle of the night. Often she left the night light on. Yet the panic underneath remained.

This is no good, Dolly Jacobus said to herself, wonderingly: this is no good. Pulling herself together, she stuck the key in the ignition and decided to visit Grandma Haya.

If the weather outside was still behaving strangely, none of it was noticeable in Grandma Haya's house, which had a weather all its own. Meir had remarked that Grandma Haya was the last ecological person in the family. She would never have dreamed of buying parsley and other spices; she grew them herself, planted by the fig tree and the lemon tree in the courtyard. The idea, Grandma said, of buying a lemon in a store. The balsam with which she scented her linen closet was picked by her in the hills, or by one of her granddaughters when her back hurt too much to go look for it. An egg was a meal for her, and who could explain to her, pray, why people ran around as they did nowadays and caused themselves all kinds of diseases of the liver and the heart? People don't live by human proportions any more, she would say: they build too high, live too high and talk too high. It's an insult to creation. Offices, everyone must have an office.

It was indeed Meir's and Bilhah's good fortune that she had never been to their office, because if she had, who knew whether she wouldn't have taken a stick to them on account of the unopenable windows, fraudulent windows, an arrogance of a building. Once, when she went to town to buy fabric for a dress, Grandma Haya took one look at the prices and threw the cloth back on the counter. "The nerve of you," she said to the salesgirl. "The nerve of you." Then and there she swore that she would never buy another thing until impudence passed from the world. Over her dead body would the speculators get rich. Several years before she had gone to Tel Aviv and returned in a rage; ever since, her favorite phrase of dismissal was to say, "That's from Tel Aviv." If someone brought her a box of chocolates all becellophaned and beribboned, she would wrinkle her mouth sarcastically and ask: "Is that from Tel Aviv?" And once, when Dolly had brought her a book by some young author, she had declared after reading it: "It must be from Tel Aviv." It was common knowledge that you didn't bring Grandma Haya flowers unless you had grown them in your own garden. Flower butchers was her name for flower shops.

In the middle of the Yom Kippur War, when she had grown tired of baking cakes for the soldiers, Grandma Haya decided to step out: she had an urge to go see the Chagall stained-glass windows at Hadassah hospital. Buses either came in those days or they didn't; over half-an-hour later Dolly found her sitting on the stone bench of the bus station, and suggested that she take a taxi. "What's gotten into you, child?" Grandma Haya scolded her. Besides which, taxis were built low, you couldn't see anything out of them. Buses were built high, at least you could look out and see.

Grandma Haya no longer stepped out any more. She was tired, tired in that quiet way that marks the end of all wanting, of even the hint of a desire. I'm not afraid to die, she told her family. I've never quarreled with my body and I don't intend to quarrel with it now.

"Come on in," she said to Dolly with a bright smile, opening the door for her. "You can help me slice string beans in the kitchen." Grandma Haya never sliced string beans the lazy way, across. She always sliced them lengthwise, her knife passing right through the little seeds in the pod. It gave them an entirely different taste.

They were seated opposite the black grandfather clock in the kitchen. Through the short, starched muslin curtains the light half-filtered in. Dolly had no idea why she had come. If it was to bare her heart, she herself wasn't sure what there was to bare. There was an opaqueness in her that she failed to comprehend but that kept her from returning home. She was in that state of blind anticipation in which a man vaguely senses that things have come to a head, without knowing exactly what things or what head. Grandma Haya sliced string beans and talked.

"Once when Menahem, may he rest in peace, was alive, two young yeshivah students came to see him one Saturday morning. '*Doktor, kumt*!' 'Where to?' asked Menahem. 'Our rabbi has had a heart attack.' Menahem was already halfway out of the house with his doctor's case when I decided to open my mouth. 'Just how do you expect him to come with you on the Sabbath?' I asked. 'He won't be able to drive his car down your streets.' 'Then let him walk,' said the students. 'Oh no,' I said. 'My husband is a man of more than seventy, and he's not going anywhere on foot.' 'Just a minute,' said one of the students to me. 'We'd better talk things over between us.' So they went outside and whispered a bit, psss, psss, psss, and then came back in. '*Doktor, kumt*!' 'How is he going?' I asked. 'In his car,' they said. 'But they throw stones in your streets at cars traveling on the Sabbath,' I said. '*Doktor, kumt*,' they said. 'Just let him drive slowly behind us, everything will be all right.'

"So he got into his car, may he rest in peace, which by then couldn't have gone very fast anyway, neither it nor he, and drove slowly behind the two students, who walked ahead of him shouting '*Shaa*! *Shaa*!' to their left and to their right. When Menahem reached the police barrier blocking traffic into the quarter, the police were fast asleep, they never dreamed that anyone would try driving a car into Mea She'arim on the Sabbath. By the time they woke up, the two students had moved the barrier and Menahem had driven though. A policeman ran after them in a state of shock, shouting, 'Hey, it's *shabbos*!' So what did the two students do? They turned around to him and said *Shaa*! That's how Menahem drove into Mea She'arim on the Sabbath, with the two students shaa'ing all the *shabbos*-criers. He examined the rabbi, gave him something to feel better, and came home. We had a good laugh over it."

"How did he get back out, with the students?"

"No, by himself."

"And what happened?"

"They stoned him of course, what do you think? Dolly, you're younger than I am, throw out this garbage and put some water in the kettle. Where is Meir?"

"Meir is in Malta. At an architects' conference."

Grandma Haya made a face.

"Why on earth Malta? What can a man expect to find in Malta? When is he coming back?"

"I don't know," Dolly confessed. "He didn't say exactly. Perhaps next week."

Grandma Haya was annoyed.

"What kind of business is that? A husband goes off to Malta-shmalta and his wife doesn't even know when he's coming back. You're an idiotic generation. I suppose you don't even know what's written in your marriage contract. In a Jewish marriage contract it says that a husband mustn't go off to the end of the earth without first asking his wife's permission. Did Meir ask your permission?"

"I gave him permission, Grandma Haya," smiled Dolly, the old, habitual darkness in her heart. "And you know he would have gone without permission anyway. That's how men are." Suddenly she found the courage to add: "Don't you think it might be better if women didn't marry men at all? Perhaps what a woman really needs is another woman."

But Grandma Haya wouldn't hear of it and flapped her hands in distress:

"What sort of nonsense is that? Really, the things you people say. A woman needs a woman, feh. What is this, Tel Aviv?"

Dolly made a soft, sweeping gesture with her palms, as though gathering in with great gentleness the curly head in the post office, like gathering a flower. She rose to go.

"I'll pour you your tea, Grandma Haya, and then I'll be off. Please, you needn't get up."

Grandma Haya got up anyway. In the grave, she said, is where I'll stop getting up to say good-bye to my guests. She kissed Dolly at the door with the cold lips of a person who no longer has much vital heat. "And tell Meir that I don't like this going off of his one bit. Besides which I want him and Bilhah to close up my windows in the dining room. There's enough to do here in Jerusalem. What is he running all over the world for?"

Home, when Dolly returned to it, was warm and very clean, and smelled unmistakably of comfort and wealth. She took off her coat and sat down at the table, exhausted in advance, as though some grim and unavoidable disaster awaited her and she hadn't the strength to begin. Soon, however, God knew from where, a sharp burst of energy ran through her: now, at once, this evening, she must understand everything about herself once and for all. It was time she knew. She rummaged through the closet, took out all the albums and began feverishly looking for the few rare snapshots of herself from her refugee days. None lit the faintest spark. She could not find herself in any of them. Perhaps, she thought, if only, if only I had some picture from my childhood, from the age of four or five, perhaps then. But such a picture was not to be had anywhere on earth. It was as if Dolly had been twice-born, and her first, perhaps realer life had ended abruptly at the age of fourteen. Afterward another, post-diluvian life had begun, with its disguises and new names.

A great wave of sadistic compassion, a feeling not unlike that of a little child who plays lovingly with a doll and a minute later punishingly tears out its hair, cast the girl from the post office up inside her again. The shame of it, thought Dolly, dry-mouthedly, the wonderful shame of it. Why, I practically am in need of her. Already she was planning how the two of them would sit here, at this table, studying English together. Dolly would teach her patiently, yet sometimes not, losing her temper in a fit of erotic anger; and as the weather would be hot, and the air-conditioning was out of order, the two would take off their blouses. They would wash each other in the shower. One more step and the girl would be hers, a gutterbird, pinched and adroit.

After midnight the wave vanished as suddenly as it had come. That's the last of it, she thought tiredly, the absolute last of it. I almost made a terrible mistake. Thank God I got over it in time. The situations a person can get herself into, really. She left the night light on, took a sleeping pill, and drifted off into a deep, obtuse sleep.

At ten o'clock the next morning, without knowing a minute beforehand what she was about to do, Dolly Jacobus settled vehemently into her car, slammed the door shut with pursed lips, and drove off with a violent grinding of her gears. She parked in the usual lot, which was attended this morning by a new, unfamiliar face, and walked with quick steps in the direction of Advocate Yitzhaki's office. In her panic that she might reconsider and change her mind, she nearly ran up the steps. The lawyer's office was composed of two rooms entered from an old, peeling corridor that housed several other offices as well, in addition to a bathroom with a gigantic old key in its door and a small cubicle in which an aged, immortal-looking man sat making tea and coffee for the office workers. The older he grew, it was said, the more polished were his copper trays and the dirtier the drinking glasses borne on them.

Dolly Jacobus was still examining the name plates on the wall when the bathroom door swung open at the end of the corridor and the girl in the purple blouse emerged and stopped to turn the key twice behind her. She looked even tinier than she had yesterday in the post office. An ancient, wicked triumph shone in her eyes when she caught sight of Mrs. Jacobus. She stepped up to her, too concentrated a ball of impudence for one small girl.

"Would you like to come work for me?" asked Dolly Jacobus. She felt that her generally musical voice lacked all expression, was as toneless as a block of wood.

"Whaddam' I gonna do fa' you?" asked the girl with a trace of scorn. "I ain't no cleaning woman. I work for a lawyer, y'know."

"I know that you do," said Mrs. Jacobus. "You're Advocate Yitzhaki's messenger girl. But wouldn't you like to get ahead in the world? I could teach you English if you'd like."

The girl stared at her blankly.

"It won't cost you a penny," said Dolly Jacobus. "You can come every day to study for an hour, an hour-and-a-half."

The girl gave her head a skeptical shake.

"You'll be sorry y'ast." She seemed to hold the consonants and then spit them menacingly out of her mouth. Cheekily.

"Wouldn't you like to try?"

The girl looked at her askance. To do so she had to throw back her head, since Mrs. Jacobus was much taller. From the girl came the smell of a recently chewed sesame bar.

"When do you finish working here?"

"Me? At six."

"Fine. Be down near the Agron building at six. I'll be waiting for you in my car."

"Me? I can't today. I gotta date with my boy friend, see?"

So soon, so soon the degradation of it had begun. Dolly Jacobus could feel the knife that was being slowly, almost gently turned in her body. Already I am at the mercy of her whims, of her boy friend, who may or may not exist, most likely not. A terrible pity flooded her eyes. She placed a gentle hand on the girl's cheek.

"All right, little girl. Let's make it tomorrow."

The girl must have had no idea of how to respond to an innocent touch, for immediately she thrust out her hips like a streetwalker's, as though it was expected of her. Dolly Jacobus swallowed a hot lump, turned on her heels and began descending the stairs.

"Hey missus!" called the girl after her, leaning over the balcony. "Missus! Listen, Missus, it's okay. Let's make it today."

And Dolly Jacobus felt weak with happiness.

A letter was waiting for her at home from Meir, special delivery, as was his habit. She put off opening it. There were two telephone calls. A friend called to invite her and Meir to Friday night dinner, but said quickly when told that Meir was still away, "All right, then, let's make it some other time. Bye-bye, Dolinka, and send the man my best." Then Grandma Haya called, querulous, cross, and very old. Why wasn't Meir back yet? Why weren't her windows taken care of? Did they think she was going to live forever? She had completely forgotten Dolly's visit of yesterday.

Otherwise, there was nothing to do. Lust turned into a series of practical details: a meal ready in the refrigerator, plates on the table, a record that took a long time to choose, a new blouse that lay in its wrapper in the bedroom to give the girl as a gift. She had bought it in a children's store, since sizes that small were available nowhere else. Three times she went to town shopping and three times she came back. It all became so new, blind, and inevitable. Hurry, hurry.

The Agron building was very white in the dusky light. A gray haze rose from the acacia trees to mingle with the exhaust of many cars, against which the lampposts and yellow fences stood out strongly. Dolly Jacobus felt everything intensify: all shapes seemed more significant, as though—the white gleam of the stone that faced the office building, that street light over there that was trying to say a clear sentence—they were all in a code that had to be learned to be read. The cloud-dampened, haze-dimmed twilight did not surprise her: why, since last evening her world had been darkening—since well before last evening in fact—with that last, eerie glow that portends a certain disaster. I am waiting for my love, she told herself, for my poor, ugly love with her smell of sweat and synthetic violets. To support her in the style she will become accustomed to. I shall not skimp.

She waited a long time. The girl did not appear. A gang of boys on their way to Morasha passed by her car and peered apathetically inside at her. A young mother screamed at her son with practiced, despairing, almost ceremonial screams. Two foreign journalists whom she knew waved at her on their way to the press club. Suddenly, in a gust of evening breeze, the acacias began to touch one another, to talk back and forth. The city whirled the evening around inside it, rings within rings; soon it would be suppertime, soon it would be nighttime, soon there would be street lights and movies and people clustered around hot popcorn. The whirling rings slowly thickened into solid darkness. The girl had not come.

At seven o'clock, cold, beat, and aching, Dolly Jacobus pressed the accelerator, and headed for home. What luck, she thought, at least she doesn't know my name and address. All I needed was to have a blackmail case on my hands, she and her boy friend together, don't get wise with us, lady, we know all about you. Or some venereal disease, who knows. How could Yitzhaki even employ such a horrible girl? Why, one ought to ... one ought to ...

She hurried to enter the house, which seemed to her now all Meir's: those were his clothes in the closet, his slippers on the floor. What a disgrace, really, the things she had thought of doing in it. Even the shirt from the children's store that lay on his side of the bed. Blushingly she took it and threw it in the garbage pail. I didn't do anything, Meir, she said to herself, I only thought of it—and thoughts aren't deeds, Meir, are they? She drew open the heavy curtain, which revealed the most stunning landscape on earth: the old walls of Jerusalem, the Temple Mount and Mount Zion. It's all there, she reassured herself, it's still there, all those thousands of houses dipped now in darkness as though they, as though they alone were the only true houses and deserved to have their wishes come true. She looked around her. The pictures still hung on the walls, the books hadn't vanished, her shoeless foot sunk as sensually as always into the Mashhad carpet. My God, how could I? How? The lunacy of it.

She suddenly made up her mind to call Meir. True, he had firmly, with all the authority of a rational man, warned her not to do it, so that she feared the moment of his anger and surprise—but she must hear his voice, if only to tell him about Grandma Haya's windows, or to find out the number of his return flight, just to talk. She explained to the long-distance operator that she did not know the number, but that she wanted to get the Hotel Phoenix in Valletta. Yes, Valletta, the capital of Malta, that's correct. Once again it seemed to her the most cavalier and elegant of cities. Yet it was hard for her to imagine Meir walking its streets without his car, since he had long ago turned into a centaur, part man and part automobile. It was perhaps only in bed that he sometimes still lay peeled of his layers and defenseless. Who knew what his strength was without his car in the streets of Valletta?

While waiting for the operator to call back, she prepared herself a sandwich, which she ate sitting on the arm of the easy chair, her bare feet crossed. Soon I will speak with Meir, she thought, I will hear the wonder in his voice—the same mild wonder I always hear, as though life itself was not what he had expected. Meir Jacobus, the architect, the man who found it easier to talk about entrances for Zone Three of the Jewish Quarter than about what was going on inside him. We've drifted apart a bit lately, Meir, thought Dolly, but it will all work out, won't it? We will talk now and it will work out.

The sandwich was eaten. Dolly had just gone to the kitchen to get an apple when the telephone rang. She left the unwashed fruit by the sink and ran barefoot to the telephone.

The long-distance operator told her to wait. She heard her talking to the operator in Valletta. Then to the desk at the hotel. So many different voices talking so far away—Dolly had never been very good at understanding such things. *Attendez un moment*, said the operator at the hotel. Then: "Mrs. Jacobus, here's your call."

"Hello?" An unpleasant and familiar woman's voice sounded in Dolly's ears. For a second she failed to understand: why, it was the wooden voice of Esther, ugly, gum-chewing, wigged Esther. The secretary. Then she understood. Slowly she replaced the receiver.

The long-distance operator was persistent. She rang again. "Your call to Valletta, Mrs. Jacobus."

"I've changed my mind," Dolly said. "Please cancel it. I've changed my mind."

So that's how it is, said Dolly out loud in the empty apartment. That's how it's been all the time. I've really always known. But what actors we all are.

She turned off the light and sat on the window sill, looking out at the broad canopy of sky and many lights. Something fell away from her and dropped, perhaps the paths that henceforward would go their different ways, with cosmic speed, so that there would be no remembering even when she had still been her undivided self.

Why, one ought to, said Dolly out loud to the shadowy paintings, whose frames glittered silently in the dark room. One ought to.

Tomorrow, she thought, I'll know what one ought to do.

1980

Translated by Hillel Halkin

Questions for Discussion

1. At the very end of the story, Dolly realizes that Meir has been having an affair with his secretary, yet the groundwork for this realization is laid in the third paragraph: "There were no annoying questions in [Dolly's letter] of the how-are-you? when-are-you-coming-back? variety, no burdensome I-miss-you's or it's-so-difficult-without-you's.... Within a year or two of their marriage she had learned not to ask what would be. What will be, will be, he would quietly answer her." In what other ways does Hareven prepare her readers for the story's climax?
2. What are the implications of Meir's insistence that Dolly make no demands on his emotions or even on his time? Readers can conclude that even before the affair, Meir had distanced himself from his wife and his marriage—why did he remain married? Why did Dolly?
3. Shulamith Hareven makes an unusual statement about Dolly's feelings of self-worth: "Self-love had descended on her slowly, by degrees; it had grown securely out of that greater, more comprehensive love that she had felt for her beautiful home, her books, her paintings, her expensive shoes." Do the material possessions in which we take pride truly enhance our self-love? How?

4. Compare Dolly to Avigail of Ruth Almog's "Shrinking." Both suffer from low self-esteem (for example, both expect—and receive—neglect at the hands of men), even though Dolly's status as a well-to-do woman of society differs greatly from Avigail's status as an unmarried school teacher.
5. Dolly was once a refugee. How has this influenced her? Consider that Israel, even today, is overwhelmingly an immigrant society—comparable in some ways to the immigrant society of American Jewry in the early part of this century. Which of Dolly's characteristics have symbolic meaning for Israeli society?
6. What roles do art and creativity play in this story? Consider Dolly's batik and poetry, Meir and Bilhah's work as architects, Meir's office building, and Grandma Haya's esthetic judgments—though she is presented not as artist but as an "ecologist"! Is woman's art possible? Is any human art possible, or is the artistry of nature the only true art?
7. The omniscient narrator states: "Four consecutive miscarriages of indeterminable cause had left [Dolly] without children and with the perpetual irritation of an impatient soul that strives for wholeness and cannot understand why it has not come, what can be taking it so long?" The Jewish tradition strongly endorses the value of child-rearing, and the Western tradition certainly endorses woman's role as mother. Can a woman lead a full life without children? Can a man?
8. The young girl is presented in a symbolic way. She has "an omniscience as old as the world" and she feels "an ancient, wicked triumph." Why does Hareven choose this small, lower-class Jerusalemite to represent a sort of Aphrodite? Note that the girl's physical appearance is described minutely, though readers know nothing of Meir's external characteristics.
9. Is "Loneliness" in some way an indictment of the upper classes? Of the options available in women's lives? Of Israeli society as a whole?

Program Suggestions

1. The possibility of a lesbian relationship is presented in "Loneliness" as deviant, illicit, irrational, and unwholesome. Today, at least in America, lesbian and gay Jews have found a measure of acceptance. Invite the rabbi of a gay and lesbian synagogue to discuss issues of homosexuality within the Jewish community. OR, have the members of your study group conduct a debate on the pro's and con's of establishing gay and lesbian synagogues.
2. Meir is having an extra-marital affair, and Dolly, for about twenty-four hours, deeply desires one. Invite a rabbi or Judaic scholar to discuss Jewish laws and beliefs about sexuality, marriage, and adultery, and invite a rabbi or a Jewish counselor to discuss the effects of adultery on Jewish marriages today.

A Slight Delay

Dahlia Ravikovitch

A wicker fence. A wicker fence. Nettles from the first autumn rains. Then, two abandoned stalls of cold water showers. A row of books in a wooden case. A Japanese picture and a shadeless lamp. This was my room, and from here I was supposed to move into the office.

"Have you moved the bed into the office yet?"

"Did you take the blankets?"

"Did you bring the cakes from the kitchen?"

"You must be crazy walking around the camp in a housecoat like this!"

Dahlia Ravikovitch was born in 1936 in Ramat Gan, a suburb of Tel Aviv, and spent her earliest years on a kibbutz. She attended high school in Haifa and later studied at the Hebrew University of Jerusalem. She has worked as a journalist and teacher, and writes television reviews for the newspaper *Ma'ariv*. Her first poems were published when she was still in the army, and with her first collection, *The Love of an Orange*, in 1959 she was securely established as one of Israel's leading poets. In addition to six volumes of poetry, she has written a book of short stories, and two children's books. Dahlia Ravikovitch is the recipient of many of Israel's literary awards, including the Shlonsky, Brenner, Ussishkin, and Bialik Prizes. She currently lives in Tel Aviv; she has one son.

"I'll be back in half an hour. If there's a phone call for me...." Rachel, the Bombshell, threw the towel on her arm and left. She had a soft voluptuous body and fair hair, and she had the right attitude toward life. There was always someone whispering with her at night.

They said that there was a radio in the commanding officer's room. But it was forbidden to enter the commander's room and, in any event, any girl who entered there would have to dust the place. It was best not to go in. One of the officers lingered in the adjacent room; it was four or five in the afternoon on Friday. He had come from home on a bike. He was not planning to do any work.

"Why did you enter the commander's room, and how did you get the key?" Rachel asked resentfully, and her suitor chimed in, "Who gave you permission to turn on the radio?"

I examined the detailed map of Israel, the archeological shards, the carpet, and the enormous desk. This room retained the sunlight long after the sun had set. The commander had left his office long ago. A cascade of sunlight mixed with dust flooded the broad brown desk. It was five o'clock, and two Brandenburg concertos were playing on the radio. For a while I could not find a place for myself; then I settled in the deep chair and sat immobile across from the desk. It was as if I were asleep. I did not want to move a limb. I was thinking about the matriculation exams I had taken a few months earlier, and about the impatience and anxiety I had experienced before taking them. I remembered the first exam, and how I enjoyed myself once I realized what it was like. How powerful I became in my own eyes. A few days later, we went on a trip around the country, I and my boyfriend: we whistled in movie theaters and were uncharacteristically insolent. When all that was over, we were drafted into the army, and I despised myself because I felt so useless. The days and weeks passed, and most things fell into place. When the first concerto was over, my cheek was sticking to the desk. I shuddered when I realized how quickly the time had passed. The light in the room became brighter and whiter. The room looked hoary and no longer different from the other rooms. The concerto was over and I hastened to leave the room.

The sun had set, and I began to sing loudly. My own voice grated on my ears, but I continued to sing with gusto, all the while hoping for a change to take place in me so that my voice would sound different.

After a while I distracted myself from thinking about my voice. While I was making my camp-bed, I accidentally knocked down a pile of Lost Equipment forms. Rachel peered at me. When I bent down to pick up the scattered forms, I was beset by mosquitoes. As I straightened up, I watched the receding paleness in the west. I started to plot and scheme how to use the phone despite the prohibition. The windows turned ink-blue a moment before darkness. I trusted I could find a way to use the phone without being punished.

When I came out of the room, Rachel, the Bombshell, said to me, "If you don't bring me food, I am leaving the office."

"She's screwed up," said Rachel, the Bombshell, to the man waiting for her outside. "You can't rely on her."

At eight, I went to the Recreation Room. In the big dilapidated armchair sat Barukh Shoshani. Although he was a refugee from the Second World War and never had a proper education, he managed to rise to the rank of sergeant, and even prepared himself for the equivalency matriculation exams. I was surprised to see him seated in that armchair, with its broken springs and gray oily edges visible from behind. This armchair may have been just as filthy on the day it was brought in with the rest of the spoils from Ramla. At any rate, the springs could certainly have been repaired, but we were not deemed worthy of the effort, being an indolent and low-class service unit.

As I was leafing through the weekend papers, I noticed the spider web between the legs of the chair underneath the radio. Only then did I realize that I had missed the PX yet again. I had a great craving for candy, particularly for those triangular chocolate-covered wafers. The Sabbath stretched before me so lean and emaciated, as if my very roster duty had caused it to be thus reduced. At least I'll be able to sleep late, and there won't be any parade. Saturday duties were rare; they were also meaningless and wasteful. I knew what I wanted. I wanted to be somewhere else altogether. A hefty mosquito circled near my arm, buzzing vociferously. I shuddered.

Rachel, the Bombshell, returned to the office, her hair wet from the shower. It looked thick even when wet. I offered her some of the raisins my family had sent me, because I was afraid of her. I had just started reading a serial when I heard a train. It was a late freight train that had been delayed until after Sabbath had started, and it now rumbled by stealthily and unlit. I thought to myself: Where is it going? How far is it going? I listened to it fade out of earshot.

Suddenly a round, ruddy head adorned with a faded gray mustache appeared in the door.

"Are you minding the phone?" Major Rosenblum asked. I waited for Rachel to answer.

"Yes, yes, I am here all the time," Rachel said.

"So am I."

"I'm expecting a call," Rosenblum said. "If they call, tell them I'll be back in half an hour."

"Major Rosenblum—" I pleaded.

"What is it?"

"Can I call home? ... Long distance," I hastened to add. I was not sure he had heard me.

"Where to?" he asked.

"To the Galilee." I sounded ridiculous to myself.

"We shall see," said the major. "I'll be back in half an hour. Maybe you'll be able to call from my office."

"Thanks," I called after him, but he had already left. A sense of joyous adventure filled me. I was going to call home against standard orders. The officer on duty had agreed immediately, I was lucky.

His room was brightly lit. There were three lamps: one hanging from the ceiling with a shade resembling an enamel plate, another perched on a spiral metal stem, and a third hung from a nail by a made up camp-bed. On the table were yeast-cakes streaked with threads of jam and a pot of coffee.

"I'll dial for you," Rosenblum said.

I sat, somewhat confused, on a footstool by the table. I was wearing a grayish-pink housecoat which I realized was not appropriate. I had no idea how to start a conversation. And anyway, conversation was superfluous. The major was a complete stranger to me. But he had done me a favor, and I was beholden to him. I hoped he would understand that I was still immature and lacking in social skills, and it was up to him to decide whether or not to strike up a conversation with me.

"The operator says it will take about twenty minutes," Rosenblum said, his cheeks puffed and rubicund.

"I can go back to the office," I said, but I was sleepy and slow to get up.

"What's the hurry?

I kept silent and hunched.

"Have some coffee."

"I don't drink coffee at night."

"Then take a piece of cake."

"No, really," I said affectedly. "It's not out of politeness. I am full of cake already." I wanted to smoke but I had left my cigarettes at the office.

"How old are you?"

"Eighteen."

"I thought you were older."

"Everybody thinks so," I laughed. "But I had my birthday last Sunday." I was very proud to be so young. I felt an advantage over those older than me. Some, burdened with wife and children, had problems supporting their families, and were humiliated by their superiors. I thought to myself: What have they done with their lives? How have they wasted the years? From time to time, I was seized by fear that my youth would be frittered away. But in the meantime, I still had my youth and I was very careful with it. Every day I watched it and gave it serious consideration.

"Did you graduate from high school?"

"Three months ago," I said and thought: What an advantage!

"Do you have siblings? Older or younger?"

"I have a younger brother. He's smart as a whip, and handsome, too."

"No wonder, with such a sister."

I knew he was flattering me, but the frost around me was thawing.

"He writes me such funny letters that I roll on the floor with laughter." I decided to go and fetch my cigarettes after all.

"What's the rush? Have some coffee."

"No thanks." I felt resentment. Why does he keep harping on coffee when I have already told him?

His desk was close to the door. He got up. He was taller than me, and I felt him look down on me. He leaned against the threshold, and his hand touched my back, as if by accident. I recoiled a little. I was not quite sure he really meant it. The pinkish-gray housecoat was so obviously inappropriate. I felt as if I was wearing rags.

"Wait," he said, "why are you running?"

I stood a little shaken. "What are you afraid of?" He smiled. Suddenly the phone rang. His wedding ring was thick and crude. Everybody knew he had a seven-month-old baby.

"Mom," I cried into the phone. "How was your week? Can you imagine, I managed to call you tonight without any problems. Is Micah with you?"

My mother wanted to know if her package had arrived. I told her everything was all right with me. A complaint was lodged against me for disorderly appearance, but it was later dropped. I am beginning to get the hang of the work. Mother was very pleased.

"Have a nice Sabbath, and all the best," Mother said, and before hanging up she added, "Who stayed with you this weekend? Do you have a nice roommate?"

"What does it matter?" I answered. "I have a book to read, and I am still translating those poems. I feel great here in the office. It beats the four-hour guard shift everyone else has to do."

"Why didn't you add regards from me?" Rosenblum said in a rasping voice. "After all, I let you make the phone call."

"It's really wonderful of you."

He grabbed my arm near the shoulder. There was neither grace nor affection in his movement. I was startled and pulled my arm back forcefully.

"Stupid girl. Are you afraid?"

"No."

"What then?" He was still holding my arm.

"I am not afraid." All the pleasantries were now drained out of me. "I am not afraid at all. I simply don't want to."

He let go of me and looked at me coldly. I remained standing there.

"Okay, leave."

When I entered the room, Rachel was still standing in the window, talking to her suitor, and the room was swarming with mosquitoes. Rachel had smeared herself with mosquito repellent and was unaffected by them. The light was too poor for reading and my sadness was too overwhelming. I still had not fully grasped what had happened to me. That's why I found it hard to concentrate. There were numerous preparations before sleep, and they took forever. I filled out the duty roster and hung it on a hook. Later, I lay down on the camp-bed and rifled through old letters. Tranquillity descended on me, and it seemed as if it all had happened many months before and was already forgotten. My old thoughts surfaced and clustered together. I thought to myself that I was, indeed, eighteen, and it was an age to be proud of. I will be careful and not let this age slip away from me. Soon enough I will inherit the best life has to offer. Soon I will fall asleep and enjoy the bliss of dreaming. Thus I am preparing myself for life, and life will follow. Perhaps the coming year will be the best ever. Winter will be here soon, and the mosquitoes will disappear. Whatever I am looking for will be given to me in spades. Maybe it won't happen exactly as I plan it, maybe not even in the manner I envisage it, but I am sure I will lack for nothing. The heat started mounting from my feet up. I filled up the entire bed. It's just a slight delay, I laughed. Even my brother used to mock me in his letters. But my brother will soon change his attitude. No doubt he, too, will love me when my wishes come true. I rubbed against the sheets. I stroked my shoulder with my hand. I will get my heart's desire in spades, I thought. And then some. It's just that everything will be slightly delayed.

1965

Translated by Marganit Weinberger-Rotman

Questions for Discussion

1. What is your reaction to the narrator's statement, "[My boyfriend and I] were drafted into the army, and I despised myself because I felt so useless." How is the statement typical of any new army recruit, and how does it apply more particularly to Israeli women recruits?

2. The 18-year-old narrator, although initially confused, realizes that Major Rosenblum is making a sexual advance. She then unhesitatingly rejects him, without considering the consequences (and a hostile superior officer would definitely have negative consequences). Consider similar situations in your experience, either as a teenager or as an older woman. Is the narrator typical in her initial confusion? Is she typical in being able to tell a man "I simply don't want to"?
3. Compare the proposition by Major Rosenblum to the two passages in "Shrinking" where Avigail encounters a man in the street. Like the narrator of "A Slight Delay," Avigail reacts assertively; she says to one man, "Get lost," and she tells the other to move away. Though Avigail and the 18-year-old soldier are very different, both speak forcefully to men who threaten them. How do you react to harassment by strangers? What can we conclude about Israel based on these two characters' fearless reactions? How do sexual advances by a strange man on a city street differ from sexual advances by an acquaintance in the workplace or the home? Both stories indicate a truth of women's existence: the need to retreat from potential sexual assault. Comment.
4. In reflecting on the harassment, the narrator at first is unable to "grasp what had happened." After taking care of her tasks, however, she looks on the incident as something that happened long ago, and is able to comfort herself with optimistic slogans. Compare your own reactions to terrible events. Consider as well the sadness of this passage—the brother who "no doubt ... will love me when my wishes come true," the vagueness of the narrator's hopes. Nonetheless, these reflections following sexual harassment are remarkably free from shame. Comment.
5. The narrator says that Rachel "had the right attitude toward life. There was always someone whispering with her at night." Is this said ironically? Or does the narrator believe that always having a man is evidence of the right attitude?

Program Suggestion

Invite an Israeli woman in your area to speak to the study group about her army service. Note that Israeli girls do not serve in combat units. What is the effect on a girl of spending two years "in an indolent and low-class service unit"? Of knowing that any girl who enters the commander's room will "have to dust the place"? Does army duty foster the ideal of women's service to men, or does it merely reflect conditions that are pervasive within Israeli society as a whole?

White Lines

Dorit Peleg

I only live in hotels. Tall, white hotels with the same balcony duplicated along their breadth and height, and with their name emblazoned in large letters underneath the roof. The rooms are almost identical. Curtains of lace-like white netting or of heavy velvet, depending on the climate, sway in the wind which enters through the crack that I always leave between the glass doors leading to the balcony; an easy chair and occasionally a beach umbrella and a railing overlooking the city of that day. Inside the room, the double bed wide

---

Dorit Peleg was born in 1953 in Haifa, and spent several years of her adolescence in Ethiopia. After her army service, she completed a B.S. in Computer Science, and worked for many years as a software engineer. In 1986 she began teaching creative writing. In 1990/91 she taught Hebrew and creative writing in the Southwest China Teachers' University in Sichuan. Her works have appeared in literary magazines, and she has published a collection of short stories, *White Lines*, as well as the two novels *Una* and *Miss Fanny's Voice*. Literary awards include the Tel Aviv Foundation 1980 Writing Grant, the Dr. Haim Kugel Literary Prize, awarded to *Miss Fanny's Voice* for best prose work of 1992/3, and the Levi Eshkol Prime Minister's Literary Grant for 1993/4. She was also the recipient of fellowships from the Millay and Yaddo artists' colonies in 1985.

Editors' Note: All punctuation used in the English translation of "White Lines" is at the special request of the author and co-translator, Dorit Peleg.

enough for four. The edges of the sheets are carefully tucked under the mattress, a thick wide bedspread whose fringes reach the floor. Two armchairs and a toilette with a large mirror in its center. Two night tables, one on each side of the bed. Once the second night table used to disturb me, an eyesore beyond the bed. Not any more. On the contrary: this duplication gives me a feeling of space. Of abundance, as there is in anything superfluous. For no one sleeps in my room but me. I can spread out my arms and legs in the big bed and tuck Kleenexes under the other pillow and scatter cake crumbs in the far end, for the chambermaid to clean up the next morning. Only me alone. Always.

A bathroom gleaming with sterile whiteness, a tiled floor and a toilet seat wrapped in paper like a birthday present. Untouched. A white porcelain bathtub, so immaculate that it can only be stepped on with a sense of reverence. I always get into the bathtub very slowly, one foot after the other, carefully. Of all the furnishings in the room this is my favorite. Gives me a very clean feeling. Perhaps it's a remnant of my former days, those I do not want to remember, that inspires the feeling of sacredness I have when I am stretched out on the bottom of the shining porcelain tub, my body enlarged and a little hazy in the foamy water, and cleanliness spreads through it and purifies it. And I forcibly obliterate all the pictures that suddenly float up from the soap bubbles and linger before me in that split second before they burst, the broken toilet bowls and the corroded metal pipes spitting out sudden spurts of cold, turbid water.

Another of my favorite haunts is the lobby. Soft lights in the corners, warm shades of brown and rust, armchairs you only have to look at to feel you are sinking into them. Chameleon-like waiters hover between the seats on cushions of air, their buttocks clearly outlined through the thin cloth of their uniform trousers. If I didn't know it was impossible, I'd swear it was the same waiter in all the hotels, in all the cities. Maybe it's the dim lights that blur the lines of their faces and make them anonymous and, at the same time, very familiar. The body I've been familiar with for a long time now.

But for me the lobby isn't just a place to relax in. It's my place of work; at least that's where my work begins. They sit here, scattered around the spacious hall made intimate by its dim lights concealed in the corners. The lampshades spill rings of soft light onto the armchair beside them, turning it into a small, secret corner, a world unto itself. So I can look them over for one initial moment, seeing and unseen, in the no-man's land between the harsh light of the reception hall and the shadows of the lobby. I must scan the entire shadowy den before me with the precise, comprehensive scrutiny of a proofreader—for there won't be another chance—embrace all the corners with a glance, appraise, and make my choice. There have been missed opportunities. I had not always seen all the prospects. But over the years I've developed an amazingly accurate yardstick, a sort of sixth sense, and I'm almost never wrong.

It's a cold night and I'm alone. I don't know why I am telling all this. If the need to tell exists, it has replaced the strength I used to have. A few weeks ago at the restaurant I almost suggested to a wretched salesman that we split the check. Of course I stopped myself in time. Before diving in, remember you're heavier than water. I do nothing without first considering the consequences. The implications. The side effects.

Maybe I'll quit soon. I haven't saved much; my expenses are too high. A day's stay in a hotel like the one I'm in now would support a family for a week. My conscience doesn't bother me. A conscience is something superfluous, the tonsils of emotion. This is the only way I am prepared to live. When I quit (retire—I must say retire, like any middle-aged civil servant—what a ludicrous word), I'll have enough left to maintain me on the same level for several years. I will not give up even the smallest comfort. When the money runs out, I too will cease to exist. With no unnecessary hesitations. Quietly and decisively and without superfluous ado. A clean break. I hope.

Not like all these women. Women alone. I know them. A wrinkled velvet armchair soiled by ashes and crumbs of cake from the corner bakery. The cigarette smoke is solid in the space of the room, has been for weeks now, months, you can bite it, I feel it in my teeth when I enter. Shoes tossed into a corner, once it was bohemian, now it's sad, if you allow yourself such luxuries. My room is always clean and sparse, and I only smoke in the lobby or after a meal. Once I overheard a chambermaid say, her room is sterile. She's lived here for weeks and you won't find even a handkerchief on the armchair. True. I like lines that are straight and clean. You begin to slacken, a jacket thrown sloppily on the bed, soon you'll have holes in your stockings, you won't know how and already there are flakes of ash on the armchair. Like those women. I hate them.

This evening I approached a barbered head that looked promising, to ask for a light. As I drew near a chill went through me. His son was sitting next to him. I hadn't noticed him sooner because his head didn't reach the top of the chair. The filtered lamplight struck his hair with bright undulating glints, like those you can see at sea in the late afternoon hours. His face was thin and delicate; he looked very young. I almost forgot why I went over. Just before it became embarrassing I pulled myself together, and put the cigarette between my lips. They were trembling. I thanked the army haircut and went up to my room. The script was cut short. I should have inhaled deeply, then thanked him with a smile. One look straight into his eyes, no more. Turned around and gone back to my corner. The rest would have followed naturally. Like in the westerns. Except that I couldn't. The boy was younger than Michou by at least three years, but that didn't help.

That's what happens when you break the rules you have set yourself. Once I saw one of the waiters pull a girl into the corner of a balcony. I was standing on the balcony above, smoking a cigarette and looking out the window. It was a gray, rainy day, and I stared at the wet house opposite and at the drops of rain puffing up the dust on the sidewalk. I had a side view of them. She was very young, not more than thirteen. Beautiful, but still a child's beauty. The flattery: I remembered it well, over the years. As though a door had opened up before you and admitted you into the company of all the guests you had looked at from the lowliness of your thirteen years, as they blew gray clouds of smoke from long cigarette holders, their words shed with perfumed ease, effortlessly. But she hadn't the vaguest idea of what it was all about. She still didn't know of the game's existence, let alone the rules. The waiter was twenty-something, his black hair slicked back with cream, his pants tight. He led her into a corner and fenced her in, whispering in her ear, put his hand under her sweater. Squeezed. I saw the girl shiver. Even from afar I saw the shock in her eyes turn into shame. She started struggling with him, trying to get away, but he was used to women who knew how to play the game and, according to the rules, if you had got this far the struggle was meant to whet the appetite. Then, too, I deviated from the rules. One mustn't get involved. I went down one floor. Grabbed him from behind by the collar of his white waiter's shirt and pushed him aside. The child fled, her face flushed with tears, wiping her nose. He straightened his shirt, glaring angrily at me. He knew very well who I was but he didn't dare say a word. There's a certain advantage to a reputation like mine: what can one say.

But that was a deviation. And I cannot permit myself deviations. They're too costly. One word, one impertinent movement when dinner is served, and a week's work can be lost. The fabric I'm weaving is too fragile; these are not things that go through the mind, they filter in without you noticing, the tone of a voice, the way a plate is laid. You know without knowing what. But that's enough. Downfall waits for no one. You begin to soften up, to pamper yourself and, before you know it, you're on the outside. I don't want to be outside. That's why I'm always here, inside this little world delimited by bar, restaurant, lobby, residential floors. Here everything is clear. Everything is orderly. Everyone knows his place and the script was already written long ago and everybody has managed to learn it by heart. It's quite a large world, if you're familiar with it, almost a labyrinth, and there's a sauna and a gym and corners with potted palms in hidden corridors and original pottery ashtrays, you could wander around for days and not get back to the same place if you didn't have to eat, and eating is important. It contributes to the order. The game itself is also dictated by the place and is conducted according to the well-defined predetermined order, as it must be. The lobby: the eternal hunting ground. A chance encounter, a cigarette lit, a book forgotten. Dinner the next day. Another day. Gin and tonic at the bar. No hurry. Hurrying will get you nowhere. Or at least not where I want to go.

Seems like this is going to be a strange night. I can only lock myself in my room. So as not to go outside. Because for some reason I feel the need to go outside. To walk in the night, in the cold, dark street, to feel wet gusts breaking on my face. To lick raindrops from my lips. A cold wind blowing through my eyelashes. To move my hand over the wall of a house and feel it wet, slick, all the roughness smoothed out as though by a layer of oil. Rain.

I turn over. Can't fall asleep. Michou also sat in the chair next to his father and from afar I couldn't tell they were together. Except that his mother was there too. I didn't notice her, and when I did I was already too close. I thought I'd light my cigarette and leave, but the blue dress I was wearing caught her eye. I had to explain to her in full detail how she could get one like it, and all I wanted was to get away as fast as possible, because women have the ability to notice what men never do, the words from that far-off period that sometimes surface in the stylized sentences I have constructed for myself. But in the meantime they invited me to join them for dinner. The night was lost in any case, and it would have seemed strange if I had refused and eaten on my own. I accepted. A smile of gratitude, a woman alone. Respite from an evening of loneliness. I try to understand why this hypocrisy in particular gets to me. With the men I don't feel this way; perhaps because then it's part of the game, calculated moves like in chess, each one moves a pawn and takes a piece or two. But to pretend I'm one of them.

Women alone. Even when they try to commit suicide they disgust me. Sprawled across the crumpled bed, folds of fat swelling over the line of pantyhose elastic, their chin smeared with vomit and brandy, the room stinks of them, mumbling bits of sentences and usually a name. Moaning it, to vomit it out, too. This will not happen to me. I keep no whiskey and no Seconal, and if I ever want to go it will be clean, I tell you. I never say his name. Not even alone in my room, not even in the empty corridors with the impervious numbered doors, never. I said it when there was someone to say it to. Now it no longer exists.

✦

"Everyone calls me Michou," he said and smiled a slight, finely-drawn smile. "But I don't like it. My name is Michel."

That was when his parents went up to watch television in the games room and left Michou to amuse you a little, he's only quiet when we're here, it won't hurt him for once to talk to people who can teach him something.

"But it's hard to break people out of patterns they're used to. Particularly if they're the ones who have set them," he said. Apparently he had given a lot of thought to the matter.

"Particularly if they're your parents," I laughed.

"Yes, that's right," he said, a bit surprised, and smiled again. I liked his smile because I thought there was pain in it. How could there be pain in a seventeen-year-old smile.

It's not clear to me any more why I took the trouble. Everything he said was known and familiar, I'd long ago gone through and left behind me all that he was involved in. Perhaps that mother of his had succeeded in arousing a certain feminine malice which I hadn't thought still existed in me, after all I no longer have any need for it. Perhaps because we looked respectable together, a real family picture, and that's good for me. I think it was his smell. He had a smell I had already forgotten, of somewhat over-sweet aftershave lotion mingled with a trace of sweat, the good sweat of someone for whom physical effort is still a game, a warm body smell like earth that makes you want to put your face close and breath it in, almost a milky smell. But that's already my imagination. Thirty-four years old. It was exactly a year and a month ago. Good god, thirty-four. Two idiotic digits in blue ink smeared with Campari, two blank digits that don't mean a thing, you can play with them forward and backward, backward and forward, three four, four three. Two forevers. Two scars engraved in me by all the stampers of passports and issuers of visas and reception clerks. A succinct memorial to a succession of rooms and beds, porcelain sinks, stockings with runs, freight trains, needles of rain and the crisscross of sun, to all the slaps, the muffled whispers, the caresses, hands smoothing the brow. Thirty-four. I shudder when I think of what those two empty symbols hold.

We sat at the bar on the high stools by the counter. It was dark and cool, pleasant. Without me he couldn't have gone in; entry to the bar is forbidden to minors. I signaled to the bartender and he nodded;

a fleeting surprise appeared in his eyes and faded out, three years behind the bar and of the spark of curiosity hardly an ember remains. I saw the thought go through his mind. What's she after with him, how much pocket money can he possibly be getting, these millionaire parents are the meanest, she'll get nothing out of him. Then I saw the shrug in his eyes and he turned from us to a couple of Bacardi and Cokes for two Swedes reeking of beer. You can make a fortune from those guys who switch drinks halfway through.

He looked around him with interest, turning his head and peering into corners that shouldn't have been peered into.

"Strange, I had the impression that man was married to a blonde."

"Looks like you were mistaken."

He took his eyes off them and glanced at me, cocking his head sideways for a moment like an inquisitive bird, and suddenly his face broke into an unexpected, mischievous smile.

"Or not," he gloated openly.

I couldn't help laughing. With a trace of condescension, perhaps. At first. Then from a strange feeling of complicity, perhaps in transgression, perhaps in something else, undefined, which set us apart from the others who seemed to me distant, blurred in the wet, glazed mist of the glasses.

"What will you have?"

He hesitated for a moment.

"Scotch."

So that's what they drink when their parents clear out for a vacation in Greece or on a skiing holiday and leave the house and bar wide open. I never knew what liquor tasted like until I was twenty-one, but then I came to know it all too well.

"Straight?"

This time he didn't hesitate. "A little ice. Please."

The orchestra's playing suddenly became louder and a wave of Mantovani enveloped us, as sticky as sweet colored cotton candy. For a moment the old nausea swept over me, that which I thought I had lost long ago in the nightclubs with the bare stage and the glasses of absinthe on the tables with one short leg that always needed to be propped up with a wad of paper napkins. It's the schmaltz, I remember thinking to myself. The waiter set the gin and tonic on the table, I raised my hand to sign the check and hit the glass with my elbow and I remember thinking, unbelievable, I'm spilling a drink in the bar, when he caught it just in time and righted it. I remember being surprised, hazily, by the hand that caught the glass, decisive and firm for his age and flecked with light hairs.

"You've got great reflexes," the waiter said.

✦

I've turned on the light. I have no patience for this tossing and turning in the dark, time is meant to be used. I must start thinking more seriously about investments, otherwise the money just melts away. I wonder how much I'll get for this locket. The pearls around it look real. Beautiful antique-style work, seems almost a shame to sell it. It would go perfectly with the black velvet, but no. What I need now are government securities and bank shares. I'll buy some more National Bank shares, that's what Shipley says and he should know. If one must have a stockbroker then he should be the best, even if I am small change compared to all the big industrialists who flock around him. It's lucky he's a bit in love with me. I see it in his eyes when I come into the room, it's good, otherwise he certainly wouldn't have anything to do with such petty transactions. If only he knew. But really, in what way am I any worse than all those fishmongers?

A dealer in *objets d'art*. That was a stroke of genius, back then at that embarrassing moment in his office. But when it comes down to it, what else could I have said: any superficial inquiry would show that my main source of income is the sale of jewelry. Where I acquired the pieces would be a little more difficult to find out. But buying is the delicate part, everyone knows that, people don't like it known that they got into debt and it's obvious I mustn't be questioned. The very soul of discretion. When I think of the girls I see on the street, or those who sometimes go up in the elevator to the rooms, those who answer telephone calls, I can only laugh. I take nothing, not a cent. I don't even let them buy me cigarettes at the hotel tobacconist. That's important. It's not that I have scruples; it simply doesn't pay. How much can you charge for ten sweaty minutes between damp sheets. But a week of the greatest passion of your life—a week of madness that strikes you like lightning—that has no price. No price is too high for the discovery that everything is not yet behind you. That someone can still fall in love with you, that the pot belly and the beginnings of baldness do not matter, that you're warm and human and attractive. What price eyes that look deep into yours for a moment of intimacy whose flavor you had long forgotten, a warm hand enveloped in yours under the table, secretly. And afterward, after enough time has passed, much time, in your room, the barrier is broken, she was only waiting for a man like you, the hidden fervor bursts into flame—

I have a chambermaid deliver the pieces to the jeweler. After he has left, of course. After all there is a world, there are rules, there are a wife and three children in another town. Romance is painfully banished to the corner of memories, Tristan and Isolde died a long time ago, you can't just throw everything to the wind, things you labored to build up over the years. I quite understand. The chambermaid brings back the money with exact receipts. I make it very clear in advance that it isn't worth her while to cheat. And she gets a decent tip.

Ultimately I don't need to strain myself too hard, the world they built works beautifully for me. Vice-president of a paper-napkin company, you don't just throw that away like an old shoe for the chance of a few years of happiness. Not after all the asses you've licked and the dinners at which you stood quaking behind your chair when the chairman of the board entered the room, and your wife in the evening gown with the too-low décolleté and perhaps a blind eye turned occasionally, what's happiness. Sometimes, at first, when the affair was over, I would be overcome by nausea to the point of vomiting. Not any more. Yes, the family, I understand—my eyes wet, and I grip your hands hard—I'll get by, I promise. Even their romance has rules, a continuous function of discrete progressions, exactly fifty-four hours have to pass from the first drink to the first kiss, I worked it out, earlier isn't proper, later isn't spontaneous. Spontaneous. It's reached the point where they are no longer able to recognize the real thing when it happens to them. Nor the fake. But they did know once, that's the terrible thing, once they did know and even the worst of them once had a fragment of something real. When do they lose it. The process is so gradual, spread over years, an erosion so slow you don't feel it and at the end you no longer remember there was ever anything else.

✦

The next morning I took him for a walk around the hotel. He stood in a corner of the hall, leaning against the reception desk in faded jeans and an open shirt. His neck emerged from it slender and tanned, and I couldn't decide whether it was a vulnerable, defenseless throat, or the kind you long to lay your lips against: not to kiss, just to crush them against it so they'll absorb the texture of the muscles, the warm fragrance, the little delicate hairs on the skin. Perhaps both.

"A tour of the kingdom."

He walked beside me with a light step, effortless. In high heels you're limited, your steps are measured, you tap instead of springing, you've lost the animal in you.

We turned into one of the corridors. It led to the small terrace at the rear of the building, one whose existence was unknown to most of the guests. Our steps echoed between the walls, his muffled, a spongy rubber ball, mine sharp, short, ricocheting back to me from the walls. The corridors here are long and winding and they have unexpected twists and turns; anyone who isn't familiar with them would find it hard to believe there are such great distances here, like in the underground stalactite caves I was once taken to. The cavern went on endlessly, cold and wet in the gloom, and the stalactites protruded along the way white and still, shining with a phosphorescent light, and sometimes I longed to be standing again in the sunlight, thawing, and sometimes I wished the path would never end.

The small terrace looked out over an inner garden, a temperate imitation of a tropical forest. The green was very green in the light. The sun and the air seemed to me artificial, I remember, hard and blinding after the dim air-conditioning, hitting me in the face all at once.

"Why are you closing your eyes?"

"It makes me sleepy ... the sun."

"Strange, in the sun you don't look real. As though someone had drawn you with chalk."

"Let's go."

"You should get a tan. Otherwise you could be erased."

"Let's go, the tour is only beginning, sailor, the thread is still long—"

"—And the Minotaur is waiting for you at the end," this lightly, as if in fun, as if the Minotaur were not really waiting at the end of the road.

Sometimes I can see the Minotaur's face. It is painted with a thick layer of crude colors like a mask but it is not a mask, and it focuses and blurs at the end of the corridor, bobbing up and down in the distance like the head of a drowned man and the grin drowned in it.

"Let's go."

We walked through the wall-to-wall embalmed corridors with hushed steps. We passed the bookstore, the beauty parlor, the men's restrooms. We drank coffee in the little coffee shop. In the gloom of the carpet store we gazed at the delicate Kashmir weave, the diamond-like clusters of flowers that hill people stinking of goat's cheese had pricked their fingers on. We carefully fingered the Yemenite silver-work in the jewelry store, filigree so fine that the metal seemed fluid. We parted in the sauna and met again wrapped in white towels, weary as though life had flowed out of us and left us filled with the genuine satisfaction which is emptiness. We drank a cold drink, slowly, avidly. Come into my parlor, said the spider to the fly.

"Now I'll show you something different. The dark side of the moon."

I open an iron door in a hidden corner of the corridor and enter another world. The staff living quarters. A bare, filthy floor. Slippery. Walls repulsive to the touch, slick with the grease of the thousands of hands that have leaned against them when the electric bulb was burnt out, as it almost always is. A smell of darkness and mold, a sour smell rising from the bottom of the steps. Yes, this part too I know, I wander around here a lot. I like wandering here. Whenever I feel I'm slackening, growing soft, I come here and I get over it very quickly. It reminds me—

"Of what?"

"All sorts of places. From the movies."

I open a door. It yields at a touch. Here all the locks are broken. No need for the chambermaid's extra key. A pile of sunflower seeds is heaped on the floor. Crushed newspapers whose letters are foreign and incomprehensible. The workers here are imported from another country, raw material for the dirty work. Orange peels on the bed. There's a hole in the floor of the shower. Whatever goes into the toilet goes out through there.

"Let's go," he says this time.

And it is he who takes me gently by the shoulder and leads me away.

I lean against the iron door because I'm short of air. He stands close, very straight. How could I have expected him to be haunted by my evil spirits. Are there any evil spirits at all at seventeen. What am I doing here with him, on this side of the corridor, what am I doing at all. His buttons press into my face, and I feel the fine smell enveloping him like steam. His body is so slim, I feel the muscles and sinews in his back moving under the skin, strong as copper wires. Alive. And I let myself relax.

✦

Morning. Soon the chambermaid will come in with the orange juice and the cup of coffee. I have such reference points scattered through the day, milestones of indulgence I allow myself. I hoard them carefully during the long hours, one by one, taking pleasure in nuances, extending to the utmost this moment stretched out in bed and savoring the gamut of flavors of fresh orange juice, from sour to sweet. The taste of hot coffee in the morning.

I must get up. At nine I'll be sitting across from the clumsy diamond dealer on the dining room porch. He will shovel scrambled eggs with his fork and chew them making ugly noises. Beads of sweat will cluster on his forehead and I'll pretend not to see him take out a damp handkerchief and hurriedly dab at his face. By yesterday I should have already reached his room and I put the moment off.

Maybe this afternoon. Maybe tonight. If only he didn't sweat so much. But there's no justification for this delay. According to my schedule it should have happened yesterday, and so far the schedule has always proved itself. I built it to adapt itself to the individual, to his pace. Flexibility is the most important thing in this game. Try and rush the local bank manager, he'll panic and take to his heels. True, he'll come back to you, time and again, with a sigh that was initially mysterious and that later turned comfortable and routine, in the men's talks in the living room after the women have gone out to the porch. Nothing in it for you. His wife, on the other hand, will often hear about you in fragmented hints shrouded in secrecy. Bear in mind. I could have and didn't. This nobility of soul will poison her life. If only he would cheat on her and let her be. No, this type must be ensnared patiently, the net drawn closer bit by bit without them feeling it until it's too late. I prefer the other kind. People used to wielding real power, chairmen of boards, captains of industry. The pace is different. You can't play with them. Arouse their curiosity, yes, otherwise they won't bother, force them to make an effort, but don't overdo it. Direct and clear and to the point. Of all, that is the cleanest. But there aren't many of that kind.

"A little morning game of bridge, eh? What do you think?" The diamond dealer has finished swallowing the croissant and he wipes from his mouth beads of moisture, a blend of coffee and lust, with a napkin.

I'm an excellent bridge player. Very early on I discovered that this is a most useful skill; men who wouldn't turn their heads if you appeared on their balcony stark naked and asked for a towel, will fall at your feet after one brilliant hand. The most legitimate way to meet, the most respectable proximity. Besides, I like bridge. A cold, precise game, it's not poker. Poker is what they used to play in the small, dingy nightclubs with the lame tables. Bridge is beyond all that, raised above the smoke of the rabble's cheap cigarettes to the hushed rooms upholstered in green velvet, the white garden chairs on the balconies of the big hotels.

"Partners?" I smile a subtle, intimate smile, wasted on him. His type doesn't understand subtleties.

"All the way, ha ha." He leans forward and covers my hand with his, pressing down in a way that cannot be misinterpreted. The smirk on his face. Sometimes I think I prefer that of the Minotaur. But no, no.

In any self-respecting hotel there is a special room set aside for bridge. Square tables, green tablecloths sweeping the ground, why green. The color of foliage and money. On the wall, a large clock. You can fix your eyes on it while waiting for the next move, mint-flavored minutes trickling by. Ten-fifteen. The morning will pass quickly. That was a good idea: an unwritten pact imposes silence on those sitting here. A charged silence. The stupid or inexperienced, those who haven't been burnt yet, play with their wives. A grave mistake. Even now you can see it. Their summer safari suits are choking them in spite of the air conditioning, their hands sweat. It's easier for the women in their flimsy dresses, narrow shoulder straps cleave tanned flesh, property. Hidden looks span bridges of hatred. I told her not to go out all at once. He always makes the same mistake.

✦

Michou's parents were crazy about bridge, but they were among the experienced. Apparently they got burnt early on and managed to keep going. All in all, they seemed to get along quite well, the cautious type, don't tread on my toes and I won't tread on yours, constant and mutual alertness. Perhaps that's the only way to survive. I told them I didn't know how to play, that as a child my parents had forbidden me card games of any sort. You're missing one of the greatest pleasures in life, they protested. I saw Michou look at them. His father gave a brief summary of the virtues of bridge, but it may be said to their credit that they didn't insist too much. What with bridge and business we leave the boy too much on his own, it's nice of you that you're prepared to devote some of your time to him, that is if he's not spoiling your holiday too much—

Beside the pool. His slim body stretched out on a large towel, his toes paddling in the water. I lie on a deck chair and look at him from above. There's hardly any hair on his chest, his arms. His face is smooth. I long to touch his shoulders. They are tanned golden. A plum not yet ripe. I must call myself to attention, so as not to stare at him too much. I rub oil on my legs, the scent of almonds oozes between my fingers.

"You have the body of a real woman," he says from under the arms covering his face. I cannot see his eyes. I cannot know. In the water I see slender bodies, still tomboyish, breasts barely discernible in a minuscule bra, tanned arms cutting through the water with smooth, confident strokes. Hair hanging down to the waist. A body without flab. And in the eyes, the confidence bestowed by ignorance. Them, too, I hate. But I bow down before them, and make way, for they shall inherit the earth.

✦

Twelve-twenty. The game is coming to an end. The manager of the experimental farm in South Africa will probably go back without his wife. At the other tables too people are stretching, straightening their trouser creases, the women are fixing their hair and collecting scarves and purses. It's nearly time for lunch. What would I do without those meals. They punctuate the day. Protect it from chaos. More than that: a meal is a rite. You must be scrupulous about using the correct fork, holding the knife properly, eating with your mouth closed, not slurping your soup. A safety valve that diverts the pressure from me. I couldn't bear a world without regular meals, without bridge, without afternoon coffee, without an evening drink at the bar. To be closed in with someone in a hundred and twenty square meters of proximity. To be aware every minute of his being there. Of his knowing I'm there.

"A little cocktail to give us appetite? What?" The diamond dealer rubs his moist hands together.

"Why not?" I smile. It's already past twelve and before one, any time is good and besides, I don't drink more than a tenth of the glass. His job is to lose control. Mine is to keep it.

"Hmmm ... it's hot here. Perhaps we'll go up to my room? Or ...?"

"My room is off limits—"

How the hell can you take this liberty. Where do you think you are, at a prom. Soon you'll just get up and go because you don't happen to like his table manners. Since when have you become a princess. You need a few nights on a flea-bitten mattress with cold showers squirting from filthy walls to remember what's good for you. But the thought of it. His clumsy red body sinking into the mattress desecrating the straight lines, folds of fat on my sheets. The heat-swollen hand on my pillow. I cannot bear the thought of the whiteness violated, cannot see the straight lines disheveled. In my room there's only me alone and everything is drawn clear and straight, a clean smell of ironing drifts from the sheets. I pay the chambermaids extra to have my sheets laundered and ironed every day. They think I'm insane, scared of germs. What do I care. I want the smell of starch, this crispness that breaks when my body sinks into it.

There are also other moments. Unclean. I have needs. I try to get them over with as fast as possible so I can go on. Alone under the blankets, under the starched sheet that rustles when I touch myself, I use sentences that once existed. Someone said them someone said them to me I said them and now they are not. Now they are something that has lost its existence and has become a means, a password, a switch you touch and the light goes on.

"You want me—"

"Say you want me—"

A spongy warmth permeates me, stretches me to the last muscle. And I cry my solitary heron's cry above the desolate plain of the sheets. It rises, I hear it as though severed from me carried remote and harsh and before its peak it is cut off, and falls in the darkness.

✦

His body under the sheets was so slender it hardly disturbed the plane. A fine line drawn out in the whiteness, an imperceptible mound. Only the hair refuted the uniform white, flowing over the pillow in wild sunburned spurts. Later he threw off the sheet, tossed it to the floor and suddenly I saw him in my white empty bed, my bed and that of the chambermaids' hands, and I knew he shouldn't be there.

"I feel strange. Like in synagogue," he said and took a sip of water. He leaned his back against the wall, his legs drawn up to his chest and the tan crying out from the sheets and once more I couldn't decide. The eyes. Seventeen years old and they have a lucidity of logic that frightens me. The blue in them, the blue beyond them is clearer than anything else clearer than the light in the room clearer than the curtains clearer than the sheets on the bed and very far away in it the cold burns. A real, hewn cold, not like mine which was acquired with toil, with deliberate intent, false. It's his seal. It's stamped in him. I know this with as much certainty as if I'd put out my hand and burnt myself on it.

The small tables. The dim lights in the bar, the white latticework chairs on the balcony. They're all there and not there. And I am forcibly thrown over to the other side of the table, to the lit side of the lampshade, I lean over to take his hand. Mustn't lose caution. Mustn't lose caution. I repeat the words over and over and once more hold onto them so as not to fall, say them like a magic spell and yet they close doors instead of opening them. And I want to put out a hand and stroke, but sometimes it doesn't reach, when he looks at me with those eyes so lucid that they cut everything they touch, straight and clean and precise as in surgery.

"I thought we might go for a trip tomorrow," he says deliberately, in that slow, lazy speech of his.

"You know I never leave the hotel."

"Yes, but I thought all the same we might go for a trip. A short trip. To the park in the center of town. The Judas tree is in blossom."

I say nothing.

"We're leaving in another three days."

So much unconditioned air. Expanses of air that are not bounded within a white latticework parapet. I drown in this abundance of air. When we went out into the street it wasn't that bad, the two rows of high buildings sheltered us on both sides. But inside his parents' big car all the windows are wide open, the air flows fast and free, runs riot, swirls and eddies.

"Why are you closing the window? It's such a lovely day. Open it."

"The wind is ruining my hairdo."

He stretches a long arm over my leg, rolls down the window. The glass slides down with greased rapidity and disappears. A wave of wind assaults my face with a thousand tiny thorns. I close my eyes, slowly drawn into the game it plays with my hair, my lashes. Become aware of the flow on my face, gliding over the skin like the touch of a hand. No, far more delicately. Suddenly, by the open window, I realize the pleasure there is in pain. And vice versa. It's the same thing. All of a sudden, something grabs me by the hair and pushes my head out, beyond the window frame. I feel the full impact of the current. The wind whirls my hair wildly, locks of it whip my face with violence, causing genuine pain. I gulp mouthfuls of wind as deeply as possible, suck in the wild gusts, am swallowed into the whirlpool.

"You're absolutely crazy," he says. His hands are steady on the wheel and I feel his glance even though his eyes are looking straight ahead at the road which throws itself relentlessly under the wheels of the car and is crushed beneath them. And with a hopeless yearning I want to stop time, to freeze this moment, the wheels at their eternal pounce of conquest, the hum of the road, the smell of summer hanging in the waves of air, and preserve it, like in the old yellowing snapshots of garden parties.

We're walking along paths soaked with the mists of almost-summer. We do not touch. The Judas tree gives off a scent of pink, almost violet. I feel as though I'm inside a Japanese painting. I know I am not really here: I'm drinking a late morning coffee on the verandah. Why are we silent. Rapidly I search for something to say, dig and search and find nothing. After all I can't say, computers, how fascinating, I've heard that one day they'll replace us all. I feel lost.

"Look, ducks," he says. On the bank of the pond two ruffled ducks are standing cleaning themselves with their bills. They seem very busy. They burrow earnestly under their wings, then smooth their bills along the gray feathers as though to oil the beak. Suddenly one of them turns and in the blink of an eye delivers an evil peck to the other's plumage. Both of us burst out laughing.

"You're all right," he says and puts out a hand to stroke my hair.

A somewhat clumsy motion, hesitant, still unpracticed, and it scorches me in the soft wind of an afternoon that is slowly being consumed.

In the evening on the way back the horizon is painted a deep purple. The sky is on fire in a magnificent polluted sunset. The road is jammed, today is Saturday it turns out, and everyone is coming back to town from a day in the country. The driving turns into a slow, exhausting crawl, with sudden starts and stops. To our right is a large American car, a yellow Subaru is on the other side, and in front of us is a coach filled with high school children. The four of us move together, in tandem, as though we are all being towed forward by an unseen cable that connects us together, like the mobiles that hang from the ceiling in children's rooms. The Subaru's driver smokes cigars of strong, black tobacco whose flavor infiltrates through the window and mingles with the cloud of smoke emitted by the coach. The smoke burns my mouth, my eyes. The children in the coach make lewd gestures at us through the glass. We don't react. We both keep silent. Pretend not to see.

After the bridge at the entrance to town, which is the major bottleneck, everyone goes their separate ways. The coach belches out one last big black cloud of smoke as a memento and turns toward the suburbs in the southern side of town. The American car disappears with a screech of gears. Michou goes on driving at the same speed, unchanged, the expression on his face does not alter. He continues to look ahead. I see the white line unroll in his eyes. The evening is slowly swallowed into the road and a last soft light strikes his profile, illuminates a fine down on his cheek, chin, the slope of his nape. Creates a halo around his face, I can feel its softness from where I'm sitting. Just to stroke the ends of the hair that curl delicately, fairer than all the rest. Just to touch them with the tips of the fingers. The hand I extend trembles almost imperceptibly, lit by the same light. It's almost impossible to tell it from the evening.

Michou shakes his head impatiently. I've seen foals toss their heads with the same motion to drive away a tiresome fly that landed on their neck. He moves an arm to ward off the hand that had almost touched. The outstretched hand recoils with a jerk, torn from the fine thread that had spun it into the evening, and again becomes just a hand. A plain hand, not even tanned. You fool. How many more times will anybody touch you like that, how many more times will anybody want to touch you like that. Don't you know that they are numbered and ever decreasing. And you subtract one.

"Sorry. I didn't mean it. I just can't stand being touched when I'm driving."

I want to say it's all right, I understand, it interferes with the driving, but nothing comes out. The humiliation. Like in those days, which I do not remember.

We part in silence at the elevator door. There are different elevators to odd and even-numbered floors. In the room, I collapse on the bed and it seems to me I have never been so tired. In the troubled sleep left to me before dinner I see a labyrinth of endless paths, paths choked with wild vegetation in flaming shades of purple and red. Giant tropical leaves extend their hands over my head in wild colors of fire and I'm too hot and entangled, and I struggle against them to free myself and walk once more through the cold corridors of my mind.

✦

"Pardon me," the diamond dealer apologizes in confusion. "I don't know what came over me. Must be your perfume, ha ha. I just wanted us to be alone for a moment. All these people...." He stammers out something more and for a moment, when words fail him, he seems almost human.

"It's very hot," I say. "Better to sit outside. There's no point in being closed up in a room."

"You're right," he hastens to agree. "Stifling. Can't breath." He pulls out his handkerchief and wipes his brow. "But in the evening ... it will be cooler in the evening. Don't you think so?"

His self-confidence has been shaken. That's good.

"In the evening it might really be more pleasant inside. Maybe after dinner we'll have coffee upstairs. In your room."

And this time no postponements. No delicate feelings. I'm a day behind schedule. Eliminate all this slack.

"It's too hot to eat now. I think I'll go up for a rest. We'll see each other this evening."

He rises, pulls back the chair for me. And the expectation on his face is something I cannot bear to look at.

In the room the air conditioning is on. A pleasant gloom. I take off my dress and slip between the sheets. Divine coolness. Blessed be the inventor of starch. It's early, I came up earlier than usual and this time I don't intend to waste precious hours of sleep on things that have been and are done with. I'll get up at seven. Before dinner I'll take him for a short walk in the lobby area. By chance we'll pass by the jewelry shop. If only I accept, his victory is guaranteed. He'll plead, insist.... I've had a silent understanding with the saleslady for years now. She works on commission.

✦

A year and a month ago I got up and began dressing. Forcing myself to make up my face but failing to draw the eyeliner straight, it smears in a dark circle around my eye. I dip cotton wool in cream and remove it, start over again. What is this power he has over me. How can power derive from a deficiency. Take every year he's lacking and multiply it by all the compromises. All the surrenders. Add all the escapes. An equation of weakness. Every year he's lacking is another turn of the screw tightening the helplessness in me. How can you be a match for someone who has not yet been there.

There was the usual pre-dinner din at the lobby. The hum of tuxedo jackets rubbing against bare shoulders, quick glances of covert hotel acquaintanceships. The PA system calls from the reception desk, Mr. Graham, Mr. Graham, please come to the entrance hall. Mr. Graham, Mr. Graham. And as at that exact moment when the picture in the solution emerges from the photographic paper, he stood out from the rest of the summer suits and came into focus. His mother stood to his left in a dress cut low in the back and a lot of glitter and his father was on his other side. God I'd forgotten they existed.

"Good evening," he said and extended his hand. It was hard to decide whether he was more ashamed of his parents or in front of his parents. Maybe he was already ashamed of me too. Once things are known they are less remote, more concrete, you can be ashamed of them.

"Good evening," his mother smiled a glittering smile. Another hand was extended in turn. A courtesy touch, cool, offering no resistance to the hand that took it. "We wanted to invite you to dine with us. We're celebrating tonight. It isn't quite clear just what." From the oblique meaningful glance she threw her husband it was easy to deduce how the siesta had gone for them. Strange. People do on a weekend in a hotel what they don't do at home in a year, it's never ceased to amaze me. Change the sheets, reverse the position of the door from the bed, an anonymous closet and tiles of an unfamiliar pattern in the bathroom and you've wrought miracles. Stolen fruit. To do it in a bed not theirs gives them the feeling they have broken all the rules, you can even hear strangers' footsteps approaching and dying away in the corridor, stopping at the door. A pleasant tremor of fear. Nails digging deep into the flesh. Stop, they'll hear us, stop—

We walk together to the restaurant. Michou's mother links arms with me amicably. She really feels good tonight. Seems the endless bridge games haven't impaired her husband's capabilities.

"I don't know what you've done to my son. You've really bewitched him," she complains jokingly. "He won't be separated from you. When we told him we were to dine together this evening, a family celebration, he simply informed us he'd already arranged to eat with you. Of course we had intended to invite you anyway," she hastens to add. "But really, you've worked wonders, you've no idea. Usually he doesn't have a word for our friends."

I smile politely.

"It's only natural."

"If I wasn't afraid of Michou I'd say he had fallen in love with you," she adds in a piercing whisper that Michou can't help hearing, and bursts out laughing.

You're embarrassing her, Margo, stop it. Mr. Milan senior takes her arm and leads her forward, pointing to a showcase window glinting with the silvery frost of jewels. I remain behind. Taking care not to look at his face. To let the moment when he hates me elapse. God I could strangle that woman. And yet a feeling of warmth pervades me. All the same. He did insist.

After-dinner sluggishness. The lights are dim, soothing, reflected in the pale luster of the liqueur glasses. Mr. Milan pushes his chair back. He finds it somewhat hard to extract himself, bridge doesn't help to reduce the paunch and the tables here are crowded together to leave room for the dance floor. He bends toward his wife, inclining the upper half of his body in a would-be chivalrous bow, half serious, half self-mocking.

"Will you honor me with a dance?"

Suddenly it occurs to me that under different circumstances I could have come to an excellent understanding with this man.

Mrs. Milan actually blushes. She starts to say something, gets confused, stops. Puts her purse on the table and gets up. He takes her arm and the two of them sail off to the dance floor.

We are left by ourselves at the table. We don't speak. The air between us is saturated with all the things that have already been said this evening. At the table next to us are two women no longer young, one the old-maid-schoolmarm type, long and desiccated, a string of black beads tightly wrapped three times around her neck like a hangman's noose. Her table partner is ample, her generous dimensions burst out of the corset which is obvious under her too-tight dress. Her cheeks are painted a harsh crimson, alien to her doughy face. Her hair is platinum blond. The shriveled teacher constantly opens and shuts her purse, shuts and opens, with a mechanical motion that doesn't stop and of which she is apparently unaware. The blond suddenly leans toward her and whispers sharply; she starts and looks at the purse in her hand with a surprised glance, stops the movements of the long, dry hands whose knuckles are like knots in a rope. But a few minutes later they unconsciously glide back to the clasp and the mechanical game resumes while her eyes are fixed, seeing unseeing, on the couples dancing on the floor, open and shut, shut and open.

I look at Michou, want to say something. Change my mind and look away. Two bored American lawyers down their martini glasses slowly but with grim consistency. Every so often one of them outputs a short sentence, grinding and swallowing his words, and the other answers in a monosyllable. With a lift of his shoulder, one gestures toward the table of the fat blonde and the teacher, raises a questioning eyebrow. For want of anything better. The other doesn't bother to hide a shudder of disgust, shakes his head decisively, forget it. There are limits. The fat lady has picked up on the glance, the shudder. She turns her head and looks as though she's about to spit in their direction, but stops in mid-motion and turns her back on them. The teacher continues to stare at the dance floor while her hands are still dancing their terrible convulsive dance, open and shut, shut and open.

Another table is occupied by a middle-aged married couple. She looks at the dancing couples with a longing that has been denied so many times it has become sterile, a longing that knows it will not be satisfied. The man appraises the dancing women with a knowing look that fools no one but his wife. His face is that of a miser, although he's staying in this hotel, although I have no doubt about the two cars, about the expensive furniture in the house. One has only to see the famished look of the woman beside him.

"These people disgust me," Michou says suddenly. There is a look of repulsion on his face. But the words are not said in anger. He looks at the people sitting around us from a distance, and his words are measured with a cold decisiveness that leaves room for nothing more to be said.

"Yes," I say.

Michou inclines his head sideways and watches me with that inquisitive look the meaning of which I do not know. His fingers drum on the table.

"In another fifteen years I'll be like that too," he says. "More or less. I'll have a little paunch and I'll play bridge in an expensive club and in time I'll betray my wife with someone like you, if I find one. That's the way it is," he says and the lucidity of his eyes is a wall in its very lucidity, and equally impenetrable.

"Shall we dance?" he asks and doesn't wait for an answer but takes my hand and leads me to the floor. The dancing couples are mostly middle-aged, they're used to each other and to the old Frank Sinatra tune the band is playing. They pay a lot of money to protect themselves from surprises. We are not used to each other, his hand has to search for mine in order to hold it, uncertain movements of adjustment. At last his right hand holds my left, his other hand around my waist, my hand on his shoulder touching not touching. The band switches to La Marguerita. Our rhythm is still uncoordinated, and every now and then our feet collide. His parents' faces flash by for a moment, his mother waves at us, they disappear. The other couples spin past like a carousel. I close my eyes and let the music envelope me, let his hands guide me. California dreaming. I want very much to sink, I must get a grip on myself so as not to let go. My face is pressed against the suit jacket, I know that if I open my eyes I'll see nothing but this rough fabric. I smell the warm smell of earth and the too-sweet aftershave lotion. The only two solid sensations in a medley of motions and sounds. I try to hold on to them, for I know that if I let go I will no longer have any foothold, like the astronauts who are slowly, in hovering circles, drawn into space.

Five fingers dig into my back to the point of pain and they break through the hoarse whisper that lulls me, through the protective layer of the smell of freshly washed hair and eau-de-cologne, and tear me back to the wooden dance floor, the evening dresses, and the false notes of the saxophone. All at once I focus. I see his mother. She's leaning slightly forward at the table, in her hand is an empty glass of whose existence she's unaware, and she is looking at us.

We move with the rigid and unavoidable movements of puppets. I feel as though pinned through my back to cardboard. I cannot alter even a single movement. My movements are guided. Every one of the formal, doll-like steps is an effort.

We walk to the table in silence. Sit down. The silence crawls over us, heavy and sticky like an octopus. The dim, discreet lights, the ceiling fashioned in relief, the dancing couples, all the familiar scenery suddenly seems to me remote. Almost alien. A place not mine: there are no unplanned silences in my world. Sometimes it's necessary to keep silent, in the dark, it's appropriate then. I have no control over this silence. I long for my world which is governed by an artificial order laid down in advance, in which nothing happens that isn't calculated.

Mrs. Milan makes an attempt at a smile.

"It's very late, children," she declares with false gaiety, stumbling over the word. Not a successful choice. "Time for bed." Again, the wrong word. She resolutely gathers up her purse, her scarf. We all get up. A scraping of chairs. Mr. Milan goes to settle the bill. Nobody looks at anybody else. At the elevator I recognize her goodnight. I don't need any explanations. And I think to myself that only a woman could grasp with her senses alone, in a moment, in a brief glance, one touch, an imperceptible relaxation of the body.

✦

Again I woke up. It's not yet six, two hours until dinner. Lately I've been finding it hard to fall asleep. Maybe I need a rest, it might be better to take my vacation earlier. Once a year I go on vacation. Two weeks without working. There's a small, old-fashioned hotel, the sort that's called a family place. I go there every year. They know my peculiarities. Long ago they stopped wondering at my aloofness from the other guests. They've also learned to turn a blind eye to the occasional waiter who happens to stray into my room at night. I shan't travel within the next few weeks, I haven't yet reached the quota I never leave unfilled. But for some reason I feel tired.

The walls of the lobby in that hotel are covered with oak panels. In the evening I usually relax in one of the armchairs and sip a glass of hot wine. The wood has a warm shade that has deepened over the years, and it blends with the brown of the great logs from which the bar is made and with the tawny light that seeps through the thick glass of the lamps. Sometimes it seems to me I'm inside an old yellowed print whose edges have faded to a dull shade of brown. The whole room looks like a copy of one of the old photographs hanging on its walls, photographs that show the very same room and people in old-fashioned attire, holding beer steins and bearing a look of profound gravity. Flakes of cinnamon are scattered over the hot wine and a yellow ring of lemon clarifies it and lends it the transparency of a precious stone. I take small sips, watching the light that breaks and is diffused in the red, examining the photographs on the walls. Time passes slowly, flowing into the heavy wine and sinking in it. I see the hours slowly drifting to the bottom of the glass like sediment. When nothing is left on the bottom of the glass but the hours that have yellowed in the light of the wall lamps, I leave the armchair and go up to my room.

Hotel staff changes very frequently and sometimes there's one whose body, outlined through the seams of the tight white shirt, arouses in me a brief desire, the residue of faded needs. From the moment I first look at him he knows what I want and I know that he knows. There's no need for words. He gives me back one brief look and it's all been said. When I leave the lounge at night after I've finished my glass of wine he's there, in the corridor, or going down the staircase I'm about to climb. There are nights when I gesture to him with a curt nod, without looking at his eyes. He continues on his way. But a few minutes later I hear his footsteps on the stairs, and the low cough outside the door of my room.

The room is a mass of obscure impermeability that knows what is to come. The curtains are drawn. Dark air stands densely in the space of the room. We struggle in silence, crushing each other in wordless resentment. The sweat trickles off our bodies and is absorbed in the sheets. At the end of the act, we move apart at once as though that had been the goal toward which we were striving throughout all that mute wrestling. For a few minutes we lie, exhausted, in panting defeat. Afterward he gets up, buttons his shirt. Puts his shoes on. Slicks back his hair with a mechanical gesture, as though there is a mirror in front of him, and leaves.

I am left alone in the sweaty darkness. I lie for another few minutes in the absolute emptiness which is what I strove for, seeing nothing, feeling nothing other than the sticky touch of the sheet. Against my will, slowly, my body is replenished. Finally I get up and take the extra sheets out of the closet. Remake the bed, tug at the ends of the sheets so that they stretch straight and tight over the mattress. And then I turn out the night light and sink into a deep, dreamless sleep. I would like to sleep like that now. But now my sleep is haunted with dreams. The same dreams float up in my sleep with stubborn persistence, and in them I am always wearing my beautiful nightgown, the white one.

✦

I am wearing my white, beautiful nightgown. The one I wear for myself in bed. I brush my hair and wait. And when I hear the light tap on the door I get up and cross the room on bare feet. I open the door and stand at the entrance. He stands on the other side. We stand at the two sides of the doorway frozen in that timeless, motionless moment, and do not touch. And then he makes a small gesture with his hand, as though about to enter. The moment cracks and is broken, splinters trickle from his hands and shatter on the floor.

"Mother wants us to go back tomorrow."

"Was there a lot of fuss?"

"A whole scene. I wasn't supposed to hear, but when my mother raises her voice ... she's corrupting our boy, and so on, and so on." He flops down on the bed, hugs his knees to his body in the familiar crouch.

I'm still standing facing him, leaning against the door. Supported by it, not daring to ask.

"It's lucky father has a business engagement tomorrow. Even my chastity can't compete with that."

Is that bitterness in his voice.

"So I'm being taken tomorrow on a shopping trip. Buying sneakers, a new tennis racket, and me."

"And in the evening?"

"In the evening I'll come. I've thought of something."

I don't want to hear any more. From the open crack in the balcony door there flows toward us a pale lunar light that floods the room. Lights and sounds from other rooms filter in through the slats of the blinds, a distant revel. We're entangled in each other, I see our bodies twist in the sparse light that trickles in through the shutters, interweave, envelope each other, separate. A sinuous movement. Arches curve and cave. A snake dance without flute in nocturnal light. The stripe of light from the door falls on him obliquely and draws a relief map. I can see all the hills and valleys of his body rise and fall. But I don't want to see. I close my eyes and hug him to me with all my strength, burrow into him so as not to see.

The next morning I sleep until noon. I order a meal in my room, a packet of cigarettes. The day goes by. At five I go down to have coffee on the balcony, perhaps they've already returned. They are actually there. He and his mother. I smile the smile of a hotel acquaintanceship that knows just how far it can go, a smile that acknowledges but takes care not to get too close, not to impose. I nod politely, sit down at the other end of the balcony. Grip the white railing under the table. Forbid myself to look. She too. But our glances clang against each other like two metal balls and I know that I should get up and go. I do not get up.

Two of her friends arrive and drop into the seats beside them, uttering sharp staccato birdlike cries. They rustle the wrapping paper of the parcels they've bought, tear the string with long crimson nails. Michou gets up, makes his apologies, leaves the balcony. The lady friends rustle the wrapping paper more loudly, what a gorgeous kid, and what a build. I swear, if only I were ten years younger. I bet the girls chase him like mad.

"The young ones are not the worst."

His mother's voice cuts through the hubbub and the rustle of wrappings, sharp and clear. She enunciates each word separately. Each word drops on its own, frozen and clear like an ice cube. I know now where his cold is quarried.

"It's the older women who're the worst. Grab whatever comes to hand shamelessly, they have five minutes till closing time, and they're in a panic to make use of every minute because later will be too late. They should all be locked up. No child is safe from them. Instead of staying put at home doing charity work, they haven't a scrap of self-respect. I wouldn't be surprised if they paid them."

The latticework of the railing presses into my hand but I feel no pain. The words are heard as though they had nothing to do with me, part of the general feeling of the table, the dress I'm wearing, the afternoon breeze.

"But don't think for a moment that they manage to turn his head," her voice rises, limpid and frozen. "He's far too clever for them. Takes what they can give him and moves on. He's already had several like that," the voice continues, but the path the words traverse grows narrower and they roll along, the distance between them grows and grows and they disappear and are lost to me.

"Come on," he says. I don't see his face. His body is outlined in black against the light of the corridor, framed in the doorway.

I don't ask where to. We go downstairs and quickly cross the lobby, go out through the revolving door. He opens the door of an unfamiliar white car with rental license plates. Hertz. I ask no questions. I get in and sit beside him.

The night air assails me with great, cool waves. This time I don't try to fight it. I turn my face to it, trying to swallow it in deep gulps perfumed with street smells and night lights. The illuminated shop signs and the street lamps go by with intoxicating blindness, touching not touching. I see people, young girls wearing skirts that are already not winter and not yet summer, frizzy dogs on long leashes. People in groups and alone, people streaming in opposite directions, crossing each other's path, people in the street. I am a part of this night and also a spectator, passing it by in the traffic-lit slowness of the cars.

The shop signs have disappeared and the street lamps also become rarer. The taste of the air has changed and it no longer has the smells of the little stalls and the mixture of perfumes and sweat. It is cleansed and sharpened and from a potpourri of smells it turns into something else I once knew and can no longer remember. The headlights slice the white mist with bright beams, waver in a will-o'-the-wisp dance on the road that unrolls before us. Thin tatters of mist float before them, sway, dissipate and dissolve like night moths. I know: the sea.

We drive for a long time in the thick mass of darkness that does not change. Impossible to distinguish between where you were a moment ago and where you are now: the same obscurity, the same white beads strung and unstrung, the same feeling that behind the car window something waits, alert, biding its time until you come out so it can snatch you. The car stops at some point in the dark space. A moment of stillness, silence. Doors slamming.

The night all around is open and black. An abyss breaks against itself with a dull thud that sprays salty drops of foam on my face. Everything is so open. Exposed. A cold sea wind penetrates the coat I pull close. It surrounds me, wild, biting, nobody's property. I know I shouldn't have gone out. The walls of the bar are now enclosing the seated people with the soft diffuse light of the little wall lamps. The air is warm and dense, there's a smell of cigars and the armchairs sink under you with submissive willingness. I don't want this wild space.

I pull my coat even tighter. But the wind is stronger than I am, it whips my face with sharp, burning lashes, blows prickly volleys of sand at me, penetrates through sleeves and collar and finally sweeps me into its whirlpool. I know that there is no point in pulling my coat around me. I don't want it any more. I throw it off. The wind seizes it and lifts it into the air, and it soars for a few seconds and then falls slowly, spinning like a wounded bird. I'm free before the wind. Gulping in as much as I can from the wet night air, from the white splinters, throwing my head back to let the wind play with my hair. And suddenly I start whirling with outstretched arms, a great bird caught in the wind.

Michou catches me as I sink to the sand, carefully sets me down on the blanket. He hugs me to him, and when I lean against him a great relief spreads through me.

The lights emerge from the darkness with increasing frequency and hurt my eyes. I shift uncomfortably on the seat, crossing and uncrossing my legs. The taste of the sea is fading from the air. Again, the smells of asphalt, the open lighted door of a gas station exuding a fatty aroma of grilled meat.

"When did you rent the car?"

"This afternoon. When they were asleep."

"Must be very expensive."

"Not too bad."

"No, it's very expensive, I know."

A moment goes by. And then:

"After all, you're still in school."

He's silent. A silence that cannot be misunderstood, a warning silence. And yet I cannot avoid saying the words I know must not be said.

"Perhaps—"

"Stop it."

He cuts me off short and sharp. I knew and nevertheless I said it. Something forced me to try, although it was absolutely clear to me how I would say the words, his face, the different quality of the air between us. I had to say what my role required. The script was written long ago and I have no control over it. There are rare moments that may be outside all this but they are rare, and ultimately all words are unavoidable.

In my room, the stripe of light from the balcony and the moon filtering between the cracks of the blinds merge with the white sheets, skip over us, illuminate the curve of a hip, a shoulder, a breast. I love to see his head appear in the patch of light as though it had just materialized from the darkness, his mouth stretched in an expression of almost pain. His eyes are closed. I hold his head in both my hands and force him to open his eyes. I want him to see me. I want to brand in him my face in the light falling from the shutters, among the echoes of distant laughter drifting up from the garden chairs. He gives a little sigh, like that of a dog you've held for too long in the air, or a child, and buries his head in my breast. I didn't even hear him when he went out before morning into the empty corridor humming its eternal air conditioning, and I hope it was only at home that he found the chain I had slipped into his shirt pocket when he fell asleep, because I needed him to keep something of me.

✦

The summer lies swooning over the manicured lawns around the pool. They are such a violent green that they seem artificial. How could any growing thing look so green in this heat wave. Maybe they're made of plastic. The heat evaporates my thoughts and blows them away in a hazy cloud. I cannot concentrate. And I must concentrate. This is the right time for a preliminary survey of the scene, a leisurely survey hidden behind dark glasses. This is also a good opportunity to present the new guest: a tanned body curved in the right places, an almost imperceptible line at the corner of the mouth, no longer eighteen but not bad at all. Worth checking out.

Now at least I feel human. When I arrived the heat was simply too much and I gave up lunch and its prospects. I felt sticky and dirty and all I could think of was a cold shower and bed and the pleasant hum of the air conditioner through the sheets. I slept for three hours. Now everything is closed. I must send the ring to the jeweler's first thing tomorrow morning. Sapphire and white gold, it's not the crown jewels but it ought to bring in a reasonable sum. I hardly have any cash on me. I left in a hurry. Now when I think of it, I don't understand how I allowed myself to just get up and go. Not to go: to flee. After the first night. I never leave before the affair has died its natural death: tears, a last parting embrace, a wave of the hand at the cab as it moves away. And yet there have been far worse than him. I know: I couldn't stand the thought of any more nights. But since when do I allow myself to be unable to stand anything. The word "unbearable" was erased from my dictionary so long ago that I no longer remember how it's spelled. And yet.

At least I wasn't swept away by this hysteria to the point of losing control. I had the common sense to send myself a cable from my children. "Ben very sick. Come at once. Love." The diamond dealer stood stunned, feeling a vague desire to protest against this landslide of events, against the hasty way I was slipping out of his life, but he didn't dare. A sick child is not something you can protest against. Thank goodness for children.

The clamor on the lawn makes me tired. Children go by like colorful stains, their mouths wide open in a constant scream. The mothers shout to the children to come back. They are very well groomed, deeply bronzed with the tan acquired over many afternoons in deck chairs beside the pool, a tall cocktail glass shedding frosty drops onto the table at their side. After they've finished shouting at the child they lean back comfortably; they've done their duty and now they're at leisure to get back to conversation. Feminine voices rise and fall in repetitive waves, monotonous, one voice replaces another without any difference. Identical words fall from lips painted a deliberate red. Manicured nails remove stray hairs from the brow. A group of boys clusters around a little beauty whose hair is worked into a myriad of braids and whose nose is tiny and irresistible. She laughs loudly, openly enjoying the uproar around her. I get up and go. It's already late. Time to dress for dinner.

The lights in the lobby are dim and soft. They spill onto the people sitting next to them like a mist, flowing over the profiles, blurring, softening. This kind of light is good for my face. I'm not afraid of wrinkles; there are good wrinkles, lines of laughter at the corners of the eyes, lines of sun. And after all I don't try to look younger than my age. At least not by much. It wouldn't suit the type of person I'm interested in. No: what frightens me is this hardening of my face I've recently discovered in the mirror. The lines have become harder. A certain bitterness has appeared around the mouth. And this must not happen. Because I do not sell my body. I sell a dream. I deal in an illusion of tenderness. A delusion of intimacy. And in the candlelight the lowered gaze must not be hard. The delicate, hesitant smile cannot be distorted by a shadow of bitterness. A few months ago I read a book called *The Picture of Dorian Gray*. What wouldn't I give for a picture like that. All the stores of disgust, all the hatreds, all the great contempt piled up in me I would transfer to it. But I have only a mirror. I've begun using more nourishing creams. I read about a new cream based on mineral oil that's supposed to work wonders. Tomorrow I'll send a chambermaid to look for it in all the beauty shops.

I leave the cover of the corridor and enter the lobby. Walk straight over to the far corner of the hall. The man hidden there in the armchair by the window seems the best prospect. The suit he's wearing is made of a fine weave. An expensive wristwatch. And the loneliness is evident in him. In the way he huddles into himself, in the meticulous folding of leg over leg, the careful turning over of the pages. A half-empty drink is placed beside him. I don't make much noise when I sit down in the armchair opposite him, enough to let him know that I'm here. I put down the book, take off my scarf. Signal to the waiter.

He raises his eyes, scrutinizes the book I'm reading. *Bridge: The Art of Thinking*. I need a light.

No, I'm here on holiday.

I can stay as long as I like, there's nobody waiting for me. My husband died last year.

Computers. How fascinating. I've heard that one day they'll replace us all. Do tell me.

1982

Translated by Malka Moskowits and Dorit Peleg

Questions for Discussion

1. As Lily Rattok states in the Introduction, prostitution is used as a metaphor in "White Lines." Discuss the following topics, both as they apply to the narrator of the story and as they apply to actual women's lives: emotional manipulation of men, hatred of women, isolation and alienation, economic power, love as a commodity.
2. The narrator must exert a vigilant command over her every interaction with other people, constantly playing a role that in no way reflects her own feelings or desires. Professor Rattok argues that the narrator "achieves absolute control of her life because she forfeits it," that by denying her every emotion, she has effectively deadened all life within her. What is your reaction to this portrayal of control, to the narrator's minutely-detailed script? Is such control ever appropriate in human relationships? When? Is it ever appropriate in other areas of life? How much control is possible in real life? In what ways do we "forfeit" our lives by exerting control?
3. Dorit Peleg exercises extraordinary control in constructing her short story! Examine how she uses phrases illustrating control and phrases illustrating relaxation to convey her theme.
4. The narrator asks herself why is she attracted to Michou, but does not find a satisfactory answer. What is the reason?
5. Consider the episode when the narrator joins Michou and his parents at dinner. Why does Peleg introduce the "schoolmarm" and the "fat blonde"? Why does she introduce the "miser" and his wife?
6. Analyze any of the following motifs: whiteness, cleanliness, air and wind, light and dark, hot and cold, the many scents, lines.
7. "White Lines" is a disturbing story. Why? To what extent is the message of the story troubling, and to what extent are we troubled by the depiction of a *Jewish* prostitute? In other words, would the story be just as disturbing if it were translated from Italian or Czech?
8. The protagonist of "White Lines" is never named. The protagonists are also unnamed in seven other stories: "Excision" (the narrator and the first divorcée have no names), "The Truth,"

"Votes for Women," "A Slight Delay," "A Room on the Roof," "Ummi Fi Shurl," and "Apples in Honey." What purposes are served by avoiding names? Is the avoidance of names in half of the stories in *Ribcage* merely a coincidence? If not, what can we conclude about Israeli women's literature?

9. The narrator wants to have a picture like the one painted of Dorian Gray, so that her face will not reveal the disgust, hatred, and contempt that she feels. Discuss parallels and differences between Oscar Wilde's character and Dorit Peleg's narrator.
10. The narrator has worked out that "exactly fifty-four hours have to pass from the first drink to the first kiss," because "earlier isn't proper, later isn't spontaneous." Although fixing one particular time for the drink-to-kiss period is clearly a literary exaggeration, rules of courtship do exist and are sometimes as ridiculously extreme as this. What are some of these rules? To what extent can the rules be broken? Whom do the rules serve? How do we learn them? Consider the passage describing the waiter and the young girl who does not yet know that rules exist. How have the rules changed in your lifetime?
11. Compare the narrator of "White Lines" to Dolly in "Loneliness" and to the narrator of "Ummi Fi Shurl." Discuss the themes of isolation and alienation as explored in these works. In what ways might these be particularly Israeli themes? In what ways might they be particularly female themes?

Program Suggestions

1. In the early part of the century, prostitution was known as the white slave trade, and feminists (including prominent American Jewish feminists) worked to abolish it. Even today, most accounts portray prostitutes as victims rather than as predators. However, in a spate of recent books and plays written by successful prostitutes, women describe the sex-for-money exchange with almost as much cynicism as Dorit Peleg's protagonist. Organize a program on the early feminists' battle against prostitution and on contemporary attitudes toward prostitution.

2. The images of control, mechanization, and lifelessness found in "White Lines" re-explore the images found in Dahlia Ravikovitch's famous poem "Clockwork Doll" (1959).[1] Read the poem out loud and discuss its relationship to the short story.

1. Dahlia Ravikovitch, "Clockwork Doll," translated by Arieh Sachs, in *The Modern Hebrew Poem Itself*, edited by Stanley Burnshaw, T. Carmi, and Ezra Spicehandler (Cambridge, MA: Harvard University Press, 1989), pages 186–187.

La Promenade, Triptych

Michal Govrin

"For the time being we can rest here," said Moniek Heller when they reached the bench at the edge of the beach. "It's nice here, opposite the sea." And the soft sound of the Polish words in his mouth was accompanied by an interrogative lilt.

"Fine, fine." Lusia Taft nodded, the little smile on her face below him expressing partly submission, partly uncertainty, and partly an effort to convey thanks.

"We can wait here for the others to arrive," said Moniek, hastily pulling a large handkerchief from the pocket of his light-colored suit and sweeping it over the bench before indicating to Lusia, with a ceremonious flourish, that she could sit down.

He smoothed his pants and sat, straightened his slender back, crossed his legs, and placed his hands one on top of the other on his right knee. Then he raised his chin and surveyed the broad beach,

---

This was originally published as the first part of a three-part story entitled "La Promenade, Triptych." Michal Govrin was born in Tel Aviv in 1950. She studied at the University of Tel Aviv, and received a doctorate in the history of theater from the Sorbonne in Paris. She teaches drama at the Hebrew University in Jerusalem, and works as a stage director. She also translates and adapts works for the stage. She is the author of a collection of poems and a collection of short stories.

which was covered with mist and bedecked with a string of little flags at the water's edge, dancing in the breeze in the distance.

Lusia carefully straightened the skirt of the suit she had had specially made for the voyage and sat down on the light green bench. A woman has to try to look her best, and she set her bulky purse down neatly, next to the knees peeping out of her skirt.

"A beautiful day," said Moniek, and he went on looking at the ocean lying motionless at the bottom of the slope, as if it had been put to sleep by the mist that had shrouded the seaside resort all day long.

"Yes, a beautiful day," confirmed Lusia.

And they sat for a moment without talking, gazing in front of them at the sea. The white sand came all the way up to the bench, penetrating the little holes in the weave of Moniek's leather shoes and sticking to the heels of Lusia's broad shoes. Moniek straightened his hands neatly on his right knee, and Lusia held her full body a little more erect than was necessary.

"Really, everything is beautiful here," she suddenly announced, shifting in her place. "I don't know how to thank...."

"No need, really, no need." Moniek Heller drummed with the fingers of his right hand, and the signet ring on his finger glittered.

"The beach is so big," continued Lusia, a shade dramatically, turning her head from the glitter of the ring to the glint of the water at the edge of the beach. "After so many years a person forgets."

"Yes, yes," replied Moniek, and after a while he added, "I'm here every weekend regularly from April to June, twelve years already. In the summer I go for the cure to Montecatini, and last winter I tried the baths at the Dead Sea. It was nice there. No question about it." He shook his head slightly from side to side and then added, "And we met there too. That was also nice."

They both smiled, as was only fitting at such a moment. Moniek patted Lusia's right hand lightly with his left hand, after which he replaced it on his knee.

"Very nice what they've done there. Every convenience," Moniek recommenced.

"Yes, yes, very grand," replied Lusia in an animated tone, taking care to keep her purse upright.

"No question about it, they've done great things there in Israel!" summed up Moniek.

"No question about it," replied Lusia.

And neither of them had anything to add, especially since the country in question appeared no more real at the moment than the tiny figures of the bathers moving like dots at the edge of the water.

"I didn't ask yet how things are at the shop," said Moniek, and his fingers resumed their drumming.

"June isn't the best time of the year for wool," replied Lusia, "but as long as the shop stays open I'm not complaining."

"That's right," agreed Moniek.

"A person needs a break every now and then. After a while you get tired—you know how it is. It isn't easy with all that tension all the time," said Lusia, and her heavy voice stood in the air for a moment around the light green bench at the edge of the shore.

Behind them rose the cliffs with their grand summer houses, preserving a nostalgic *fin-de-siècle* royalty in their ornate facades. And on the beach the white planks of the walkway led right down to the changing booths at the edge of the sea.

"No, it isn't easy," repeated Lusia after a moment.

"It isn't easy," said Moniek too, and after a while he asked, "It's not too hot for you—" He almost said "Mrs. Taft," but thought the better of it and concluded on a more familiar note, "Lusia?"

"No, it's very nice here," replied Lusia, and she went on to ask the question that was expected of her, "And how are things at the shop?"

"Could be worse," said Moniek. "We're busy with the new autumn models already. Plenty of worries, as usual, but for the time being, not bad at all."

He raised the hand adorned with the signet ring, tugged at the knot in his fine woolen tie, and straightened his crossed knee. Then he replaced his hand, and finally he let his knee fall back into its former position too.

"And why not?" he went on. "The children are fixed up. And ever since Rouzia died I try to do whatever the doctors say."

And after a short pause, during which he made a number of little pecking motions with his sharp chin, he said, "And now we can begin again together, no?"

And only the drumming of the fingers of his right hand on his left went on moving the signet ring up and down.

"Yes. There's quite a lot in common," said Lusia.

"*Nu*, like we already said, wool and ladies' wear go together quite well," said Moniek with a laugh, uncrossing and recrossing his thin legs.

Lusia laughed too, and then there was another silence, which was not even oppressive, so peaceful was the expanse of sand receding into the water. For a moment Lusia lifted her orthopedic shoes out of the sand, and then she sank them back again.

"Good afternoon to Mr. Heller and Mrs.—"

"Taft!" cried Moniek, making haste to rise to his feet and turning to face the roly-poly person approaching them along the esplanade at a pattering kind of run. His full face, almost completely hidden behind his sunglasses, beamed all the way up to the crown of his bald head, and his whole appearance proclaimed that he was on vacation: from the perforated white shoes teetering rapidly to and fro to the open mesh of the shirt flapping around his thighs and the white hairs peeping through it on the broad expanse of his sunburnt chest.

"Sitting on the beach, eh?" he called as he approached. "Just the two of you!" And a burst of heavy laughter rocked his body.

"The lady is from Israel. From Tel Aviv," said Moniek when the laughter of the holiday-maker had somewhat subsided.

And Lusia turned herself around with the erectness appropriate to the occasion and put out her hand: "Pleased to meet you."

"Hirshel Feingold!" Moniek hurriedly announced.

The latter skipped from his place and lowered himself rapidly over his round belly to Lusia's hand. "The pleasure is mine entirely, mine entirely," he said, and he went on, smacking his lips admiringly, "So, she's from Israel? Very nice, very nice!"

"This is Hirshel Feingold, who I already told you about," said Moniek, as if for Lusia's ears but loudly enough to let him know that his name had already been mentioned between them.

"Oho! What did you tell her already?" cried Hirshel in mock alarm, and although he made a sign with his hand as if there were no need for them to tell, it was evident from his smile that he was waiting eagerly to hear.

"*Nu*," Moniek shrugged his shoulders in mock resignation. "I told Mrs. Taft a little about your business interests on an international scale, your branches in Hamburg, New York, London, South Africa—*nu*, the whole list, more or less. Also how right after the war, still in the DP camp, you already began making money in real estate."

"You shouldn't talk about it!" exclaimed Hirshel Feingold, swinging himself around the bench, and before Moniek had time to finish saying politely, "Sit down with us, Hirshel," Hirshel was already sitting and wiping the sweat from his brow with a pudgy hand. And leaning forward stiffly over his paunch he went on in the same breath, "They didn't open La Promenade yet? It's already after five! Everybody should be here in a minute. Henrietta's arriving in a minute too. I went out first. I couldn't stand it shut up in those four walls any more. When we come here I always say: 'You have to get the most out of the sea air, and not stay shut up in your room!'"

And after breathing in a noseful of the air, he turned to Lusia Taft and said, "So, the lady has come to us for a little rest?"

Lusia was embarrassed, and Moniek began to mutter, "No, the lady...."

But Hirshel Feingold went on without waiting for a reply, "Nice, nice, very nice. And I'm just leaving next week for my hotel in Netanyah! You know the Hotel Repose there? Not bad, eh? I put it up in sixty-two. *Nu*, I've got in Eilat and Nahariya too. We have to support the state, no? Not a bad living. But plenty of problems, as usual in Israel. *Nu*, so how can you do business with Jews already?" And he burst into laughter, which wobbled his shoulders, convulsed his belly and legs, and in the end set his hands shaking too, at first opposite each other and then clapping one against the other. Moniek too hurried, if a little late, to join in the laughter, and Lusia nodded her head after them

"Henrietta! So you got out at last!"

Hirshel reared his head and waved his chubby hand at a tall woman in a narrow-skirted suit, who was limping toward them along the esplanade. Even from a distance it was evident that it was an effort for her to put one foot in front of the next, and it was clear that in spite of Hirshel's explanations they had set out from the hotel together.

"Come on, come on, meet some new people!" Hirshel went on calling out toward her, without rising from his seat.

Lusia watched with pursed lips as the woman approached, and then she stood up and held out her hand. "Lusia Taft. Maiden name Mandelstein."

"Pleased to meet you. Henrietta Feingold," replied the woman, and her handshake drooped.

Moniek rose and bowed. "Hello, Mrs. Feingold."

And the haggard woman limped around the bench, passing close to her husband's back in order to sit down in the empty place beside him. But before she got there Hirshel cried, "I saw Arlette riding on the beach!"

And turning quickly back to Lusia and Moniek as if he were addressing an audience, he said, "Our daughter's fantastic! She knows how to live!"

"Arlette's riding?!" cried Henrietta, and sat up in alarm.

Hirshel dismissed her cry with a downward flap of his hand and was about to turn back to his audience when the sound of a shutter being rolled up was heard, and immediately afterward iron chairs being banged down on the terrace: At last the La Promenade café had opened its doors for the afternoon session which, more than anything else in the seaside town, was taken as supreme proof of the fineness of the weather.

Hirshel Feingold leaped to his feet and said, "Over to La Promenade, everyone!"

And he hurried off to make sure to get their regular corner on the terrace. Right behind him, Henrietta lifted her body from the bench and limped after him with an expression of concentration on her face.

Lusia Taft and Moniek Heller remained sitting where they were a moment longer, but Hirshel Feingold was already urging them on from the café terrace: "Moniek, Mrs. Taft. What's the matter? What are you waiting for?"

He himself was busy dragging the round iron tables together and waving chairs about in his short arms.

"Coming! Coming!" called Moniek Heller in reply, and he went on sitting on the bench with Lusia Taft, facing the white sand and the little fleet of sailing boats whose solid bellies were cut out like blue silhouettes in the mist. In the end he bent over Lusia and offered her his arm.

In the meantime Hirshel Feingold had completed his arrangements in the corner. The chairs stood untidily around the tables, as if at the end of a party. In the corner, next to the canvas partition that marked the boundary of the café premises, Henrietta sat erect, preoccupied, and silent. And as if to fill the vacuum left by her silence, Hirshel sent cries of encouragement toward Moniek and Lusia, who were coming up from the beach with heavy steps, and waved both hands at two couples who were approaching along the esplanade. "Over here! Over here!"

Among the other people strolling up and down the esplanade, bordered on one side by the café facades and on the other by the expanse of sand stretching into the mist and the sea, there could be no mistaking the destination of the two couples who were making for the corner of the weekend regulars at the La Promenade café. The deliberate tread, the way in which the ladies gripped their purses as if they were traveling bags, the embarrassment with which the man at the right buried his hand in the pocket of his loose-fitting suit, or the determined air of recreation surrounding the checkered cap set jauntily upon the head of the man at the left. The latter approached arm in arm with his yellow-haired wife, the bright pink of whose costume matched her husband's vacation air. Next to them, the couple at the right appeared somewhat ill at ease.

"I see we have new visitors today!" Hirshel Feingold declared happily.

And the owner of the checkered cap hastily dropped his wife's arm and pushed the new couple forward as he announced: "Mr. and Mrs. Harari from Ramat Gan."

"Mrs. Taft from Tel Aviv." Hirshel promptly took his turn as sponsor.

And in the hubbub of greetings and handshakes filling the café terrace with Polish sounds, Moniek bent over to explain to Lusia, indicating the man in the checkered cap and the woman in the pink suit, "The Honigers, from Paris. In synthetic underwear. A first-class business."

Hirshel Feingold made impatient gestures with his hands. "Sit down, sit down!" he cried. "Why are you standing?" And he pointed at the circle of chairs standing chaotically around the tables.

Mr. Honiger gallantly pushed the chair closest to him toward Mrs. Harari, whose gray hair was gathered into a bun behind her head. Mr. Harari drew in his legs and folded himself into the chair next to his wife. Mrs. Honiger sat down beside him like a genial pink chaperone. Last to be seated were Moniek Heller and Lusia Taft, and Lusia turned her chair carefully around so that she could see the sea from where she sat. Only Henrietta did not get up while all this was going on; she remained in her place next to the canvas partition in the corner. Mr. Honiger jumped quickly to his feet again and held out his hand to Henrietta over the tables. And Hirshel Feingold called out to the assembled company, "*Nu*, what's everybody drinking?" He beckoned the waiter with a proprietary air.

The waiter, who was apparently well acquainted with the week-end regulars, folded his hands across the white napkin over his arm and waited while Hirshel counted off the orders one by one:

"Tea, coffee, lemonade," and in the end he turned to Henrietta, who said, "I'll have tea with lemon," as if she were committing herself to a fateful decision.

Hirshel sent the waiter off, and all agog at the new audience he turned toward them and made a number of unclear, agitated motions with his hands. In the end he burst into a long laugh of contentment. When he had finally calmed down, and all the others too had finished signaling their participation in the mirth, Hirshel wiped the moisture from his forehead and said, "*Nu*, not bad here in Europe, eh?"

Marek Harari nodded his dark, pointed head and lowered it with a smile. "Not bad at all."

"Good, good," continued Hirshel, without paying any attention. "Good, all this reminds me of the joke...."

But Gusta Harari, who felt the need to add something to her husband's words, leaned over to Henrietta and said, full-throatedly, while Hirshel was still telling his joke, "We only came because of the Honigers. They insisted we should come here to them for a rest on our way home."

And when Henrietta made no response Gusta continued, turning to Lusia and smiling at her confidingly, "Otherwise how could we possibly have afforded it?"

Hirshel burst out laughing, and his laughter was echoed by Mr. Honiger and Moniek Heller. Marek too stretched his face, but his eyes remained sunken. And Henrietta, who had almost disappeared behind her husband's gleefully agitated limbs, dismissed the joke with a pursing of her lips and shifted slightly in her chair.

The waiter arrived with a nickel-plated tray loaded with jugs of tea and coffee and tall glasses of lemonade. He put the orders down in front of the people seated around the table according to their instructions. Hirshel placed his thick hand on the bill and closed his fist around it.

"It's on me!" he cried.

Mr. Honiger and Moniek Heller attempted to protest. Hirshel Feingold waved both his hands in the air and proclaimed again and again, "No arguments! It's on me!"

They all smiled in enjoyment and stirred their drinks. The mist on the beach thickened and brightened, almost hiding the glitter of the sea from the eyes of the people sitting on the café terrace. A number of vacationers strolling along the esplanade turned their heads curiously at the sound of the hubbub.

Mr. Harari lowered the china cup from his mouth to the saucer and said, "The espresso is really very good here."

"The lemonade, too." Mrs. Harari followed suit.

Hirshel gave the little cup of coffee engulfed between his hands an energetic stir and said, with the self-satisfied air of a man who has just brought a business deal to a successful conclusion, "Yes, yes, not bad. Not bad at all."

And Henrietta, bending her whole height over the table, squeezed the lemon in her glass with tiny movements, making innumerable clinking noises with her spoon against the side of the china cup.

Mr. Honiger took advantage of the pause in Hirshel's stream of words and began, "A government auditing committee came to my factory—five Jews, can you imagine?"

"I'd rather not..." began Moniek Heller, wrinkling his forehead slightly, but Hirshel replaced his little cup on its saucer with a bang, slapped them both down on the table, and burst tempestuously into the conversation. "Ten days ago when I flew...."

"And what was your maiden name, may I ask, Mrs. Taft?" Mrs. Honiger turned with a gold-framed smile to Lusia Taft.

"Mandelstein," replied Lusia, and she leaned over the table. "Lusia Mandelstein."

"Mandelstein?" repeated Mrs. Honiger, thrusting her pink-clad bosom toward her. "And where are you from, Mrs. Taft?"

"Tarnów," replied Lusia. "And you, Mrs. Honiger?"

"Chrzanów," answered Mrs. Honiger.

"My late husband had family from there," said Lusia.

"What was the name?" asked Mrs. Honiger.

"Romek Taft," replied Lusia.

And Mrs. Honiger nodded her head. "We were in Israel until fifty-five, and then we moved to Paris."

"Yes, yes," Lusia too nodded understandingly.

Hirshel's laughter drew to an end like a roll of thunder receding into the distance, and rubbing his fat hands in satisfaction he turned his attention to the newcomers.

"So what brings Mr. and Mrs. Harari to us at La Promenade?" He flung this out of the corner of his mouth at Henrietta, who was still squeezing the lemon against the side of her cup. "They're from Ramat Gan. Having a little vacation in Europe, eh?" He answered himself, and he was already turning to Moniek Heller, about to begin a new subject, when Mrs. Honiger said suddenly, "Tell them! Tell them!"—and her pink earrings swayed excitedly on the lobes of her ears.

Hirshel turned to face her with an air of pleasurable anticipation, and cried, "What, not for a vacation? So you came to get rich at our casino, eh? We have to beware of our Israelis—one of these days they'll break the bank!" He waved a fat finger at them.

"It's not important, Hella," said Mr. Harari to Mrs. Honiger. "Really, it's not important."

"What's the matter? It's nothing to be ashamed of! You can tell them," Staszek Honiger joined in, from the other side of the table.

"We're in a free country here!" And he tried to laugh in order to make his encouragement more emphatic.

Marek Harari lowered the long head sticking out of his suit, and the skin of his neck tightened. He shrugged his shoulders and said in a reflective tone, "What difference does it make? We were in Munich." And again he concluded with a weary shrug of his shoulders. "Now we're on our way home."

"Really, there's nothing to be ashamed of!" cried Hirshel gleefully. "The mark's a strong currency, and in business you do whatever's necessary. It's nothing to be ashamed of!" And his last words were swallowed up in loud laughter, which tossed both his hands about and ended in a rapid, triumphant glissando.

Moniek laughed loyally with him, and Lusia smiled too. But Mr. Honiger persisted in his explanation nevertheless. "No, they—"

"We gave testimony in Munich," said Marek Harari, and he concluded with a limp, downward flap of his hand, "You know what it's like."

"We came on Monday," continued Gusta Harari, "and finished on Thursday. On the way back the Honigers offered us a rest in their villa by the sea."

"On Thursday it was all over, and we went to Paris," said Mr. Harari again.

"Who was the case against?" Moniek Heller asked quickly, in an apologetic tone.

"Heineke," said Marek Harari, and he shook his pointed head.

"Heineke?" asked Lusia Taft.

"What?" asked Moniek.

"No, I thought..." said Lusia.

"He wasn't there!" exclaimed Gusta Harari bitterly.

"Who wasn't there?" asked Moniek Heller uncomprehendingly.

The Honigers, who were already acquainted with the facts, shook their heads in an aggrieved way. Gusta Harari clutched her purse, although it was already firmly ensconced in her lap, and said as if she were reciting, "When we arrived they told us that he was sick and couldn't stand up to the strain of the trial. We waited in the hotel for two days without going out. They told us to be ready to testify the moment he recovered. On Thursday they said they didn't know when he would recover. They took us to the court, and they wrote our testimony down in the protocol. They said that in the meantime they were collecting background information. Then they let us go, and it was over. Fela and Abel Gutt were with us too. From Holon. You know them maybe? Also from Bochnia. They went back on Thursday. We're going back tomorrow. It's over," concluded Gusta Harari, and after a moment she suddenly burst out with a fury ill-suited to the pleasantness of her gray bun, "What good did it do anyone? Tell me—what?"

"Don't say so, Gusta," said Marek Harari rebukingly, as if continuing an old argument.

"Yes, I know." Gusta took a firmer grip on her purse, and her face woke momentarily from its darkness. "It's important, but who to?"

"What are you saying, Gusta?" asked Mr. Honiger in a soothing but perfunctory tone. "What are you saying?"

"The Germans? They dragged us all the way there to tell us that he was sick," continued Gusta Harari obstinately. "Our children, perhaps? Better they shouldn't know. And anyway, they don't care. They're too busy with other things."

Marek Harari nodded his head, as if he knew all about it and was resigned to the situation.

"Yes, yes," said Lusia Taft to herself.

"Gusta, really, you shouldn't upset yourself." Mrs. Honiger threw all the weight of her genial presence into the calming efforts. "It's enough!"

Hirshel Feingold drummed his short fingers restlessly on the table top and burst out laughing. "They wrote about my painting collection in the papers! You know what they said? The condition for a good investment in art is ignorance!"

"We've never spoken about it to Arlette!" Henrietta Feingold's voice cut through her husband's laughter. "Never!" She jabbed her head forward for a moment and then relapsed into her stiff-backed silence.

"Yes." Mr. Honiger quickly confirmed, without knowing exactly what, as long as it put an end to the embarrassment. "Yes, today it's something else again; you can't go on forever living ... with...." And since he didn't know how to go on, he fell silent.

Moniek Heller said, crossing his legs more firmly, "We deserve a little peace and quiet too, don't we?" And he smiled carefully at Lusia. But she did not notice his declaration, because at that moment she was absorbed in the movements of the tiny figures on the edge of the beach.

Mr. Harari put his lemonade glass down next to the flask of water standing on the table. His glass was dry, and the water flask was empty. He shifted slightly in his chair and drew in his neck again, as if he were trying to fold himself up inside his loose suit.

Mr. Honiger straightened his checkered cap and directed a polite and perfunctory "Hmmm" toward Hirshel Feingold.

In the end Moniek Heller said, "I think we'll go to eat now. What do you say, Mrs. Taft?"

Lusia looked back from the beach and replied, "Yes, yes."

"Excuse us," said Moniek, and when he stood up he too saw the figures gleaming in the dense light of the sun hanging low in the yellowish mist.

Lusia carefully straightened the skirt of her costume and patted her hair into place with a heavy hand. She bent down and shook the hands of the people sitting around the table, and when she parted from the Hararis she said, "If we don't see each other again, have a nice trip."

Hirshel, who stood up in order to supervise their departure, made haste to intervene. "You'll see each other, you'll see each other," and he concluded with a patronizing laugh: "We don't say good-bye so quickly over here."

Moniek stretched over Henrietta's hand. "Mrs. Feingold." And he escorted Lusia out of the café terrace.

No sooner had they taken a few steps away than they heard Hirshel turning to the people left sitting around the tables: "What's the matter? Why shouldn't Moniek marry Mrs. Taft from Tel Aviv? Maybe he should better start running after young girls at his age?"

"Not so loud, Mr. Feingold." Mr. Honiger tried to silence him.

"What's the matter? What's the matter? It's nothing to be ashamed of," Hirshel went on obstinately shouting.

Lusia Taft turned her head away from the esplanade for a moment and saw the Hararis sitting between Mr. and Mrs. Honiger on the terrace of La Promenade, shrinking a little between the checkered cap and the bright pink suit.

They walked up the esplanade, climbing steeply above the bluff. Lusia Taft tugged at her jacket, which tended to crease at the back. With one folded arm she clasped her purse to her body, and with the other she beat time heavily as they walked, as full of concentration as if they had just set out on a long-distance march. Moniek Heller walked beside her with long steps. His head nodded to itself, and his fingers rubbed incessantly together as if he were rolling something between them.

"What time is it?" asked Lusia.

"After seven," replied Moniek.

"I've lost the sense of time." Lusia lifted her head. "I'm not used to such long evenings any more."

"Yes, yes," said Moniek, and he contemplated the sea, which had grown somewhat darker and bluer. His fingers went on rubbing against each other, and the signet ring shone as it traveled back and forth. He nodded his head and seemed about to say something to Lusia. But he merely smiled distractedly, and she smiled mechanically back. Her swollen feet, supported by the buckles of her orthopedic shoes, clattered and dragged alternately on the esplanade.

At the top of the bluff they passed a stone balcony jutting out from the heights of the esplanade like a platform suspended in midair. A black iron mast pointed at the shifting clouds above it. They passed it without stopping.

"That's the Wind Rose observatory," said Moniek, and he laughed a little, as if to apologize for the fact that they had walked all the way up the hill without exchanging a word.

"Yes," replied Lusia, as they started down the hill toward the row of restaurants.

The sea air was dense and briny, and the foreign voices spread over the esplanade. She tightened her grip on her purse and looked at the people sitting on the restaurant balconies, at the festive little flags, and at the slender women walking in front of them along the esplanade on their high, pointed heels. Then she looked at Moniek Heller walking by her side, his head lowered to the pavement.

"We'll eat out tonight, eh?" said Moniek in the end. "We're on leave from the hotel, we only took half-board." And he creased his lips in an effort to laugh.

"*Nu*, gefilte fish they won't give us, but we'll try to make do with the French cuisine." He went on, stressing the words "make do" and tightening his tie in order to affirm his membership in the world of the seaside resort.

But the restaurants were full, and the tables outside on the pavements were all occupied too. The diners sat crowded together nibbling at shellfish piled in white heaps, and it was evident from the satisfaction with which the waiters turned Moniek and Lusia away that business was prospering this weekend at the beginning of summer.

"Here!" Moniek pointed at an empty restaurant, where the tables were all set for dinner, and signaled Lusia to go in front of him. The waiter who hurried out to meet them shrugged his shoulders and said unwillingly, "We're waiting for an organized group, but if you like we can set one more table for you outside." He pointed to a table for two standing at the edge of the terrace, close to the glass wall of the restaurant.

"That's quite satisfactory," said Moniek, and cleared a way for Lusia between the tables. He brought up the rear and helped her pull up an iron chair and slide it beneath her, as she straightened the skirt of her costume. Then he pulled up the chair on the other side of the table and sat down.

Lusia sat up straight in order to announce that it was a very nice restaurant. She hesitated for a moment, and decided in the end against hanging her purse on the back of the chair. She placed it on her knees and clasped it to her bosom.

"Do you think we'll see the Hararis again?" she asked.

"Why?" asked Moniek.

"I want to give them a letter for Israel. For the children, you know," said Lusia.

"Don't worry about it." Moniek dismissed the subject with a smile, picked up the menu that was standing on the table, and presented it ceremoniously to Lusia. "I'll translate for you," he announced, emphasizing the importance of the occasion.

"Yes, yes." Lusia opened the folded cardboard menu. "Because if something happens they won't know where to get in touch," she said, and stared at the list of names in the unfamiliar language.

"Don't worry, really. We're here now. There's a beautiful view, and also...." But Moniek did not finish the sentence.

"Yes, beautiful!" Lusia quickly agreed, turning down the corner of the menu.

Moniek took his eyeglasses out of his jacket pocket and put them on. The thin lines of the gold frame gave him a scholarly air, arousing speculation as to what he might have become if he hadn't gone into ladies' wear. For a moment he concentrated on trying to find the exact Polish equivalent for the names of the dishes on the menu, while Lusia bent stiffly forward, all attention. In the end she said, "Really, it's all so expensive. The meal, the trip...."

Moniek interrupted her with a complacent air. "*Nu*, please. There's no need...." And he beckoned to the waiter.

Lusia folded the menu and replaced it carefully on its stand, just as it had been before.

The waiter wrote down the order, removed the two menus, and rapidly poured water into their glasses. Moniek smiled in satisfaction at the efficient service, and glanced at Lusia like a wealthy man showing off his possessions. Lusia took a slice of bread and pinched off a piece between her fingers. She filled her mouth and chewed slowly.

Moniek smiled and said, "*Nu*, it's not easy to find the right woman."

"What?" Lusia stopped chewing.

Moniek rested his hands on the table, but quickly drew back when the waiter arrived and deposited their orders before them on the table.

"Bon appétit!" he said to Lusia Taft, as if they were in the habit of exchanging such civilities. He poured a little wine into his glass, tasted it, and then poured for Lusia.

"Good, the wine is good." He smacked his lips like a connoisseur.

Lusia stuck her fork into the steak and began cutting it slowly across.

"We can still begin again!" said Moniek.

"Yes," replied Lusia. She put the meat into her mouth, praising it as she did so. "The meat is very good."

"Yes, it's good," said Moniek, stretching his legs under the table, and he addressed himself to the plate in front of him.

They sat chewing, on either side of the table, then sipped their wine, and resumed their chewing.

"Nothing like this in Israel, eh?" said Moniek, scraping the meat from the bone. He straightened his woolen tie and continued, "Everything is so tense there. A hard life. Here at least a person can live in peace. Afford to take a break in a seaside resort from time to time."

The waiter stopped a number of people who were about to sit down on the terrace of the restaurant.

"Inside if you wish. Outside all the tables are booked!" he said as they tried to argue with him, pointing in an aggrieved way at Moniek Heller and Lusia Taft.

When their dessert was placed before them the sun had already set, and the bluish light of the long evening had enveloped the terrace. The esplanade was full of weekend vacationers, and their light clothes were also covered with the blue dust.

They had already placed their spoons next to their glass dishes, and Lusia had opened her purse and removed her lipstick in order to freshen the makeup that had smeared on her lips, when a large tourist bus drew up in the street in front of the restaurant. It maneuvered heavily until in the end it parked right outside the terrace, completely hiding the fishing harbor on the other side of the esplanade and the play of light and evening on the clouds.

The waiter hurried to the entrance of the terrace in order to welcome the people descending from the bus two by two and talking loudly to each other in German. At their head marched a short, plump man who seemed to be the tour organizer. The waiter ran behind the tourists and showed them to their places. The organizer made jokes, and from time to time he slapped the shoulders of the seated tourists. And in the space of a few minutes the terrace was packed full of couples sitting in crowded rows. And all alone in the corner, as in a tiny enclave, stood the table of Moniek and Lusia.

The manager of the restaurant came out. He was wearing a black suit and a bow tie in honor of the occasion. He too received a friendly slap on the back from the organizer, and then he hurried off behind the waiter to collect the orders from the diners and to see that everything was to their satisfaction. The waiter deposited bottles of beer and wine along the tables, which was greeted with cheers and an outbreak of loud chattering.

Moniek screwed up his napkin and wiped his mouth with it several times. The waiter banged their glasses of tea down in front of them and hurried off with his tray to serve the German tourists.

"Comment-ça-va?" The man sitting closest to their table at the end of the row of diners turned his face toward them with a broad smile.

His words attracted the attention of the people next to him to the couple sitting on the terrace, and they all turned smiling faces toward Moniek and Lusia.

"Non parler français." A second man, wearing a brown-checked suit, joined in the conversation, laughing with the full weight of his body.

The wives of the two speakers stared at Lusia with the respect due to a native of the place. One of them, whose hair hung like a fair ball around her head, pointed to her lips in order to indicate that she did not speak the language, accompanying this gesture with a low laugh.

The first man, who apparently knew a greater number of words, went on. *"Nous bataillons ici, comprenez, bataillons, Krieg."* He pointed to the people sitting around the tables and, broadening his smile and shaking his head from side to side in an exaggerated way as if he were telling a story to children, he continued, *"Maintenant ici. Visite. Visite. Avec Frau. Comprenez?"* he asked, and burst into friendly laughter.

And as if waiting for a signal to join in, the man in the three-piece brown suit and the two women also laughed, nodding their heads at Moniek and Lusia.

The waiter returned and unloaded his tray.

When Moniek picked up the bill lying on the table, the Germans were already tackling their first courses. Moniek placed some bank notes on the saucer with the bill and rapidly counted out the coins for the waiter's tip. He stood up. Lusia stood up too, and gathered her bulky purse to her bosom.

The man with the square chin turned toward them, smiling through his chewing, and said, *"Au revoir Madame, au revoir Monsieur!"* He waved his hand at them.

The two women also turned their heads, and the man in the brown suit quickly wiped the grease off his lips with his napkin before calling out in a broken accent, *"Au rouvour! Au rouvour!"*

Moniek and Lusia squeezed their way to the exit along the space left between the outer wall of the restaurant and the chairs of the diners. Moniek went first and Lusia, treading heavily in his wake, had difficulty finding a place to plant her orthopedic shoes. Sounds of satisfaction and chewing filled the terrace. Laughter accompanied the raising of beer and wine glasses and the jokes and anecdotes. The people seated next to the wall of the restaurant turned their heads to look after them with expressions of enjoyment at the food and the cheerfulness of the occasion.

They walked away along the esplanade, and the German voices from the restaurant terrace were gradually swallowed up in the noises of the evening. The restaurants were still full, and the empty shells of the white shellfish stood in piles. A troop of youngsters in black leather jackets and tight boots passed them. Moniek and Lusia made their way through the people standing next to the brightly lit show windows, and when they approached the Municipal Casino they saw women in evening dresses and fluffy fur capes stepping out of black limousines and disappearing up the marble staircase like huge moths, leaving a train of darkness behind them.

As they reclimbed the bluff opposite the observatory Lusia glanced at Moniek and saw that he was looking down at the pavement. They walked without saying a word. Lusia's heels clattered in the intervals between his steps, and she clutched her bulky purse tightly to her bosom still, as if she were leaning on it for support as she walked.

The darkness spread toward the street lamps, and down below, on the beach next to the water, the twilight trembled. Lusia shifted her purse from hand to hand and drew the lapels of her jacket together to arrest a sudden, chilly breeze.

"Did the doctor send you to have tests?" she asked.

"Yes," grunted Moniek.

"What were the results?" continued Lusia.

"He said there was nothing to worry about in the meantime. But still, I should start taking things a bit easy. Get used to the idea that things aren't what they used to be."

"But he was optimistic, no?" persisted Lusia.

"Yes, I think so," answered Moniek, as they passed the balcony of the dark observatory.

After a second Lusia said, "That's encouraging."

The lamp on the post rising from the observatory was unlit, and the balcony with its shell-shaped stone balustrade hung over the sea like the shadow of an obsolete grandeur.

"I don't know what kind of world we're living in!" Moniek suddenly burst out, and his sharp chin trembled. "How they can come here without being ashamed, I don't understand!"

"Don't think about it," said Lusia, almost to herself.

"There are some things I just don't understand," continued Moniek, striking his head passionately with the palm of his hand. "I just don't understand!"

"Romek also used to say that people should learn from the past. He was a man with values," said Lusia. "But how long can you go on thinking about the same thing?"

"The cheek of it!" continued Moniek, and his voice grew tired.

"Really, Moniek, you shouldn't upset yourself," said Lusia, and there was a certain tenderness in the way that she beat time with her free hand.

"Yes," said Moniek, and he tugged distractedly at the hem of his jacket.

They descended the esplanade from the top of the bluff and the observatory, and Moniek's steps resumed their subdued tapping between Lusia's heavy strides.

"Yes, there are still a few good years in front of us," he said.

"Yes," said Lusia, and nodded her head.

When they turned their backs on the light that was still clinging to the sea, Lusia continued, "Whatever happens, I'm getting some repairs done in my apartment. The marble on the sink top in the kitchen, and the balcony blinds."

"Whatever happens," Moniek repeated after her.

They walked along the spacious street of the seaside resort. The ornamental trees planted between the street lamps on the avenue swayed in the evening breeze coming from the sea.

"Remind me to take a sleeping pill when we get to the hotel," said Moniek.

"All right," said Lusia.

When they were approaching the hotel, in the light of the elegant display windows, Moniek Heller turned his head and stole a quick glance at the woman who was walking beside him with a heavy tread.

The next morning Moniek knocked on Lusia's door, as arranged.

"Mrs. Taft. Lusia." He bent over the door in the passage.

"Yes, yes," answered Lusia, who was already awake in her bed.

"Sorry I have to hurry you up," continued Moniek behind the door, "but Hirshel Feingold called and invited us to a celebration. I didn't understand exactly of what."

"I'll be ready in a minute," replied Lusia, and she sat up in bed among the big pillows and the sheets, which were still starched although she had already slept in them for two nights. The big room was dim, and underneath the high ceiling strange smells drifted. The night had left a murky residue in her. She supported herself on both elbows and descended slowly from the high bed. She pulled the curtains apart and pushed the balcony shutter open. On the sunlit wallpaper countless shepherds and shepherdesses with their flocks rested under pale blue trees. They climbed to the ceiling and disappeared behind the big wardrobe.

She went into the bathroom and rummaged in her old toilet bag in order to take out the toilet articles that for some reason she hesitated to leave displayed in the place intended for them, on the glass shelf glittering underneath the mirror. She turned her back—for years now she had avoided looking at herself naked in the mirror—and mechanically finished fastening her corset and pulling on her orthopedic stockings. Then turned around, and with a few vehement strokes she painted the vivid color over the slit of her lips. When she had finished powdering her forehead and cheeks she threw her things back into the toilet bag and straightened her crushed coiffure.

When she had finished dressing she sat down for a moment on the corner of the high bed ready to leave, with her bulky purse already in position on her knees. For a moment she ruminated on the Sabbath day here, which stretched on into the Sunday after it, and then she immediately bent stiffly over her purse, with her short legs dangling, and made sure that she had not forgotten to put in her compact. And while her hand was busy delving into the bag, she also made sure that she had her medicines. She stood up, wondering apprehensively whether she had creased her skirt, and straightened the bedspread, whose design of sailing ships affirmed the holiday atmosphere. From the balcony window she saw the two trees in the hotel garden. She crossed her hands under her bosom around the strap of her purse, and went out of the room.

When they had finished eating breakfast Lusia took the lipstick out of her purse again, and roughly repaired the drawing around her lips. Moniek crumpled the napkin and placed it on the table. He rose from his chair and approached Lusia to offer her his arm. A heavy smell of perfume rose from her body. He was wearing his brown silk tie today, and it shone smoothly and darkly between the lapels of his jacket.

When they stepped outside he was troubled by the pressure on his chest, which had grown worse since the chestnuts had come into blossom. This morning too the sky was covered with a mist, and the air was not yet really warm. Only a few bathers had ventured onto the white beach, and the little flags strung between the lifeguard stands waved limply. They hastened down the wooden walkway on the beach in the direction of La Promenade. Moniek leaned over to tuck his hand in Lusia's arm, together with the strap of her purse. Lusia patted her hair, and every time she put her heels down on the wooden planks the noise of their dragging dissipated the air of uncertainty that accompanied her deliberate tread.

At the other end of the wooden walk Hirshel Feingold, who had come out to meet them, was already waving his hands at them, like a bright, capering dot on the open beach. He covered the distance between them at a scampering run, and the coconut trees emblazoned on his shirt this morning swayed violently from side to side.

"They wrote about it in the newspaper!" he shouted, spreading a big sheet of paper out in front of them.

When he reached them he grabbed Moniek by the arm, pumping it up and down in his agitation. "I took the Hararis to the casino last night, to let them have a look. But with Hirshel there's no such thing as just watching. I started playing with a hundred, and ended up by breaking the bank! They shut the casino down when I won!" He burst into expansive laughter, and hit the rustling paper with the back of his hand. "Take a look!"

Lusia and Moniek bent over the newspaper and saw a dark picture of Hirshel embracing two uniformed croupiers against the background of the roulette table, his round face beaming.

Still laughing, Hirshel snatched the paper away, disappearing for a moment behind the sheet spread between his two hands and emerging again with a gleeful face after he had folded it. Once again he grabbed Moniek's arm and started pulling him behind him.

"First we'll have champagne at La Promenade," he announced, "and after that lunch at the Excelsior. Hirshel never misses a chance for a celebration!" And he was off again, running in front of them with his low shoulders swaying from side to side, and with them the coconut trees on his shirt.

On the terrace of La Promenade Henrietta stood tensely, twisting and untwisting the strap of her purse. Next to her stood a man in a striped suit and a brown hat. Moniek presented him to Mrs. Taft. "Allow me to introduce—Lusia Taft, Mr. Tzuker."

"Pleased to meet you," said Lusia with her polite smile, and she shook hands with Henrietta, placing one foot in front of the other in order to indicate that as far as she was concerned the walk was over.

"He was with us in the same DP camp," whispered Moniek into Lusia's ear. "Also in ladies' wear. He never comes before Saturday night—can't afford to shut his business down earlier."

Lusia nodded her head understandingly and went on smiling at the owner of the brown hat.

"Arlette hasn't arrived yet!" Henrietta burst out.

"But Mrs. Feingold," said Mr. Tzuker soothingly, obviously for the umpteenth time, "You know what the youngsters are like today. Really, there's nothing to worry about."

But Henrietta was not appeased, and she went on wringing the strap of her purse with small, rapid movements.

Hirshel, at the table, clapped his hands. "Mrs. Taft, Mr. Tzuker, Moniek! We're all waiting for you!" and he signaled to the waiter, who hurried to uncork the bottles of champagne standing on the table.

They sat down in their usual places, except that this morning Mr. Tzuker seated himself helpfully between Lusia and Henrietta. Hirshel rose to his feet and poured the frothing liquid into the glasses with a flourish.

Marek Harari choked a little and coughed. Gusta Harari hurried to pat him on the back. Marek's sallow face flushed like an elongated copper dish. When his coughing had subsided he raised his face apologetically and smiled at Hirshel Feingold, who was already refilling the glasses. Hella Honiger laughed, and her broad bosom looked more authoritative than ever inside its pink jacket. Mr. Honiger nonchalantly emptied his second glass of champagne, and Lusia whispered confidingly to Moniek, "I'm not used to drinking so much."

"A little celebration never did anyone any harm," replied Moniek, clinking his glass ceremoniously against hers.

"Us too! Us too!" Staszek Honiger called out from the other side of the table, stretching across to clink his brimming glass against Mrs. Taft's and half rising to his feet as he said, "Really, you should only be...." But he sat down again without finishing his sentence. "They haven't said anything official yet, so maybe it's better not to be in too much of a hurry," he muttered to himself, and in order to cover up his over-hasty gesture he addressed the rest of his toast to Henrietta: "They should only be happy, the young ones!" And he gulped down the rest of his champagne, holding his jaunty checkered cap in place with the back of his hand.

Hella Honiger chipped in quickly, "Yes, the young ones should only be happy!"

Mrs. Harari too raised her glass in a burst of emotion and announced, "They shouldn't suffer; they should live in peace! That's the most important thing. In peace and quiet!"

"Drink up! Drink up! Don't be lazy!" urged Hirshel Feingold, lifting another bottle from the tray, which was already covered with a puddle of champagne, and impatiently filling the glasses. "You should have seen the people in the casino last night; they were fit to burst!" he said, pouring the champagne onto the table without paying any attention to what he was doing. He added, shaking with laughter, "I think they won't let me into the casino again! Ha ha!"

Marek Harari leaned toward Mr. Honiger and said something to him. Gusta Harari nodded quickly in agreement. Mr. Honiger agreed too, and hastened to say, "We have to start moving already. The Hararis have to be at the railway station."

"Yes, yes," said Marek Harari, jumping up from his place. Gusta rose immediately after him and stood beside him, ready to go.

Hella Honiger said, summing up with an official air, "It was a pleasure!"

Lusia Taft made haste to rise after them. "I'll give you my telephone number. If you could get in touch...."

"Out of the question! You're not going like this!" Hirshel cried, clapping his hands for the waiter. "We're all going to see our Israelis off. *Nu*, *nu*!" He urged Mr. Tzuker on, signaling him to support Henrietta, fumbled with his wallet, and rapidly placed the bills in the waiter's hand.

Lusia Taft finished writing the telephone number down on a piece of paper and bumped into a chair as she hurried around the table to Gusta Harari. The waiter folded the bills into the pocket of his coat, highly satisfied with the generous tip he had received, to judge by the number of times he bobbed his head at the celebrants as they withdrew. Moniek smoothed his brown silk tie and waited for Lusia Taft.

Henrietta Feingold rose to her feet and announced, "I'm not going. I'm waiting here for Arlette!"

"But Mrs. Feingold, really, there's nothing to worry about." Mr. Tzuker, who depended on the good will of Hirshel Feingold for his living, immediately renewed his coaxing. "Nothing has happened!"

Hirshel bustled the company out between the tables and ran on ahead of them up the esplanade, his hands churning at his sides. After him Mr. Tzuker hurried to give his arm to Henrietta, who rose obediently to follow her husband, and it was evident that he was torn between his desire to run loyally side by side with Hirshel Feingold and his duty to keep up with the limping pace of Henrietta, who kept her head back in the effort to locate Arlette.

Mrs. Honiger, a cordial guide, sailed beside the embarrassed, slightly charred figure of Marek Harari like a heavy pink ship. Lusia threw her pencil back into the belly of her purse, and Gusta Harari closed her own purse on the envelope with a sharp click. Gusta, in her old traveling costume, hurried after Mr. Honiger, who thrust out his head in order to emphasize the carefree holiday air proclaimed by his checkered cap. And the last to leave were Moniek Heller and Lusia Taft, who brought up the rear of the little procession.

Marek Harari hurried behind the limping Henrietta and the swaying Mr. Tzuker, as if he were taking shelter under the shade of Hella Honiger's bosom. His narrow forehead stretched, giving his whole figure a questioning air. "I hope there won't be any problems," he said.

Mrs. Honiger turned both hands toward him and began encouragingly, "But Marek, everything will be all right. You'll arrive in time. You'll take off in time. And this evening you'll be at home already." Her bosom forged ahead like the vanguard in front of the troops.

"Yes, yes," Mr. Harari submitted.

"It's good that you came for a little rest," said Staszek Honiger behind them to Mrs. Harari, pulling his cap backward and forward on his head.

"Really, there are no words to thank..." said Gusta Harari, "It was all such an effort—"

"It's good that you came!" Mr. Honiger cut her short. "A wonderful opportunity to see the villa we bought here. *Nu*, so we achieved something in the end. If we'd stayed in Israel, who knows...." He looked a little pityingly at Marek Harari, and returned the checkered cap to its proper position on his head.

Marek Harari bowed his head to the pavement, and the skin of his neck tightened. "I don't know how we'll go back to everyday life after all this," he said, and his chin reached out to the sea, distant at the bottom of the bluff. "It won't be easy. No, it won't be easy,"

And Mrs. Honiger pursed her lips in disgust and made no more efforts at encouragement.

Lusia was tired of running back and forth, first from the hotel to the café, and now from the café to the restaurant. She tightened her grip on the purse beneath her bosom, dug her heels heavily into the pavement, and made an effort not to lag behind in the climb up the hill. Moniek smiled wryly, perhaps because of the fast pace, which was quickening his breathing, and perhaps as a result of the debate taking place inside him. "It's all coincidence," he announced to Lusia, as if he were making a confession, "why we landed up here instead of somewhere else." He fumbled with his tie, and the square signet ring on his finger wandered to and fro. "In the beginning we wanted to get established, and afterward the children were already used to it."

"Yes, yes." Lusia swung her arms heavily and concentrated on the effort of walking.

"That's the way it is," continued Moniek. "A person doesn't always end up where he wants to." Lusia shrugged her shoulders and tightened her hold on her purse.

"If we start thinking about what we really wanted..." said Moniek, and let out a laughing groan. After a moment he made a couple of bobbing movements with his head as a sign of cheerfulness, tucked his hand into Lusia's elbow, and said, "So what? We've still got a few good years in front of us, eh?"

Lusia's broad shoes beat the pavement heavily, and she said, "As long as we've got our health. That's the most important thing." And she shifted her purse to her other hand.

The people strolling along the esplanade turned their heads to gaze after the cavalcade advancing between the calm seaside villas and the bright signs of the delicatessen shops. At the head the coconut trees emblazoned on Hirshel Feingold's shirt waved frantically to and fro. After them dragged the limping Henrietta, with Mr. Tzuker bursting coaxingly forward. Bringing up the rear in sudden spurts were Hella Honiger's pink bosom, Gusta Harari's little face, and the stubborn figure of Lusia Taft.

When they reached the top of the bluff, next to the balcony of the Wind Rose observatory and the mast sticking out of it, Henrietta suddenly stopped. The people coming up behind almost bumped into her, like the ragged tail of a carnival dragon. “I can’t go on!” she said firmly.

Hirshel, several paces ahead, came back at a run and went on jumping from one foot to the other on the spot, as if the sudden halt had not interrupted his running at all.

“I can’t run any more!” Henrietta flung at him. Then she pulled her hand from Mr. Tzuker’s arm and dragged herself to the stone parapet of the esplanade. She leaned against the parapet and scanned the beach anxiously.

The unexpected halt cast the Hararis into confusion, and they opened feverish consultations with the Honigers about the amount of time left before they had to catch their train.

Moniek and Lusia stood where they were, as if waiting for instructions.

From the other side of the bluff the German tourist group advanced on the observatory, and the echo of their laughter and loud voices rose in the street.

“I think we’ll have to go,” announced Marek Harari apologetically, pointing to the watch peeping out of his sleeve.

Gusta chimed in like an echo, “Otherwise we’ll be late.”

On the balcony of the observatory the war veterans crowded. They pushed toward the shell-shaped balustrade in order to examine the old Wind Rose carved into the stone with its arrows and its famous pictures of towns. Peals of laughter accompanied their exultant shouts: “Hong Kong! New York! Berlin! *Ja, ja,* Berlin! *Auch* Düsseldorf!”

Hirshel Feingold skipped across the space between him and the Hararis, and the coconut trees waved in agitation. He shook the Hararis’ hands rapidly. *“Bon voyage! Bon voyage!”* he cried, slapping Marek Harari on the arm. He capered up and down and announced, “I’m going on to tell them to expect us at the restaurant.” He waved at the little group with a chubby hand, crying firmly to the Honigers, “This afternoon as usual at La Promenade, eh?” And, turning his head, he charged toward the observatory, where the veteran warriors were at that very moment emerging, accompanied by their wives. Hirshel waved the folded newspaper tucked beneath his arm at them in passing, as if to say, Yes, yes, that's me! And, his short, bright figure disappeared into the dense stream of tourists.

Gusta and Marek Harari made haste to take their farewells from Henrietta, and after them the Honigers too took their leave.

"I hope that nothing has happened to Arlette." Henrietta stared distractedly.

"But really, Mrs. Feingold," said Mr. Tzuker reprovingly, in a louder voice than usual, in order to make his words heard above the vociferous conversations eddying around them, like a current flowing past some small obstacle in its way.

"Don't forget to call," Lusia Taft thrust forward in the direction of the Hararis.

"The minute we arrive!" said Gusta, smacking her purse as she spoke.

Moniek approached to say good-bye, but he gave way to Mr. Tzuker, who ran up to shake hands, bowing and making his brown hat bob up and down.

"*Nu*, good." Mr. Harari shook hands with Moniek Heller and Lusia Taft, who was standing next to him

A moment of confusion ensued as the Hararis got ready to leave but were prevented from doing so by the organized group of German tourists blocking their way.

"Good luck for the future," said Gusta Harari in the meantime, and she and her husband nodded their heads in the direction of Moniek Heller and Lusia Taft.

Hella Honiger crossed the road with a confident air. Staszek hurried after her, calling out to the Hararis to follow them down the road disappearing between the buildings of the little seaside town.

The esplanade emptied of the group of Germans, who started down the bluff in the direction of the row of cafés, and Hirshel had long ago been swallowed up behind the observatory on the other side. Mr. Tzuker was unable to persuade Henrietta to continue the walk to the restaurant, despite all his calming efforts and all the brown noddings of his hat. He left her where she was, collapsing against the stone parapet, and stationed himself a couple of paces away, like a bodyguard. His face was turned half to the esplanade and half to the sea, as if he were announcing a time-out.

Moniek Heller linked his arm in Lusia Taft's and took a few slow steps up the hill with her. Next to the observatory balcony he said, "*Nu*, in the meantime why don't we..." and he pointed to the two steps.

"Really, the beach is so big," said Lusia, clattering her shoes on the steps and approaching the balustrade.

"Yes," said Moniek.

Lusia leaned her elbows on the carved stone balustrade, between the miniature etching of the churches in Stockholm and the one of Negroes bathing in the sea in Cape Town. Moniek too rested his hand on the balustrade and called out at random: "Shanghai!"

"Tarnów we won't find here, and Tel Aviv didn't exist when they built the observatory," he said, and laughed.

Lusia contemplated the mist covering the beach and the bay. Moniek fingered his signet ring limply, and after a moment he placed his hand over Lusia's between a picture of Brussels and one of Amsterdam.

"Yes," he said, as if in continuation, "the main thing is that we're here." And without waiting for an answer he added, "That's already a miracle."

Lusia nodded her head mechanically. "Yes, yes."

And she turned her head from the beach to the street. For a moment, she saw the regulars of La Promenade scattering to the four points of the compass—Hirshel Feingold bouncing like a brightly colored ball in the direction of Moscow, where the arrow pointed; the Honigers and the Hararis disappearing into the shadows of the street between the old hotels in the direction of Madagascar; Mr. Tzuker standing guard on the latitude of Sao Paulo; and Henrietta frozen next to the parapet, her face turning toward some unknown point in the distance, a mask of anxiety.

"We can begin again too. Why not?" said Moniek. The words came out of his mouth at first with animation and in the end with uncertainty.

"Yes, yes." Lusia went on nodding her head, without remembering exactly what it was that she was agreeing to.

Once more Moniek tucked his arm in hers, and they climbed the two steps from the observatory to the esplanade. And they set out again. Moniek Heller lifted his chin. Lusia Taft's heavy shoes clattered. Dutifully she breathed in the healthful air of the seaside town.

1984

Translated by Dalya Bilu

Questions for Discussion

1. What aspects of Israeli and European Jewish society are represented by the five men and four women who meet at La Promenade café? In what ways are the characters typical of Holocaust survivors? In what ways are they atypical?
2. Michal Govrin uses details of a character's dress or behavior to portray a psychological trait. For instance, Lusia Taft's broad orthopedic shoes and her clattering gait are mentioned at least five times. How do you react when you read of the shoes? Other frequently-repeated details include Mrs. Honiger's pink suit, Mr. Honiger's checkered cap, Hirshel Feingold's coconut-print shirt, Lusia Taft's bulky purse. How do you react to these? What other external details does the author use to illustrate the characters' internal life?
3. Mrs. Honiger says, "Our children ... better they shouldn't know." As the others attempt to calm her and change the subject, Henrietta Feingold cuts in, "We've never spoken about it to Arlette!" In your opinion, how much should Holocaust survivors discuss with their children?
4. Moniek Heller reacts with anger and passion after encountering a group of German war veterans and their wives. What is your reaction to this fictional meeting? How do you react when you see vacationing German tourists or German immigrants to America? How would you react if you knew the men had served

in the German army? Even today some Americans define their Jewish commitment by refusing to own German automobiles, drink German beer, etc. What is your opinion?

5. The Israelis—Lusia Taft, Gusta Harari, and Marek Harari—are less wealthy than Moniek Heller, the Honigers, and the Feingolds, who live in Europe. Yet, the Europeans all comment at some point on residing outside the state of Israel. What can readers conclude?
6. Michal Govrin never explicitly names the luxurious, French-speaking, seaside resort where her characters are vacationing. Only after many pages does the reader learn that the resort is in Europe. What is accomplished by this indirection?
7. The characters all speak together in Polish, though they make their homes in France or in Israel. Also, except for Lusia Taft, all seem to have remained close friends for about forty years after having been together in a Displaced Persons camp. What is your opinion of their continuing closeness? What is your opinion of their speaking Polish? Do you make allowances for Holocaust survivors that you do not make for other immigrants?
8. Moniek Heller states several times, "we can begin again." In speaking to Lusia Taft, he is referring to marrying again, but he, like the other survivors, has already begun again at least once. Comment on beginning again—as a survivor and as a spouse.

Program Suggestions

1. Michal Govrin gives a quiet, realistic portrait of Holocaust survivors in "La Promenade." There is no mention of the Holocaust itself, and there are no remembrances of torture, sadism, deprivation, or debasement. The author never uses the literary techniques of magical realism; indeed she uses no dream-like or fantastic imagery at all. In these ways, Govrin differs from many Israeli and American Jews who write on the topic. Using "La Promenade" and one or two other stories or novels, organize a program on Holocaust survivors in contemporary fiction. For instance, the literary styles of David Grossman's *See Under Love* (which focuses primarily on the child of

survivors), Cynthia Ozick's "Rosa," and Shulamith Hareven's "Twilight"[1] all contrast sharply with "La Promenade." What does each writer achieve through the use of a particular style? For a three-part program, you might also include a seminar on the Holocaust itself as portrayed in literature, perhaps comparing American and Israeli authors, as well as a seminar on Holocaust survivors as portrayed in other media—especially movies.

2. Approximately 333,000 Holocaust survivors settled in Israel, a nation of 3.5 million Jews. How did this massive immigration influence Israeli society? What influence did the immigration of approximately 140,000 Holocaust survivors have upon 5.5 million American Jews? Invite a scholar of Jewish sociology or demographics to speak to your group about survivors, their lives, and their impact upon Israel and America. (A number of survivors and survivors' children are themselves expert speakers on these topics.) Discuss William B. Helmreich's *Against All Odds: Holocaust Survivors and the Successful Lives They Made in America.*[2] What do similar studies show for Israeli Holocaust survivors? In Michal Govrin's story, all the characters have successful businesses (and some are extraordinarily prosperous), and most have children who, the reader can infer, are leading full lives of their own. Is this typical?

3. Adam Dickter asks in *Hadassah Magazine*: is American Jewry suffering from "A Holocaust Obsession?"[3] Many of the educators and community leaders whom Dickter interviews regret our nearly exclusive focus upon commemorating the Holocaust. Read the article and arrange for a debate. Ask study group members to argue the different sides, or invite leaders of your community to debate the issue.

---

1. David Grossman, *See Under Love*, translated by Betsy Rosenberg (New York: Farrar, Straus and Giroux, 1989); Cynthia Ozick, "Rosa," in *The Shawl* (New York: Alfred A. Knopf, 1989); Shulamith Hareven, "Twilight," translated by Miriam Arad, in *Twilight and Other Stories* (San Francisco: Mercury House, 1992).
2. William B. Helmreich, *Against All Odds: Holocaust Survivors and the Successful Lives They Made in America* (New York: Simon & Schuster, 1992).
3. Adam Dickter, "Monumental Question: A Holocaust Obsession?" *Hadassah Magazine*, vol. 75, no. 8 (April 1994), pages 19-21.

A Room on the Roof

Savyon Liebrecht

That summer she sat on the patio under the rounded awning of the Italian swing, as the straw fringes intertwined with the edges of the cloth dome rustled softly, sounding like forest noises, her eyes on the red glow flowing from the western horizon at sunset, her baby already standing on his own two, widespread legs, his fat fingers grasping the bars of the square playpen made of interlocked wooden bars. The lily-like hibiscus waved its circlet of toothed leaves bound in an envelope of buds, only their heads looking out of the long, laden calyxes, pouting like the lips of a coquettish girl, the abundant tranquillity all about deluding merely the part of her that was asleep in any case, not the part that was driven, tensed toward something beyond the apparent silence, knowing the restlessness of someone under eyes constantly prying but always unseen.

Savyon Liebrecht was born in Munich, Germany in 1948, the child of Holocaust survivors, and came to Israel as an infant. She began writing seriously at age 18, while serving in the Israeli army, and later studied philosophy and literature at Tel Aviv University. Her work, however, failed to attract a publisher until, at age 33, she began attending a weekly writing workshop led by Amalia Kahana-Carmon, who gave one of her stories to an editor. Savyon Liebrecht has published three collections of short stories, and has also written scripts for television. She lives in Tel Aviv with her husband and two children.

That early winter—the mud, the puddles of cement, and the rusty fragments of iron—already seemed distant and impossible, with the three Arab men giving off the stench of wood smoke and unwashed flesh. The men with their bad teeth and mouths, with high-heeled shoes that were once fashionable, now looking over-sized, with the leather crushed under the heels.

In her dreams they still visited her sometimes, coming too close to her, which, perhaps, where they live too, could be interpreted as what they might have meant to hint, though perhaps it was done inadvertently. For a long time she wondered about it: did Ahmad draw close to her unheedingly, touching her legs with his rear as he dragged a sack of cement, with his back to her? And later, was it by chance that his elbow touched her breast when he passed by her, balancing a bag of lime on his shoulder, while she raised her arms to the lintel of the door to check the concrete rim as it dried? And did Hassan really believe that she would invite him inside the apartment on that black night when he came back for his coat?

That summer, for a long time after they went off without ever reappearing, she avoided the roof when it was dark, fearing that they might pop up from behind the high potted plants. Sometimes, when she happened to wind up in the back corner, which was imprisoned within three walls and used, for the moment, as a storage area, and she saw the tools they left behind and never came back to collect, a chill would climb her back like a crawling creature with many legs, stirring a column of water in the depths of her belly like the pitching that afflicts you when you're seasick.

But there was no one to accuse. She had brought the thing down on her own head. And if her baby wasn't slaughtered, and her jewels weren't stolen, and nothing bad had happened to her—she should bless her good fortune and erase those two winter months from her memory as if they had never been.

Yoel, her husband, had been opposed to the idea from the moment she had brought it up, still just an idle word in her mouth and still lacking that fervor, that stubbornness, and that unyielding feeling of necessity which were later to possess her.

"A room on the roof?" He twisted his face and took off his glasses as he did when he was angry. "Do you know how filthy construction is? Do you have a notion how many tons of soil and rocks will fall on your head when they break through the ceiling for the stairs? And I don't see why we need another room. There are already two unused rooms in the house. And if you want sunlight—you have half a dunam of private lawn." Against her rebelliously pursed lips, which for a long time, until his patience first broke down, were to emit a defiant silence, he added: "How is it you suddenly got the notion of building? What do you need that for, with a four-month old baby?"

"So why did we take the trouble of running to the engineer and the municipality to get a building license?" she countered his argument. "And didn't we pay all the fees and the property improvement tax and all that?"

"So we'd have it in hand," he replied, "so that if we want to sell the house one day—it will be more valuable, with the license already in hand."

But the idea had already struck root, twisting up inside her with its own force, like an ovum which had embraced the sperm and was now germinating, and the fetus was already stretching the skin of the belly, and there was no way of putting that growth to sleep.

All that time she was wrapped up in her first-born son Udi, who summoned her from her dreams at night. She would come to him with her eyes almost closed, as though moon-struck, and her hands turned over the tiny baby clothes of their own volition. On her walks, pushing the baby carriage across broken paving stones, past piles of sand, she found herself lingering around houses under construction, raising her head to see the men walking with assurance on the rim of high walls, amazed, learning how stories grow, windows square themselves in dark frames, shutters fan out panel by panel from an enormous yellow device looking like arm-bones with the flesh scraped off them.

From one of the yawning holes that would be a window, someone shouted at her with an oriental accent: "You looking for someone to service you, lady?" She blushed as though doing something wrong and pushed her baby away in a panic. Near a building which she often passed, as he looked into the carriage, a contractor told her, "Excuse me for saying this, but this is no place to wander around with a baby. Dirt and cinderblocks or pieces of iron sometimes fall around here, and it's very dangerous."

After she started leaving Udi with a baby-sitter in the mornings, a woman who took a few infants in her home, she would go to those places in her old trousers, worn at the knees, climb up the diagonal concrete slabs, supporting herself on the rough rafters, grope in the darkness of stairwells still floored with sand. Here, she would later say to herself, she saw them face to face for the first time, in the chill damp peculiar to houses under construction. They came toward her from corners that stank of urine, all of them with the same face: dark, boiling eyes, sunk in caves of black shadows, hair cut in the old-fashioned way, shoes spotted with lime and cement, and dusty clothes. Here too their peculiar odor came to her nostrils: sweat mingled with cigarette smoke and soot. While she exchanged words with the Jewish foreman, the Arab workers would cast oblique glances at her; down on all fours laying floor tiles; panting as they transported sacks of cement or stacks of tiles; running to ease the effort; ripping out hunks of food with their teeth; half a loaf of bread in one hand, an unpeeled cucumber in the other.

Some foremen were irritable, refusing to answer her questions, dismissing her with a contemptuous gesture and continuing to give directions to their workers, ignoring her as she stood behind them, abashed, feeling how the Arabs were laughing at her inwardly, in collusion with their Jewish foreman. But sometimes the foremen answered her willingly, watching as she took down what they said in her notebook, like a diligent pupil. As she turned to leave they would say with amusement, "So we have to watch out for you, huh, you're the competition!"

In her notebook the pages were already densely packed with details about reinforced concrete, the thickness of inner and outer walls, various gauges of iron rods, a sketch of the way the rods had to be fastened for casting concrete pillars, the ceiling, plaster, flooring, conduits for electricity and water, tar, addresses of building materials manufacturers. She hid her notebook from Yoel in a carton with her university notebooks. Once, when he said, "What's going on? Zvika said he twice saw you coming out of the building they're putting up on Herzl Street," she looked straight at him and said in her usual tone of voice, "Probably someone who looks like me." And he responded, "It's about time you changed your hairdo. Last week I saw someone from behind, and I was sure it was you. She even had the same walk and the same handbag."

Afterwards, when everything was ripe, like a girl come of age, Yoel came back from work one day, and his eyes were troubled. He said: "They want me to go to a training course in Texas for two months. We're getting a new computer. I said I couldn't leave you alone with the baby. Let them find someone else." She answered firmly, alarmed at the swift feeling that leapt up in her like the shock wave of an explosion: "I'll be quite all right—you should go." And when the tempest had died down within her she thought: a sign had been sent from heaven.

The day after she saw him to his plane, David, the Jewish foreman, came accompanied by three Arab workers, members of the same family, looking amazingly like each other. They all wore old woolen hats. They sat on the edges of the chairs, careful not to dirty the upholstery, with their eyes cast down most of the time. Only occasionally would they raise their eyelids and cast a quick glance at her and the apartment, squinting at the baby on her lap. David wrote down some kind of agreement on a piece of paper, explaining some sentences in Arabic, and they nodded their heads in consent. David copied their names from a form he'd brought with them and their identity numbers from the creased documents they took out of their pockets, a description of the dimensions of the room they were to build, detailing the thickness of the walls, the number of electric sockets and their place in the room, the break through the opening for the stairs, the type and color of the plaster, and beside these, the amounts to be paid as the work progressed. Before signing, she insisted that a final date be clearly written, obligating them to finish the work within two months, before Yoel's return.

Then the three of them stood up at the same time and headed for the door. There, on the threshold, after she thanked him for his good offices, David answered: "Think nothing of it, dear lady. It's because I can see you're a fine girl, with a sporting character. Not many women would do something like this. So here's to you! And if you need something—ask for David in the Hershkovitz building any time. Good luck! They're good workers, up on scaffolds from the age of fifteen," and in her ear softly, "Better than ours, believe me."

Sitting on the open roof that summer opposite the sky spread above her with rows of painted white clouds, hearing her baby babble, his voice rising and falling as he tried out his vocal cords, she thought: how did things go so far that those men, whose gaze avoided her eyes, who shrank in her presence with shoulders bowed, as though narrowing their bodies, answering her questions with a soft voice, as though forever guilty, how did it happen that in November they sat on the edge of the chairs that first evening, and by December they were already marching through her house like lords, turning on Yoel's radio transmitter, opening the refrigerator to look for fresh vegetables, rummaging through the cabinet after fragrant shaving cream, and patting her baby on the head?

At first they still seemed to her like a single person, before she learned that Hassan had elongated eyes, whose bright color was like the band of wet sand at the water's edge. Ahmad had a broad nose, sitting in the middle of his flattened face, between his narrow eyes his lips thick like those of a Negro. Salah's ears pricked up and his cheeks were sunken. Only the pimples on his face gave it some thickness, making it look like the thick skin of an orange.

On the first day, they arrived in an old pickup truck that had once been orange, but now on its dented face there were only islands of peeling paint, and its windows were missing. They got out and unloaded gray cinderblocks near the parking lot. Then the truck pulled away with a grinding noise, returning in a short while with a long wooden beam on top. After a short consultation among themselves, the truck was parked in the parking lot and the beam laid on an angle, the lower part leaning on the back of the truck and the top rising above the edge of the roof. Until the baby started crying inside the house, she stood at a little distance, her hands in the pockets of her slacks, and watched how one of them drew out a tangle of ropes with a saddle-shaped yoke at the end. He stood on the roof and harnessed himself with knots, looking like a coolie in a historical film. One of his mates loaded block after block in the basket on the rope, and the worker on the roof pulled them up along the flat beam, while the third worker, standing on the edge of the roof, leaned over and gathered the bricks one by one. Examining them from below, she saw how their faces grew sweaty with the effort, and their hands got dusty and were scratched by the rough blocks. By the time she had put the baby to bed and come out again, she saw they had unloaded the rest of the blocks on the lawn and disappeared with the truck, though she hadn't heard the sound of the motor. The next day, after turning the matter over during sleepless hours, she decided she must demonstrate her authority over them, and she was ready and waiting for them in her window, cradling the baby in her rounded arms, anger breathing force into her movements. From the window she shouted at them as they approached: "Why did you leave work in the middle yesterday? And today...." She looked at her watch with a clumsy movement, stretching her neck over the baby lying at her breast. "Today you come at nine! You said you'd start working at six! This way you won't finish in ten months!"

"Lady," said the one with the gilded eyes, insulted, "Today was police roadblocked. Not possible we leave early before four morning, lady."

Something in her recoiled at the sight of the beaten dog's eyes he raised up toward her in her window, at his broken voice. But she, tensing her strength to suppress the tremor that awoke within her, threatening to soften her anger, shouted: "And yesterday what happened? Was also roadblocked?" Maliciously she imitated his grammatical error. "You went away and left half the blocks down there on the grass."

For the fist time she saw the movement that was later to become routine: the jaws clamping down on each other as though chewing something very hard, digging a channel along the line of his teeth. Later she was to learn: that's how they suppress anger, hatred. They clench their teeth to overcome the wild rage that surges up, that only rarely breaks out and flashes in their pupils.

"Yesterday my friend Ahmad, he hurted his, the nail his finger."

Behind him his companion raised a bandaged hand, and she looked out of her pretty window, framed with Catalan-style curtains, feeling how the three men in their tattered work clothes were defeating her, looking up at her from their places.

And two hours afterwards, when she had fed and changed the baby and put him to sleep in his cot, her mind was constantly on the uncomfortable feeling that had dwelt in her ever since her conversation with them, when she had spoken to them with cruel irony. Now, knowing full well she was doing something she shouldn't, but still letting the spirit of the moment overcome the voice of reason, she went out of the front door carrying a large tray, with a china coffee pot decorated with rosebuds, surrounded by cups with matching saucers and spoons with an engraved pattern, and a plate of round honey cakes. She stood there holding the heavy tray, her head raised, debating whether to put the tray down on the marble landing of the stairs and climb up the wooden ladder that leaned against the building, reaching the edge of the roof, and to invite them down for coffee, or perhaps it would be better to call them from where she was. Constantly aware of her ridiculous position, she suddenly discovered she didn't remember any of their names. Then a head peeked over the edge of the roof, and she found herself calling to him quickly, before he disappeared: "Hello, hello, I have some coffee for you." Ashamed of the shout that had escaped her, she put down the tray and got away before one of them came down and brought her offering up to his companions.

That afternoon, placing her wide-awake baby in his cot, she put on old jeans and Yoel's army jacket and climbed up to the roof to see how they were getting along with the work. The tray with the rosebud pattern coffee pot and the pretty cups stood in a corner of the roof, cigarette butts crushed in the remainder of the murky liquid in the saucers. She stood and looked for a long while at the sight, which she would recall afterwards as a kind of symbol: the fine Rosenthal china from the rich collection her grandmother had brought from Germany heaped up carelessly, lying next to sacks of cement and heavy hammers.

"We finished the concrete rim," said Hassan, who seemed to have taken upon himself the task of spokesman. "Now we have to put water and it dry."

"Is it twenty centimeter?" she spoke like them.

"It twenty to the meter," he took a metal measuring tape out of his pocket.

"Is it two centimeters over the edge of the floor?"

It seemed to her they exchanged hurried glances, as if they had conspired together before she came, and she grew tense and suspicious.

"Did you bring it up two centimeters above the floor?" she repeated her question, her voice sharp and higher than at first.

"It twenty to the meter," he told her again.

"But does it come out above the floor or not?"

"Level with the floor," he spread out his hand to emphasize his words, with a satisfied expression, like a merchant praising his wares.

"That means it's no good," she said.

"Why no good, lady?"

"Because the rain will leak in," she said impatiently, her anger rising at the game he was playing with her while the concrete band was drying steadily. "It has to be two centimeters higher. That's what David said to you, and that's what's written in the contract."

"We say David twenty centimeter."

"At least twenty centimeters," she corrected him, her voice rising and turning to a shout. "And of that, two centimeters above the floor."

"There is twenty centimeter, lady," he said again, his voice like a patient merchant standing up to a customer making a nuisance.

She pursed her lips as if to demonstrate the conversation was useless. She threw her legs over the low wall around the roof and placed her feet on the rungs of the ladder.

"I'm going to get David," she said to the three men standing and looking at her, anxious to see how things would turn out. "If that's the way you're starting—then it's no good," she added. She went down the ladder with a rush to show them the bellicose spirit that animated her steps, inwardly calculating how long it would take her to get to the building on Herzl Street and locate David, and whether it would be better to take Udi with her, or leave him in his cot and hope he was asleep. Planting her feet on the ground, she strode vigorously toward her car, determined to call David in before the concrete band dried. Then she heard a thick voice calling to her from the roof: "Lady, you don't need David. We add two centimeters."

She turned her face upward, suppressing the feeling of relief and victory that surged up through her anger, seeking the three dark heads bunched together. "Quickly then, before it dries," she said in a loud, hard voice.

That evening, her sister Noa told her, her voice coming from Jerusalem mingled with those of other people: "You made a mistake about the coffee. Let them make it themselves, and don't serve them anything any more. If they get into the house—you'll never get rid of them."

"Don't worry. No one gets into my house without an invitation," she shouted, over the strangers' voices.

But the next day, in the doorway, smiling to her with his eyes as yellow as the winter sun, Hassan, whose name she had learned, said to her, with gentle bashfulness in his voice: "Yesterday lady make coffee. Today I make coffee like in my house." From a plastic bag he withdrew a container of coffee that gave off a fragrance like that in cramped spice shops where coffee grinders crush the dark beans into aromatic grains.

Taken aback by the friendly gesture, as though they hadn't sparred with each other the day before, as though she hadn't been racked all night long with worrying how she would mobilize the police and the courts if they tried again to violate the agreement they had signed, she took a step backward, and before she grasped what was happening, he slipped through the space between her body and the doorjamb, stepped over to the range, and put the plastic bag on the marble counter. With precise, expert movement, he took out a long-handled blue coffee pot and a spoon, took a spoonful of coffee, added sugar that he poured out of another bag, and filled the pot with water. Then after fiddling lightly with the lighter and the knobs on the stove he lit and placed the coffee pot on the glowing ring. She observed his motions with astonishment, stunned at the liberty he took in her kitchen, her eyes drawn to his graceful, pleasing movements, knowing danger was latent in what was happening in front of her.

He stood on one foot, his other foot to the side, like a dancer at rest, peeking into the coffee pot now and then. A hissing rose from it, heralding the onset of boiling, and the spoon in his hand stirred without cease, with a fixed circular movement. He said: "We put two more centimeter of cement from yesterday." And she answered:

"Fine. I hope there won't be any more problems. David told me you were good workers—so do things right."

Then she combed her hair and washed her face, and before she could change out of her soft mohair shirt, that had once been burned in the front by a cigarette, so she only wore it around the house, she found herself sitting at the table with his two fellow workers, for whom Hassan had opened the door with a hospitable gesture while she was spreading a cloth on the table in the breakfast nook.

"That's coffee like in our house," he said, looking at her, the smile on his lips not reaching his eyes She sipped the thick, bitter beverage, and smiled involuntarily: "You mean the coffee I made yesterday wasn't good?"

"It was good," he answered quickly, drawing the words out, alarmed at her insult. "Thank you very much. But we like it this way, strong coffee." He clenched his fist and waved it toward her with a vigorous motion, to emphasize his last word.

She heard Udi crying in the next room. This was when he usually had his first bottle of cereal. She excused herself and got up, feeling their eyes on her. She took Udi out of his cot, wrapped in a blanket decorated with ducklings, and carried him into the breakfast nook. Then she placed the bottle of cereal that had been standing on the windowsill in his hands, and it was already lukewarm. Ahmad looked as though hypnotized at the sapphire ring Yoel's parents had given her for their engagement, and the others looked at the baby curled up at her breast in his bright blanket, drinking the cereal with his eyes shut. Hassan suddenly smiled, and his eyes brightened. He enjoyed the sight of the tranquil baby, and he brought his face close to him and said fondly, "You eat everything—you be strong like Hassan."

Months afterwards she would remember that morning with dismay, when she had sat with them for the first time, as though they were at home there, drinking from cups like welcome guests, eating off the violet lace tablecloth her mother-in-law had brought from Spain, looking at her baby over their cups. She sipped the bitter liquid and only part of her, the part that didn't laugh with them, thought: could these hands, serving coffee, be the ones that planted the booby-trapped doll at the gate of the religious school at the end of the street?

Her heart, which had been on guard all the time, began to foresee something, but it still didn't know: this was just the beginning, appearing like a figure leaping out of the fog. From now on everything would grow clear and roll down like boulders falling into an abyss. The future would clearly be a fall—and no one could stop it.

In the afternoon, as she gathered up the toys Udi had scattered on the carpet, there was a knock on the door. Hassan appeared with a sooty aluminum pot in one hand and a plastic bag imprinted with the name of the supermarket on the main street in the other, a friendly smile of familiarity on his lips, and he said: "Excuse. Can put soup on fire, lady?"

She stood in the doorway, guarding the border, with her hand extended overhead on the doorframe as if halting all entry. But the warm smile on his face and the way he had asked the question didn't leave room for refusal. The blocking arm slipped down, and with cordial hospitality, as though to mask her first hesitation, she moved her hand in an arc and said, "Please, please." Anger at herself welled up inside her for treating him, despite herself, as a welcome guest.

She went back to gathering up the toys, stealing a look at the way he put the pot under the tap with steady movements, like an expert, boiling water in the blue coffee pot that he pulled out of the bag, finding the barrel-shaped salt cellar in the right-hand drawer, knowingly manipulating the knobs of the range. While she arranged the toys in Udi's room, as he slept between the duckling blanket and the Winnie the Pooh sheet, there stole into her—still faint, still resembling discomfort—the fear born of having people trespass, pushing her boundary back and pretending they were unaware.

When she returned, the other two were already with him in the kitchen. One was cutting vegetables into her new china bowl. The other was standing at the open refrigerator, his hand in the lower vegetable drawer. By the look on his face she could tell he'd been caught in the act. His hand, rummaging among the vegetables, stopped where it was.

"Need cucumber, lady," he said, stepping back.

She went to the refrigerator, slammed the drawer home and took a cucumber out of a sealed bag in the rear of the upper shelf.

"Take it," she said.

"Thank you very much, lady." He took the cucumber from her hand. "Lady drink coffee?" asked Hassan from the stove, stirring his coffee pot and smiling at her from the side.

Confused, fighting to control the muscles of her face, she said, "No thanks."

"Is good coffee," Salah, who spoke only seldom, tried to persuade her.

"Thanks, I don't drink coffee in the afternoon."

"Afternoon, morning—is good coffee." He wouldn't let up. She, already feeling the teeth of the trap closing on her, said, almost shouting: "No!" She saw Hassan open the china cabinet and take out three plates.

A moment before she abandoned her house and her baby, fleeing to the bedroom and locking the door behind her, breaking out in silent, suppressed, helpless weeping, into which dread was already creeping, she told Hassan in a soft, commanding voice: "I'll thank you not to make any noise—my baby is asleep." A few minutes afterwards, when she left her room, her eyes already dry and her voice tranquil, though her heart pounded within her, she said: "Maybe you could cook your soup up there. I'll give you a small camping stove. It's inconvenient for me here." Salah threw a malevolent glance at her over his steaming bowl of soup. And Hassan said politely, "If you please, lady, thank you very much."

For five days she heard them arriving, but by the time she had fed Udi and put him to sleep in his cot, her workers were no longer on the roof. Angrily she calculated that in the past two days they hadn't raised more than a single row of blocks above the stone rim on top of the window. Suspicion stole into her heart that they had taken on another job and, so it wouldn't slip through their fingers before they finished in her house, they had taken it and bound themselves to another boss. That was the way they did things, as the bank teller who knew about her project had taken the trouble to warn her. But in the afternoon, shaken at hearing the familiar noise of the pickup truck and, in her head composing a few harsh sentences to reproach them with, she saw the truck was laden with iron rods, thin and thick. The three of them got out of the cab and set about unloading the truck and passing the iron rods from hand to hand up to the roof. Calm now, from her window, she watched them at their work. She decided to rest until Udi awoke from his afternoon nap.

For a while she heard them walking around the roof, dragging loads, their voices reaching her through the closed blinds of her room. Later, there was a lot of stubborn knocking which she first took to be part of a dream, and then she heard them at the door. When she opened it the three of them were standing close to each other, with Hassan half a footstep in front. He said, "Hello, lady, how are you?"

Inwardly bridling at the familiarity he permitted himself in asking that polite question for the first time, and keeping her face frozen, she ignored his question and asked: "Yes?" guessing they would ask permission to heat up their meal.

"Lady, we need money."

Her sister had warned her about that in their last conversation: you mustn't pay them before they've done the work as agreed. She tensed. Her voice rasped more than she intended: "Did you finish putting the iron in place for pouring the concrete?"

"We put band around roof."

"You did the band, but I'm asking about the iron. Did you get the iron ready for pouring the concrete?"

"That's tomorrow, lady."

"You'll get your money tomorrow."

"We need some. Maybe you'll give us lady...."

"Tomorrow," she said firmly. "Anyway I don't have so much now. I have to go to the bank."

"Really, lady," Hassan said, looking straight in her eyes and pounding his chest with his fist. "Lady believe. We coming tomorrow, money or no money."

"No money," she said, knowing how Yoel would smile when she told him about this occasion. Hassan turned to his friends, and they put their heads together and whispered. From where she was she saw the back of his neck, his dusty hair, looking gray under the woolen hat with the tattered edges, frayed yarn twisting down. His mates' brows darkened. They put their heads close to each other, taking counsel. One of them pulled a creased wallet from his pocket and seemed to be counting the bank notes in it. He had a worried expression. Within her she was already prepared to withdraw her position and say: "Look, if it's something pressing, I'm prepared to give you what I have in my purse now...." He suddenly turned to her and asked, "Can wash hands in water?" He surprised her so much with the question that, like the morning when he had stood before her with a cooking pot in his hands, she said: "Certainly, certainly," pushing the door open wide, while her only wish was to slam the door in their faces.

They entered hesitantly. Now she saw that Salah was holding a large army knapsack, the kind that Yoel used to extricate from the storeroom when his unit was called for maneuvers. Hassan led the way to the bathroom, looking at her as though asking permission, and the three men made their way in and locked the door: for a long while she heard the sound of running water and the men's boisterous voices. She, walking to and fro in the living room, looked out at the large garden, across from which no other house was visible, and was gripped by sudden fear, thinking of what might be in that big knapsack. Perhaps they were assembling weapons there, spreading the steel parts out on the carpet, as Yoel had done once, kneeling on the floor and joining the shining parts one to another. Maybe they would come out in a little while with their weapons drawn and threaten her and her son? Perhaps they would take them as hostages in their pickup truck? And what about Udi? She had already run out of his special flour, and she wouldn't be able to feed him when they kept them there in their broken-down shacks in Gaza, among the muddy paths. They had shown those shacks on an American television documentary. Maybe, the thought flashed through her like lightning, she should snatch Udi out of his cot and flee with him, lay him in the back seat of her car and drive immediately to the police station on the main street.

Hassan came out first, and she was startled at his appearance. For a second she imagined a stranger had come out. For the first time she saw him without the woolen cap pulled down over his forehead. His hair, surprisingly light, freshly combed and damp, was brushed to the side, well-combed, and pulled over his temples. He wore a dark, well-pressed jacket over a white shirt and tie. His black dress shoes were highly polished.

He told her: "My friends come out minute, lady."

"Aren't you going home?"

"Have wedding from our aunt in Tulkarem. We today in Tulkarem."

At that moment the baby let out a screech more piercing than any she'd heard since the morning he had burst out of her in the maternity ward: high and prolonged, followed by a sudden silence. She herself let out a scream and rushed to the room, pushing his rolling highchair out of the way as she ran. Udi was prostate on the floor, lying on his stomach, his face on the carpet spread at the foot of his crib, with a toy between his fingers. She bent down and picked him up, carrying him in her arms, and he looked at her with cloudy eyes. She hugged him close to her body and started murmuring things without knowing what she was saying, her heart pounding wildly, making her fingers tremble. After a long while he burst out crying, resting his head on her shoulder in sobs.

"Is okay, lady," Hassan said from the doorway, and she looked around in panic, not realizing he had followed her.

"What?" she asked fearfully.

"Is okay he like so, lady," he traced his finger along his cheek and made a crying expression. "Is nothing. He good that way."

"What's good?" she asked as the baby trembled in her arms.

Hassan approached her and gently lifted Udi from her arms. "Lady get water," he said softly. "He need drink."

In the kitchen, her hands still trembling, she stood still for a long time, trying to remember where the sugar bowl was. She heard Hassan talking softly to the baby in Arabic, like a man who loves to talk to his child, in a caressing voice, the words running together in a pleasant flow, containing a high beauty, like the words of a poem in an ancient language which you don't understand, but which well up inside you. Udi, lying tranquilly on his chest, reached out toward Hassan's dark face, and Hassan put his head down toward the little fingers and kissed them. She, stunned by the sight, stood where she was and looked at them, as the tremor inspired by fear gradually died down, and another, new kind of trembling, arose within her, seeing something which, even as it happens, you already long for from a distance, knowing that when it passes, nothing like it will happen again, and, as though dividing themselves, her thoughts turned to Yoel, whose eyes examined his son from a certain distance. He was careful not to wrinkle his clothes or have them smell of wet diapers.

Hassan looked up at her and said, "Hassan have like this at home in Gaza."

"You have a baby?" She was astonished. "You're married?"

"Also like this. Four years," he said proudly, placing his hand parallel to the floor to measure the height of his son.

"You okay," Hassan said in his soft voice, turning his face to the baby. "You big—you doctor like daddy, yes?"

With the bottle of tea in her hand, she was shaken as though by a distant alarm. Troubled by the suspicion that he knew more than he should, she said, "You can read Hebrew?" and he laughed. "I read one word, another word. I see Doctor on door in English."

"You can read English?" There was some mockery in her voice, like an adult talking to a child about grown-up things.

"I can," he answered in English, smiling, for the first time, with another smile, hidden, without the forced humility she was familiar with.

"Where from," she asked, also in English.

"From the University."

"Which one?"

"The American University of Beirut." She recognized his good accent from having heard it on television when Arabic-speaking intellectuals were interviewed. She hadn't been able to shake off her Israeli accent in the two years she had lived in Texas, while Yoel finished his degree.

"Really?" She returned to Hebrew.

"Really, lady. I in Beirut two years. Maybe I be doctor that way, of babies."

"Why didn't you complete your studies?"

"Hard. Can't talk." He looked down at his hands, whose nails were free of lime. "Life like that."

Shortly after he left, joining his comrades who were waiting for him and watching him from the door, also scrubbed. She thought: they're nameless and ageless for me, in their faded black sweaters and their dirty elbows and stocking caps. They had a single face and uncouth words came from their mouths. Suddenly they were different: in white collars and jackets, their cheeks shaven, with a wife and baby and a child of four at home.

Even before she heard the bell ring she knew he had returned.

"My jacket, lady," he said and went to take his jacket, folded carefully on the back of the chair. And, at the door, with his back to her, he turned around with a carefully planned motion that made itself out to be spontaneous. "If lady want I stay now."

"Where?" she asked in astonishment.

"With lady," he answered seriously. "Mister of lady no here. Maybe need something...." And she, stunned at the very words and frightened that he knew of her husband's absence, wondered if he meant what she thought she had heard. She said, "But you're going to a wedding, aren't you?"

"Going to wedding. But if lady want—I can be here...."

After she had locked the door, still staggered at his suggestion, she suddenly noticed: Yoel's smell had come from the delicate odor of the fragrance on the shelf of the right hand cabinet next to the mirror. They had used her husband's toiletries, dried themselves on her towels. She carefully put Udi down in the cot and hurried to the bathroom.

With convulsive movements, like a madwoman, she gathered up the towels and threw them all, averting her head with a bilious feeling, into the washing machine, throwing the new soap into the garbage pail. She began polishing the taps and sink and scouring with disinfectant the floor which their bare feet had trod on.

But toward evening a tense quiet descended on her, something new. At night, before falling asleep, she remembered how Hassan had held Udi close to his chest and spoken to him in Arabic that sounded like a song; his long fingers, clean for the first time of spots of paint; the English he had spoken, sounding like human language for the first time instead of the broken phrases he knew in Hebrew. Only she preferred to set aside his offer to stay with her and not consider it. She thought back over things, seeing that she had been hard on them. They had gone to a wedding in Tulkarem. Maybe they had asked for money to buy a present for the newlyweds, and she had behaved unfeelingly with them. The unease that gripped her was assuaged when she promised herself that early the next morning she would take Udi in his carriage and go out to the main street and, in the elegant store that had recently opened, she would buy clothes for his two children. Then she thought: it would not be right to offer him a gift, as a declaration of a special relationship, and not to honor his cousins. Generously she decided she would buy something for them as well. Maybe cologne like the kind Yoel kept on his shelf. If the weather was stormy, she'd take Udi in the car. An hour later, she suddenly interrupted herself as she read: if it rained hard, she'd leave Udi at the baby-sitter's.

She waited for them until noon, their gifts in pretty wrapping paper, tied with curling ribbon, lying on the cabinet next to the front door, and the white envelope with their money next to the packages.

At noon she began to worry: maybe they had drunk too much and had an accident. What if the police came? She panicked. Maybe it wasn't legal for her to employ them. If they were badly injured and couldn't continue the job, the construction would be delayed and maybe not completed by the time Yoel returned. In the afternoon, tired and angry at her helplessness and concern about the future, she decided to go to the building where David was working. Maybe some members of the same family were working for him, and they too had been invited to the wedding in Tulkarem, and she could find something out from them. For a long time she waited for David, pushing the carriage back and forth on the battered pavement in front of the building site. When he came he told her that the wedding hadn't been in Tulkarem at all, but in a village near the Lebanese border. They would be coming as usual the next day, he reassured her, seeing her worried face. Afterwards he scratched the nape of his neck and asked: "So it's okay, the job they're doing?"

"I hope so," she said.

"What are they doing now?"

"They're setting up the iron rods to pour the concrete."

"Are they doing it right?"

"I don't know. I trust them."

The next day, anger making her fingertips tremble, so troubled her breathing was affected, she waited for them on the roof in the morning after leaving Udi with the baby-sitter and arranging to do so again during the coming days. Hassan got out of the cab and smiled brightly at her. With his filthy woolen cap and his shoes down at the heel he was once again what he had been.

"Something happen, lady?" His voice betrayed his surprise at finding her on the roof at that early hour.

"A great deal has happened," she shouted to him, leaning over the wall at the edge of the roof.

"What's the matter, lady?" he asked, climbing the ladder on his way up to her.

"First of all, you lied to me."

"Lied?" The shadow of his smile was erased.

"The wedding was in Tulkarem?" She flung out the words, her hand on her hips, like a mother arguing with a child caught out in a lie.

"No lady. Wedding not in Tulkarem."

"That's what you told me."

"I said: my aunt from Tulkarem. The wedding not. There in village near Kibuss."

He turned to face his comrades, as though asking, and Ahmad said, "Kibuss Ga'aton."

"Ga'aton," Hassan repeated the name of the kibbutz, looking at her again.

"But you didn't say you wouldn't come to work yesterday."

"We think sleep in Tulkarem and come work yesterday. No possible."

"That's one thing," she ignored the explanation. "Another thing, David was here yesterday and he said you didn't do anything well. You didn't raise the concrete band two centimeters the way we said. And you put in number eight iron rods instead of number twelve, and you made one wall with fifteen centimeter blocks instead of twenty centimeters...."

"That wall has window, lady. Must be little."

"You need a number three block near the sliding window," she exploded at his effort to fool her. "But the wall is an outer wall. You were supposed to use twenty centimeter blocks...." she added, scolding him, watching the color ebb from his face, and how his comrades froze behind his back.

"We do everything good. Lady want—David come here. We talk."

"I don't want you to talk!" she screamed. "I want you to work. You've been working for a month. What you've done could have been done in a week. You just drink coffee, slip away, and work somewhere else."

"Somewhere else?" he asked in amazement.

"On Monday. Where were you?"

He wrinkled his forehead in thought. "Monday we bring iron."

"Fine," she said, raising her chin and walking forward with vigor and sitting on the edge of the wall. "I want to see how much you get done today."

For seven hours she sat on the wall, without moving, not going down to turn off the water heater she had lit in the morning, suppressing the hunger that awoke within her, the need for a cup of coffee at the hour when her body was used to one, and, in the afternoon, fighting the pain in her back, which cried out for something to lean on, watching as they worked angrily, talking little, boiling water in an empty can on the camping stove she'd lent them, sitting down to eat with their legs crossed, close to each other, whispering to each other. All those hours she watched them as though riveted to the spot, only occasionally looking away from them, allowing her eyes to wander to the tops of the cypress trees and the purple mountains in the distance, the view of which, at a peaceful hour, she would enjoy. Later, when she recalled that morning, she would tremble as though the event were not irrevocably in the past: how had the courage to treat them that way been born within her? They could easily have come and pushed her, and she would have fallen and broken her neck. By the time anyone found her among the iron rods in the backyard, she would no longer be alive.

Occasionally Ahmad cast a glance at her, like a fearful child checking to see whether the ghost he had seen was still hovering in the area. But Hassan didn't look at her once. Seeing him, his clamped lips, and the line drawn behind his jaw, above his clenched teeth, she knew she had deeply wounded him, but she felt no remorse for doing so. Only the sweet consolation of someone who deals justly with himself, a feeling that rose and fell within her great anger.

They raised the iron rods over the edge of the masonry walls and laid them crisscross at regular intervals, tying them with thin wire. Afterwards they crowded steel struts into the room to support the wooden forms under the network. When they finished, they consulted among themselves for a moment and headed for the ladder, parting from her with a slight nod.

"Wait," she called to them. "You've earned your money." She followed them down the ladder and went into the house. When she came out she put the envelope in Hassan's hand. Only after they had left without a word did she remember she hadn't asked them to sign a receipt for the money or given them the wrapped parcels from the cupboard.

The next day, after leaving Udi with the baby-sitter despite a reddish rash on his skin showing he hadn't been changed in time, she was already waiting for them on the roof as though spoiling for a fight. Today, she thought, stunned at the idea, they'll pour the concrete for the roof. The network of iron rods was prepared and the steel struts were in place. The wooden forms were raised, the buckets of gravel and sand were covered under plastic sheets, and the sacks of cement were arranged next to them. Today they would pour the roof, and the weather was fine. The transparent clouds didn't herald rain.

When she heard the sound of the pickup truck she leaped to the edge of the roof, and even before she actually saw them she noticed his absence. Three men sat in the cab, and he wasn't one of them. Salah and Ahmad got out of the left door, wearing gray woolen hats. Then a man with a shaven head got out of the truck, looking like a fugitive she had seen in an Italian movie, who had made his way to a widow's home in a village and laid siege to it. In one look she took in his black eyes, like the maw of a coal mine. His eyebrows meeting over the bridge of his nose. A strange feeling overcame her, like when all her girlfriends had been asked to dance, and she was left alone sitting by the wall, looking at the legs moving in the dark.

"Where's Hassan?" she asked Ahmad.

"Hassan no come. This one come, Muhammad."

Observing from her corner on the wall, trying to repress the desolate feeling that grew stronger within her, she watched them put on rubber boots and mix the concrete with shovels, adding sand and gravel and pouring water, stirring it to produce a thick gray mixture in the square they had enclosed with wooden beams. Then Muhammad climbed up to the edge of the roof. Ahmad handed him bucket after bucket, brimming with the gray concrete and he swung and emptied them in big arcs over the network of iron rods, while Salah quickly filled in the space between the two wooden planks below, to stop the concrete from dribbling out.

Sitting erect on the edge of the roof, her knee swinging, her arms crossed, she felt her anger give way to disappointment at Hassan's absence. Suddenly it became clear to her that he had come between her and them, serving as a kind of protective barrier for them. Here she stood exposed to the three of them: Salah stole furtive glances at her, as though already hatching a foul plot in his mind; Ahmad smiled right at her, baring his yellow teeth like the fangs of a beast; and the new worker, standing high on the upper concrete band, his body tense, his hands on his hips, stared at her openly. From where she sat his figure looked mighty, and his shaven head resembled a crooked egg against the background of the sky above him.

She sat where she was for hours, no longer strong with the anger that had gripped her the previous morning, making her decide to sit and see with her own eyes how well they would work under supervision, but now out of fear to get up and raise her legs over the edge of the roof in front of them. They worked without stopping, diligently, bringing up the contents of the big pool of concrete and spreading it on the network of rods. From time to time they would consult each other, exchange shouts in Arabic, sing a line or two, laughing out loud into their hands. And she, sensing they were laughing at her, was angry, insulted, and fearful. She watched them cook their meal, kneeling next to each other on the torn mat, tearing with their teeth at loaves of bread they held in their hands.

"What now?" She turned to Ahmad, keeping her voice steady.

"Now must dry."

"If it rains?"

"Now two hours—good. Not two hours—no good."

"The roof is twenty centimeters?"

"Yes, yes," he said, and she thought since that morning she

hadn't heard them say "lady." She turned, pointed at the floor they had left spotted with cement. "Wash that down before it dries," she ordered, pretending she still had strength.

"No dry. We put water."

She stepped to the edge of the protruding ladder and grasped the wooden rung and, as though incidentally, turned to them, "What's the matter with Hassan?"

"Hassan no come."

"I see that."

"This one Muhammad come."

"Will Hassan come tomorrow?"

"Tomorrow, tomorrow, tomorrow—Hassan no come."

"Did something happen to him?"

"He not here."

She carefully raised her legs, and when she had descended, even before her feet touched the ground, she heard their deep, guttural laugh, and she blushed. That's how men laughed at women when they spoke ill of them.

The next day, waiting at the window, she knew why her legs had taken her there, why she had arisen early to prepare the kitchen, why she had checked how much coffee was left in the bag he had brought with him from home.

Salah and Ahmad came alone. She, knowing in her heart she wouldn't see Hassan again, was glad the shaven-headed Muhammad wasn't with them. Swallowing her pride she went out and stood before them.

"Is Hassan sick?" she asked.

"No sick."

"He won't come to work?"

"He work someone."

"Why isn't he working here? Three will finish faster."

Salah, perhaps seeing through her deceptive sentences, smiled somewhere in the depths of his eyes, the mockery of someone careful not to be tripped up.

"He no want come to lady."

"He doesn't want to get his money?"

"No want," said Salah, and she imagined she heard an echo of triumph in his voice.

"He doesn't want to get his money?"

"No want money, no want lady," he said. She no longer had anything to say after that sentence, but she spoke in her normal voice: "Very well, then finish by yourselves. You can make coffee in the kitchen if you want. There's still some of the coffee you brought."

Salah and Ahmad kept coming for a few more days after the concrete on the roof had dried, removing the steel struts that held up the forms. They put in the door and bars over the window and broke through the upper room into the breakfast nook. She didn't ask about Hassan again, but they sometimes volunteered that they had met him. She, stirred by the sound of his name, gave in and made the final payment before they finished the work. Perhaps they would run into Hassan and tell him of her generosity. But they never came back. They left the walls unplastered and forgot their tools behind the wall. Shaken with fury, again pushing her baby carriage, she roamed among the construction sites and hired workers to finish the plastering: they tarred the roof, and installed the electric wiring.

By the time Yoel returned she had a new hairstyle. They stood on the stairs leading to the bright, pleasant room on the roof, with three barrels in the corners from which palm trees sent up sharp bayonets all about, their fronds growing like a conjuring trick. He stood in amazement before the new structure and then burst out laughing. "Well, I'll be.... You leave a woman for two months, come back—and the world's changed!" On the roof, his arm around her shoulder in a gesture of respect, he wandered from one corner of the roof to another, inspecting the landscape, and sliding his hand along the walls: "I didn't want to do it, I admit, but it's really nice. Was it very dirty?"

"Not so terrible."

"You found the workers?"

Stroking the rough wall unawares she said, "They were relatively decent, workers from the territories."

"What, Arabs?" he asked, looked at her reproachfully, getting serious.

"Arabs. You can't find anyone else. But every day a Jewish foreman came to keep an eye on them, the one working in the building at Herzl Street."

"They behaved all right? They didn't make trouble?"

She took a quick, deep breath, with a whistling sound, and—restraining the whirlpool of emotions stirring within her, looking away, clearly seeing Muhammad standing on the edge of the upper roof, staring at her with hatred, and the flash in their eyes when she got up and stood in this very place and accused them—seeing Hassan's fists clench and the crease along the line of his jaw when he clasped his teeth shut, hearing the rumble of the men's laughter when she raised her legs to climb down the ladder—she said, "They were fairly decent. Once Udi fell down and I was really alarmed. One of them picked him up so gently and calmed him down, you wouldn't believe it. He spoke to him softly and kissed his fingers. Then it turned out he had studied medicine for two years. He wanted to be a pediatrician but for some reason he didn't finish his degree. He has a baby Udi's age and another boy of four...." Suddenly she noticed the softness flowing into her voice, betraying herself to herself, and she added loudly, more stridently than she intended: "But once they made some trouble about the money and tried to trick me by putting in iron rods that were too thin. Arabs, you know...."

1986

Translated by Jeffrey M. Green

Questions for Discussion

1. The central theme of "A Room on the Roof" is the personal relationship between Israeli Jews and Arabs. How do you react to the protagonist's treatment of the workers? How does your attitude toward Arabs affect your attitude toward her?
2. Do you sympathize with the Arab construction workers? What is your opinion of the men's characters?

3. The protagonist lets "the spirit of the moment overcome the voice of reason" and she brings the workers coffee and cakes. Later, "anger at herself welled up inside her for treating [Hassan], despite herself, as a welcome guest." Comment on the protagonist's struggle between her desire to maintain a superior, authoritarian status and her desire to treat the workers as equals. (Mark Twain explored this theme in *Huckleberry Finn.* Huck believes that he is damning his soul when he helps Jim escape from slavery. Yet Huck does help Jim, because his own knowledge of right and wrong is more powerful than the slave-owning morality that Huck has been taught. Discuss parallels to "A Room on the Roof." For thought: Huck is a young boy and Liebrecht's protagonist is a woman. How might the conflict between social conscience and inner conscience be portrayed if the main character were a grown man?)
4. Both Palestinians and women are "the other" in Israeli society. In what ways does Liebrecht emphasize the similarities between the position of the Arab workers and that of the woman protagonist and in what ways does she emphasize the differences?
5. The urge to build an extra room is first described as a "fetus [that] was already stretching the skin of the belly," and later, as "ripe, like a girl come of age." Why is the growth of human babies and children used as a simile for an idea about home improvement?
6. The protagonist favorably compares Hassan's tenderness toward the baby to her husband's coolness and distance. Comment on men's involvement in child care. Consider also the stereotypes about child care in different social classes. Do we expect that the "primitive" father will be more familiar with babies, while the "civilized" man will have more important responsibilities? Yet are we also more likely to expect that the primitive father will beat his children?
7. What is the significance of Hassan offering to stay the night? Why does the protagonist put the proposition out of her mind?
8. Consider the protagonist's lie to her husband: "every day a Jewish foreman came to keep an eye on [the construction workers]." What are we to make of this?

9. Compare the mother in "A Room on the Roof" to the childless Dolly in "Loneliness." Both are the wives of well-to-do professional men, and both feel a passionate need for something out of the ordinary. Why?

Program Suggestions

1. Organize a joint Zionist Affairs/Jewish Education program on relations between Palestinian Arabs and Israeli Jews. Consult the National Speakers Bureau or your regional Speakers Bureau.
2. In 1991 Hadassah and the Anti-Defamation League of B'nai B'rith produced a three-part package of materials on Arab-Israeli relations that provide historical background for today's challenges in the Middle East: the videotape *Search for Solid Ground: The Intifada Through Israeli Eyes*; the revised Hadassah study guide *Between Arab and Jew: Unraveling the Knot* by Yosef Olmert; and the pamphlet *After the Gulf War: The Arab-Israeli Conflict Revisited*. Arrange for a showing of the videotape, and discuss some of the questions raised. (All materials are available through the Hadassah National Order Department.)

Ummi Fi Shurl

Orly Castel-Bloom

One morning I couldn't stay in the house any longer and I went out. The walls were closing in on me, the living room got me down. I went outside and began walking. Look, I'm paranoid—no question about it. Stuck at home, I suffocate. A plane flies over, and I freak out.

I sat down on a bench, arms stretched along the backrest, legs crossed, and stared in front of me in infinite boredom. I was sitting on a lawn, one of those plentiful in my neighborhood. Lawns you're allowed to step on, but not to spoil. It was ten o'clock, and I knew that the day would pass, and that I had to make it pass quietly until night came. At night I was allowed to take a tranquilizer.

So I sat on the bench and thought to myself what kind of a world was it with nobody on the lawn except for me. Winter, I thought to myself. Clouds. Yesterday it rained. Not today. Maybe tomorrow. Winter. Cold. Coats. Umbrellas. Mushrooms. Winter. Nothing special. Ordinary, everyday thoughts, until I felt something stinging

---

Orly Castel-Bloom was born in 1960 in Tel Aviv, where she lives today. She studied film at Tel Aviv University. She has published three collections of short stories as well as two novels, *Where I Am* which received the 1990 Tel Aviv Prize for Literature, and *Dolly City*. In 1992 she was awarded the Prime Minister's Prize for Literature.

me. I lifted my foot and saw the sting swelling with the speed of an animated cartoon. I jumped up in a panic and looked for the culprit. I was sure it was a snake, or a Black Widow, or some kind of scorpion, but under the bench lay a woman of about sixty, who claimed that she was my mother. It turned out that her husband was really dead, and ever since then she had worn black only, ten years going back from now.

I persuaded her that she couldn't be my mother, because my mother would never lie under a bench as long as she lived, and she allowed herself to be persuaded, and in the end she even sat down next to me and lit a cigarette.

She stank of pee, and I turned my nose in the direction of the wind and felt sorry for anyone standing to her east. But nobody was standing there. I kept quiet, and the woman asked me where I was from, in other words, what ethnic group I belonged to.

"I'm not a Holocaust survivor," I replied, "but lately I've been dreaming that I am. As a matter of fact, my parents are from Cairo."

She said nothing and stared straight ahead. I looked at her—dressed totally in rags, with the stench coming off her reaching cosmic proportions. "Are you going to die?" I asked her.

"What kind of talk is that? If I haven't died up to now—I'll never die."

I thought that she was crazy, and lost interest in her.

She asked: "What are you writing about now?"

"Who are you, some kind of ghost?"

"I told you who I am—*ana ummek*[1]—I'm your mother."

"*Ummi? Ummi mush huna, ummi fi shurl*—My mother? My mother isn't here, my mother's at work."

"*Ana ukhtek*—I'm your sister."

"*Inti mush ukhti. Ukhti fi shurl*—You're not my sister. My sister's at work."

"*Ana ummek*—I'm your mother."

"*Inti mush ummi. Ummi fi shurl*—You're not my mother. My mother's at work."

1. The foreign language spoken here is Arabic.

And she went through the same routine with me about twenty times. In the end she said: "What do you do with yourself in life?"

"Uhhh ... nothing."

"So you've got time to look after me, right? To take me home with you, give up your room for an old woman?"

"No."

"*Ya sater, ya rabb*—God save us," she said and got down under the bench again. I felt uncomfortable, and I was a little scared that she might bite me again too. On the other hand, I felt awkward about getting up and going away.

1993

Translated by Dalya Bilu

Questions for Discussion

1. What aspects of Israeli life does the narrator represent?
2. Who is the old woman? Is she real, or is this Black Widow (widow in black) a creation of the narrator's paranoia, much like in Kafka's *Metamorphosis*?
3. Yigal Schwartz, in *Modern Hebrew Literature*, describes Orly Castel-Bloom's writing style: "the infantile, sociopathic attitude; the apathetic, provocative tone; the mechanical, alienated rhythm of speech."[2] How does this style affect readers? How does the style enhance the content of her work?
4. The widow in black asks: where is the narrator from? The reply is: "I'm not a Holocaust survivor, but lately I've been dreaming that I am." Why does the narrator dream of this? Does the narrator *want* to be a Holocaust survivor? Why? What identity does the narrator desire?
5. What questions does "Ummi Fi Shurl" raise about homelessness, economic and class hierarchy, and social neglect?

---

2. Yigal Schwartz, "Alice in Tel Aviv: Review of *Where Am I* by Orly Castel-Bloom," *Modern Hebrew Literature*, 1989, page 18.

6. Consider the disgusting stench and the violent act of biting. What point is the author making?
7. What is the effect of the Arabic language? How does the use of Arabic relate to the beggar's question about the narrator's ethnic group? Discuss relationships between Israelis of Middle Eastern ancestry and Israelis of northern European ancestry. How would your opinion of the story change if the characters spoke Russian?
8. Is the narrator a woman or a man? Does the sex of the narrator matter? How does your interpretation of the story change with the narrator's sex?
9. The narrator refuses to take the old woman home, yet feels awkward about leaving her. Why?
10. Yigal Schwartz writes of the literary controversy that surrounds Orly Castel-Bloom. Some Israeli critics see her works as "a deviant growth, culturally indigent, stylistically meager and deliberately provocative," while others believe that Castel-Bloom "has broken new ground, that she poses an emotional and intellectual challenge and that she is a breath of fresh air."[3] Where do you stand? Do we, as American Jews, find Castel-Bloom's flat tone and violent imagery particularly troubling because we want Israelis to write movingly of heroism and self-sacrifice?

Program Suggestion

Orly Castel-Bloom forces readers to confront issues of social justice. In what way is this typically Jewish? Organize a seminar on poverty, homelessness, and Jewish responses. Speakers might include a rabbi or Judaic scholar discussing biblical, rabbinic, and modern Jewish viewpoints, a homeless advocate (many synagogues operate shelters during the night; you might invite volunteers to speak of their work), and an expert on Israeli life—perhaps a visiting Israeli professor or journalist.

---

3. Yigal Schwartz, page 18.

Apples in Honey

Yehudit Hendel

That summer, I'd go there sometimes, and this week, I went again. It was a hot day at the end of summer. A hot wind blew from time to time, stopped suddenly and returned suddenly, full of dust, and when I entered, the place was empty. Not a living soul. I thought of wandering around a bit and then, on the other side behind the shed, I saw the gardener standing and talking with a young woman who sat bent over the stone, moving her head as she spoke, a head wreathed in balls of red curls, glowing like balls of fire in the *hamsin* light.

As I said, the place was empty. The paths had just been swept, sharpening the clean orderly lines of perspective, and in the heavy *hamsin* light it looked more colorful and shining than ever, wrapped in a thin pink coat of fresh watering and new blooming, almost a shining sheath of shining lacquer. And it was very quiet. Not even a sprinkler moved. But as I went along the path everything seemed full of rustling and talking and raspy sounds, rising from both sides of the path from the colored patches of the dense vegetation, as if someone there were grinding glass under the earth.

Yehudit Hendel was born into a rabbinic family in Warsaw in 1926. She left Poland as a young child, and grew up in Haifa, where she lives today. She is the author of a number of novels and short stories, most recently the collection *Small Change* (1988) and the novel *The Mountain of Losses* (1991).

That was in the most beautiful section, the newly flourishing section of the Lebanon War, which was laden with a rich growth of living flowers and silk flowers and velvet flowers and flowers of thin copper plates and flowers of burlap and flowers of gauze and rust-colored bandages and long serrated cacti with fleshy shoots like explosive caps and tops shaped like an axe.

The woman lifted her face to me.

Do you have somebody here? she asked.

She clasped her knees to her body, didn't take her eyes off me.

I've got somebody here too, she said.

Her knees were really up to her body, and she didn't take her eyes off me.

My husband, she said.

I understand.

Yes, my husband.

I understand.

She turned half her body to me.

My husband, she repeated a third time.

It was quiet. Her eyes were fixed on me, pale, very bright, wide open in dark brown lashes that had nothing to do with the balls of fire, and I don't know, maybe because of the quiet, I said I came here sometimes, hadn't seen her.

Yes, I come once a year, she said. Her voice was low-pitched, almost masculine, almost basso, and she spoke like someone continuing a conversation that had been broken off.

And it usually falls on a hot day like this, a *hamsin*. Always on a hot day like this, a *hamsin*. She banged her knees together, clutched her leather bag to them. And I sit alone. Sometimes with the gardener.

I said I had met him here, the gardener.

She fixed me again with bright, wide-open eyes, raised her hand in the air with a quick movement.

I'm talking to you like I know you, she said.

Maybe we did know each other once.

She laughed, repeating the nervous gesture in the air.

Yes, could be.

Maybe, I said.

She laughed again, covering her knees with both hands. Then

she shifted her eyes from her knees and moved closer to me on the stone frame surrounding the small, beautiful garden. She smiled. He's a good man, the gardener.

The sun apparently blinded her, since she was facing the wrong way, and she closed one eye, and now she looked at me with one eye, round as an animal's eye.

I said: Yes, a good man, the gardener.

She changed eyes, blinking, bent farther over the stone, and opened a cactus coiled up near the stone pillow. Apparently she saw me looking at the date on the pillow. No, no, I come on our anniversary, that's the day I come here, once a year.

Now, too, she spoke slowly, emphasizing every word.

I don't come on any other day. Why should I come any other day?

It was quiet, and even quieter between one word and the next.

And I said, it always falls on a hot day like this, a *hamsin.* In fact, it was a hot day like this then too, a *hamsin.* She banged her knees together hard, pressed the palms of her hands on them, and said it was impossible to talk about it. I said she didn't have to. She said: I can't talk about it.

You don't have to.

Yes, but when you think.

Better not to think.

That's it, better not to think. That doesn't always work. You understand.

Yes, I understand.

It was quiet. She bent over a bit, leaning forward, unzipped her purse, pulled out a pair of big gray glasses, and put them on.

Believe me, you learn it, and aside from that, time—

I couldn't think of anything else to say.

It was quiet. She zipped up her purse and put it back on the stone.

Yes, time. You think time can?

I could see her dark lashes drop and open all at once through the big glasses. She took them off a moment and straightened up again, looking around leaning her head back, the way you look out a train window. In the meantime, everything, almost alive, years, almost alive, she said, turning around to me, and the word *almost* was doubled in the empty garden, hit the air like a pneumatic hammer, and I felt something heavy in my ears and some desire to cover my ears. It seemed that was what she did too, but the wind waved her hair, exposing her ears and they suddenly looked small, almost like a little girl's ears. Her eyes moved slowly, wandering over the garden, as if the garden were fleeing behind her, and I thought I should say something but I didn't know what. The light became even lower. The sky a bottomless dome. The blooming roses and chrysanthemums in the beautiful garden burned like scarecrows, and I wanted to tell her that there are many forms alive, and something about the length of the day and the length of the night, and the simple truth of death and loneliness when that truth comes from the earth and enters your feet and climbs on you through the soles of your feet. Suddenly I remembered the custom that women once used to measure their lovers' graves with strings, and then they folded the strings and doubled them and made wicks of wax candles in honor of their lovers from the wrapped doubled string, and at night, in little cans, they lit the wax candles and all night the long wicks burned in the cans and the wind was forbidden to put out the fire in the cans, and I wanted to tell her something about the cans. But she sat quietly, gathering up her hair that was waving from side to side on her neck, moving her fingers slowly through her hair as if the strength had gone out of her hands.

That's it, she said. Her hair was now gathered on the back of her neck and she put her hands back on her knees. In the light you didn't see her eyes, only the lenses of the glasses. She smiled weakly and took off the glasses, closing one eye again as if it were more and more blinded. It really was very hot. The air grew heavy, taking on an ashen color, holding the movement of a hot dry wind that suddenly approached from some unknown gate, covering that clean, well-swept expanse with a cloud of dust. You smelled a thin odor of smoke and resin. Stone tablets looked taut enough to burst. The fresh paths were filled with arteries of lead and the broken sound of broken flutes approached as if it were going into a cave. The woman facing me pressed her hands to her knees as if she wanted to say: quiet, quiet, but the sound of broken flutes just grew louder, the leaves over the garden plots folded into burned strips of paper, scattering torn petals all around like grains of oats, and I saw the slight trembling of her hands on her knees. Once again she seemed to want to say something, but I didn't hear what, only how she closed both hands on her knees. The sound of broken flutes grew even louder, the light became really low, almost touching, and in the low light the stones suddenly seemed to be moving, waving like curtains, changing that strange architecture of cut off limbs and turning into a thick dough over the colorful fermentation over the cracks in the earth, contorting the precision of the well-chiseled tablets, and the paths, the markers, the signs at the corners of the paths, the cracks of radiance and the broken screens, and you couldn't identify any stone now. The roses seemed to be plastic, and the grass full of heat worms, and when the wind passed as it had come, the black inscriptions on the stones still ran around in the air a moment and after a moment only the young woman was seen sitting alone, quiet, in the weary garden. Now too her hands were folded on her knees and she sat in silence.

She opened her eyes, looking at me with a special intimacy.

I'm lucky, there's never anybody here on this day, I'm always here alone.

That really is nice, I said.

Yes, it's nice. And I'm always scared they'll come all of a sudden. But you see, God watches over me, until today that hasn't happened, every year I'm here alone, sitting like this, alone.

Her eyes were fixed on me all the time, with that special intimacy that exists only between strangers.

It doesn't bother you that we're talking, she said.

No, of course not, it's nice, I said.

She said: Sometimes, you know—

Yes, of course, I know.

It's that, when you sit there, looking—

Of course, I understand.

She quickly rearranged her clasped hands, and asked if I had to go and I said, No, I've got time. She said: I'm glad. Then she said: Sometimes, you know, you want to talk. The light fell on her face, where two thin serpents of sweat ran down, and she wiped them off with the palm of her hand—Nothing special, just, to talk. She smiled in pain—You know, and I said certainly, I know. She smiled again in pain—You always think everything happens to other people. Even when it happens to you, it's like it happened to other people. Her face now rested between the palms of her hands and she lifted it a little, turning aside. Some noise was heard and stones rolling around as in an execution by stoning, and she straightened up, looked, and took off her glasses a moment, putting them back on immediately, shifting them as if she couldn't put them on right. She had long beautiful mocha-colored hands, and I looked at her hands which were circled with wide copper bracelets and rings, a ring on every finger, sometimes two, and when she lifted her arms, the bracelets dropped toward her elbow, linked together making a plate of thin copper. She smiled, bringing the bracelets close to her wrists while looking at me through the sparkling lenses. Then she bent over and took out a blue Hebron glass pitcher, put it next to the stone pillow, and said something about the glass and asked if it was beautiful, and I said to her it was very beautiful. Then she said she wanted to bring velvet flowers because she liked very much to make velvet flowers, especially since fresh flowers would fade tomorrow and she only came once a year, and I said yes, that's how it is. She said: Yes, that's how it is, and stopped a moment, once again moving the glasses that gleamed like two tin tablets. What can you do, that's how it is, she repeated. Her eyes lit up with a strange passion and she shook her head, passed her hand over her throat, and once again I looked at her hands and at the bracelets, and every movement changed their position, making a dull noise of copper striking. They were very beautiful bracelets, and I noticed that every bracelet was set with different stones, and there was a bracelet with yellow amber and a bracelet with red amber and a bracelet with turquoise and a bracelet with small blue lapis and a bracelet with pink coral stones, as if she had a collection of bracelets on her arms. She said: Yesterday I almost made baked apples, every year I want to do that and I don't, baked apples. She laughed a little—That's what we used to do every year on this day, baked apples. Her voice was parched a moment, and I said that was really good, baked apples. She said: With raisins and nuts, you know that, and I said it was really good with raisins and nuts. She said: And cinnamon, of course cinnamon, and you burn the sugar a little, it's very good when you burn the sugar. She moved away a bit on the stone. We didn't put in honey, but he called it apples in honey, she said. She spoke very quietly now, the shaded dark lashes grew wet from one word to the next, and I said I also make that sometimes, especially at the end of summer. She asked why at the end of summer. Her face grew tense, firm, and I didn't know why I had said that or why at the end of summer, and I felt I had to say something and I didn't know what, and I said it was best to make it with Grand Alexanders, and that I always looked for Grand Alexanders. She listened quietly, and I said it was good to peel a thin strip around the apple so it wouldn't burst when it was baking. Now too, she listened quietly. Once again her hair was undone and waved from side to side, and she pressed it, clasping it to her scalp, then she stuck her hand in her hair and wound the ends around her finger.

It's really hot, she said.

Her face was wet and she wiped it with the palm of her hand, moving her hand from her forehead to her throat a few times, then she put her hands down on the surface of the little garden and wiped them with leaves. Her head swayed a bit and for a moment she seemed to be dozing, and I thought about the plants that hoard water in their stems, producing giant thorns for defense. Suddenly I remembered a friend of mine who wanted to be buried under his café under his table, and they told him: It must be somewhere else. And he said: how can I be somewhere else? Under my table, he said, under the table, and even broken up it's all right even taken apart it's all right even with one leg it's all right, and I looked at that strange cemetery, at the stone pillows and the beautiful gardens. Within the emptiness the black letters and the white spaces ran around, moving within air pockets, and that's how she sat too. Her hair still moved from side to side and she pressed it to the back of her neck, then she leaned over, hastily opened her bag and hastily closed it again right away, and seemed to take some hairpins out of it, because she started sticking pins in her hair. It took her time to do it because the curls kept opening up again and fell on her throat, and maybe the pins weren't strong enough to hold the burden of her hair, and she plucked off a branch, smelled it, and then stuck it in her hair, then plucked another one and held it close to me. It had the sweet rotten smell of soft wood and she stroked her face lightly with it, and I said she had beautiful hair and beautiful hands. She laughed a little: The bracelets, you mean the bracelets, and

I said the bracelets really were very beautiful. She moved away a bit on the stone—Yes, every year, he would bring me a bracelet, that was his anniversary present. Her bass voice suddenly broke like a watch that falls to the ground, and she straightened up and stretched her back—But I don't wear them, only when I come here. She stopped, rotated her wrist—He loved it when I had bracelets on my hands, so when I come here—her eyes became big, yellow, an owl's eyes, unmoving, and I saw her taking out the bracelets at night and putting them on the table and arranging them in order, and in the morning putting them on in order, and looking at her arms and some bracelets are missing on her arms, and she moves them and counts the missing bracelets.

Her throat was taut and she sat, looking straight ahead.

This is from the first year, she said, pointing to the bracelet near her wrist, the one with the big yellow amber stone which her hand stroked a few times, and I understood that they were put on in the sequence of the years, and the second year he bought her the red amber, and then the turquoise, and then the lapis, and then the coral, and I tried to guess what he would have bought her the year after. Her face was still impassive and you saw only the eyes, and it occurred to me that that was what she was thinking now too and that was certainly what she did this morning and how she went to the mirror, standing, looking, and the amber and the turquoise stones, the blue lapis beads and the pink coral return in the mirror, and she doesn't get the dates right, or the years, and she counts the years, and suddenly I didn't see her but only the bracelets shriveling, narrow, thin, closing on her like handcuffs.

She turned around to me now, making a noise that sounded like laughter, but wasn't.

Usually my arms are empty, I told you, all year long I walk around with empty arms, she said. She laughed briefly again, and I said she really had beautiful arms and they were beautiful even without the bracelets, and I tried to imagine how they looked without the bracelets but I simply couldn't. The copper stabbed my eyes like needles and I felt a slight pain in my eyes, and I didn't even see her arms but only how the bracelets wrapped one of her arms, then the other, and her shoulders her stomach her chest, and she was sitting all wrapped as in a giant rack. No, no, I said to myself, it's the quiet, very quiet, it's a strong light, it's the strong light, how they sparkle, the bracelets, in the strong light, and how she's dressed up for him, living or dead, she dressed up for him, what a beautiful dress she put on for him, maybe she even washed her hair for him, its shine is so fresh, and how it waves, burning on her head, making a living crown on her head. She said: I don't wear the rings either, not the rings either, and I tried to imagine her fingers without the rings. She had mother-of-pearl colored polish on her fingernails and I saw how delicate her fingernails looked. Suddenly I remembered the story of the apples in honey and the small annual celebration. She said: For our tenth anniversary he said he would bring me one with garnets, and I tried to guess when the tenth anniversary should have been, and what he would have bought on the ninth, the eighth, the seventh, but the needles stabbed my eyes, the amber got mixed up with the turquoise, the lapis with the coral, and I said to myself: No no, so much light, you can't sit in such light, I said to myself that was what she was doing now too, the tenth, the ninth, the eighth, and like me she was counting backward and the count was short, and she was saying it will get longer, every year this will get longer, the bracelets will get short and the counting will get longer, and then the arms will get shorter too. But she sat quietly, playing with the bracelets that made the banging sound of copper and a dull ding dong ding dong and I thought I might have met her once in the street at the corner and hadn't recognized her, she had empty arms and I hadn't recognized her, and I said to myself: No no, not that, it's not her, it's the light, impossible in such a light, and it's a mistake, it's all a mistake, but the bracelets were already running around in the garden mixing with the fresh beautiful blossoming, with the black letters and the white spaces and the rings too, and suddenly I remembered empty of all body and his house empty and empty his soul and his prayer returning empty, I remembered don't leave me empty-handed, oh don't leave me empty don't come empty, and I said no no, the air shrivels and we walk empty, why did I remember that? Where did I hear that? Many years had gone by since I heard that, we stand poor and empty, I heard that, I was a little girl when I heard that, it was always in summer, when my mother would murmur that, and our hut was across from the Muslim cemetery and the windows were open and I was afraid of the cemetery, and I said let's close the windows, but she said, it's not the open windows, it's the bell it's empty it rings empty.

Something wrong? said the woman. She was playing again with the branch in her hand, and I said I was tired and it was late and I had to go. She smiled. Of course, of course, and if you come next year you'll find me here. She sounded very quiet, almost calm, and I said I would remember the date and come, certainly, I would come. Since she didn't answer, I said it really was a very hot day and that wind, and I wanted to go in the evening but I was afraid it was closed in the evening.

She went on playing with the branch in her hand, passing it over her face. They don't close a cemetery, she said.

When I left, I saw the gardener arranging his tools in the shed, lining up the hoes and the spades, the spare faucets, and a heap of new seedlings. He smiled when I asked about her. Come next year, he said, she'll be here. He locked his shed. She always comes this time, every year.

1991

Translated by Barbara Harshav

Questions for Discussion

1. Yehudit Hendel presents a meeting between two young widows. In Israel, young women who have lost their husbands to war are relatively common. This differs from America, where older widows comprise a substantial portion of the population, but young widows are extremely rare. What are the differences between younger and older widows? What difficulties does each face? What are their needs? How well are these needs met in Israeli and American Jewish societies?
2. The narrator speaks of wax candles with wicks the length of the lover's grave. Compare this candle-lighting custom to the ritual of *yahrzeit*. How do such customs help us? Discuss the place of

yahrzeit and other mourning customs in your life.

3. The story uses the word "dead" only once and the word "death" only once. What does the author accomplish by this indirection?
4. What is the significance of the apples in honey? Are women writers particularly likely to use descriptions of food to make a thematic point or to illustrate character? Is Hendel's use of food typical? How does her description affect you?
5. Yehudit Hendel uses many images of circles and roundness: bracelets, rings, apples, the young woman's eyes, "balls of fire." What point is she making?
6. Hendel mentions several times how the black letters of the gravestone inscriptions "ran around." Why?
7. Images of ice, snow, and freezing might seem appropriate for a story about widows visiting a cemetery. Why does Yehudit Hendel instead use images of fire and set the story on an unbearably hot day?
8. Consider the sounds heard by the narrator: grinding glass, broken flutes, and "stones rolling around as in an execution by stoning." What feelings do these evoke in the reader? Is it relevant that execution by stoning is the biblical punishment for adultery?
9. The word "empty" is used once in each of the first two paragraphs of "Apples in Honey," and is then used fourteen times in the very long paragraph near the end of the story. What point is Yehudit Hendel making?
10. Examine the role of memory in "Apples in Honey." For instance, the narrator implies that memory is not to be trusted: "she doesn't get the dates right, or the years." And even more, memory can become a prison: "the bracelets shriveling, narrow, thin, closing on her like handcuffs."

Program Suggestions

1. Compare the young women in "Apples in Honey" to Gail Katz, who wrote of being a young widow in *Jewish Marital Status*. Though Israeli war widows receive governmental benefits and societal support to a significantly greater degree than young

American Jewish widows, the women's emotional and psychological experiences are likely to be similar. (Also refer to the "Acting Like a Widow" chapter of *Jewish Marital Status*, which deals with older American Jewish widows.) Choose a program based on the excellent suggestions in *A Companion Guide to Jewish Marital Status*.[1]

2. "Apples in Honey" focuses on a private, self-created mourning ritual. Invite a rabbi or scholar to speak on Judaism's traditional mourning rituals, and invite widows to speak on the rituals that they themselves have created.
3. Invite speakers to discuss the impact of war on Israeli society, highlighting the effects on women and their families. Include an ICAR (International Coalition for *Agunah* Rights) representative to speak on Israeli widows who are unable to remarry because evidence of their husbands' battlefield deaths is lacking or is insufficient for the rabbinical courts. Other speakers might include Israeli experts in sociology or psychology discussing relevant aspects of their work, as well as "ordinary" Israeli women discussing the effects on their own lives of wars, army duty (their own, husband's, sons'), terrorism, coping with fear, coping with death, etc.

1. Gail Katz, "A Time to Mourn, A Time to Dance: An Unfinished Work in Progress" in *Jewish Marital Status: A Hadassah Study*, edited by Carol Diament (Northvale, NJ: Jason Aronson, 1989), pages 147-159. Rhoda Tagliacozzo, "Acting Like A Widow" in *Jewish Marital Status*, pages 160-164. Ellen Singer, *A Companion Guide to the Book Jewish Marital Status* (New York: Hadassah, 1989), pages 35-37.

About the Translators

DALYA BILU was born in South Africa and attended the Witwatersrand University in Johannesburg. She has lived in Jerusalem since 1956. An award-winning translator of Hebrew fiction into English, Dalya Bilu has translated novels by Yaakov Shabtai, Nathan Shaham, Aharon Appelfeld, and Yoram Kaniuk, among others.

CLAUDIA CHERNOV lives in New York and has worked for the National Jewish Education Department of Hadassah since 1990.

JEFFREY GREEN has lived in Israel since 1973. He has translated six novels by Aharon Appelfeld and works by other writers. With Trudi Birger, he is the co-author of *A Daughter's Gift of Love*, a Holocaust memoir published by the Jewish Publication Society, and he has recently published a novel, *Half a Baker*.

SONIA GROBER was born in South Africa, and she received B.A. and M.A. degrees in Semitics. She resides in Netanyah and is currently a Ph.D. candidate in Hebrew literature. She works as a translator and is primarily interested in women's writing.

HILLEL HALKIN was born in the United States in 1939 and now lives in a village in Northern Israel. He studied English literature at Columbia University and is the author of the 1976 *Letters to an American Jewish Friend: A Zionist's Polemic*. He is a leading translator of Hebrew prose and poetry into English. His translations include works by S. Y. Agnon, Amos Oz, A. B. Yehoshua and Meir Shalev. Hillel Halkin is also a literary critic, writing in *Commentary*, *The New Republic*, and *The Jerusalem Report*.

ALOMA HALTER is a poet, free-lance writer, and regular contributor on literary criticism to the *Jerusalem Post* and other journals. She is the Assistant Editor of the *Ariel Review*.

BARBARA HARSHAV was born in 1940 in Detroit and attended the University of Wisconsin and the University of California at Berkeley. She has translated poetry, drama, fiction, and history from Hebrew, French, German, and Yiddish. Together with Benjamin Harshav, she is the co-editor of *American Yiddish Poetry* published by the University of California Press. She lives in New Haven, Connecticut.

ARTHUR C. JACOBS was born in Glasgow in 1937 and died in Madrid in 1994. He lived variously in Israel, Scotland, London, and Spain. In addition to his work as a translator, he was a highly individual poet who honored both his Scottish and his Jewish heritage with his artistry. His poem "Yom Kippur" is included in the High Holiday prayerbook of the Reform movement.

MALKA MOSKOWITS was born in Germany in 1956. She lived in Israel for ten years and now lives in Brookline, Massachusetts. She received her bachelor's degree in Near Eastern Languages and Literature from New York University. Malka Moskowits is a translator and free-lance writer and editor.

IDA AYALA MYERS was born in Poland, moved to the United States as a child, made *aliyah* in 1988, and presently lives in Netanyah. She is a retired teacher of languages (German and English), and a free-lance writer and translator. Her work has been published in both Hebrew and English language journals.

MARGANIT WEINBERGER-ROTMAN lectures on Hebrew literature at the University of Illinois at Urbana-Champagne. She is especially interested in works by Israeli women, and has translated fiction by Ruth Almog, Savyon Liebrecht, and Shulamit Lapid, among others.

FELICE KAHN ZISKEN currently lives in Jerusalem where she works as a translator for the foreign press. She also writes about life in Israel, and has edited art catalogues for the Israel Museum.

Afterword

Barbara B. Spack

After reading each of the stories in the study guide, and other selections of Israeli women's writings that were not included, many thoughts came to mind. These were alluded to in the Foreword and in the Introduction, but they bear further discussion here.

Some readers may think that since many of the selections deal with women's issues and were written by women, that *Ribcage* is a feminist tract. That was not the entire intent of this study guide, although it is an important element. Interestingly, many of the authors would hardly describe themselves as feminists nor their works as supportive of feminist issues. Whatever our view of the feminist nature of the stories, those of us who appreciate independence in women may applaud loudly as one character successfully contracts for the building of a room on her roof and as two others work their way through the tangles of the mother-daughter relationship.

Most of us are familiar with the prominent contemporary American Jewish authors, their styles and their themes, such as finding one's Jewish identity, accepting spirituality, and coming to terms with one's religious heritage. However, you find none of this searching in the anthology, but not because we chose to avoid it. These themes were not and are not being addressed by most Israeli authors, because in Israel either one is religious or one is secular. The denominationalism of American Jewry—and the idea that individuals should choose not only *whether* to express themselves religiously but *how* to express themselves religiously—is absent in Israel. It is only with the recent influx of Conservative and Reform Jews to the Jewish State that a variety of options for religious expression have become available. Perhaps this will impact on Israeli fiction in the future, perhaps not.

If we attempt to look at what each of these stories separately and collectively tell us about Israel, its people and its culture, we see a multifaceted collage of life in Israel. Big-city life, the kibbutz experience, relationships between women and men, relationships among women, women's isolation, Israelis' cosmopolitan attitudes, the place of women in Israeli culture, and women's lack of self-esteem—all are evident in this unique collection of Israeli fiction. The authors in *Ribcage* write not only to tell their stories but to set free their fears, their desires, their needs. We read these selections and in them see our mothers, our sisters, our friends, ourselves, and we are touched by them to our very souls.

We may want to ponder what is distinctly Israeli about these short stories. How do our stories relate to other works of Israeli fiction (by, say, Amos Oz, A. B. Yehoshua, Aharon Appelfeld)? How does a particular story in this anthology relate to the other selections? Why do our Israeli authors so frequently portray characters who are both figuratively and literally alone? (The characters' isolation is especially striking when we consider that Israeli society is less individualistic, more close-knit and familial than American.) As a whole, what statements do the stories make about Israel and about Israeli women?

It may be fruitful to compare this anthology of short stories to collections of American Jewish fiction—*America and I*, *The Woman Who Lost Her Names*, or *Writing Our Way Home*.[1] In what ways are the Israeli and American stories similar and in what ways do they differ? Such questions would provide the basis for discussion either after any one story or after reading the entire anthology.

---

1. Joyce Antler, ed., *America and I: Short Stories by American Jewish Women Writers* (Boston: Beacon, 1990); Julia Wolf Mazow, ed., *The Woman Who Lost Her Names: Selected Writings by American Jewish Women* (New York: Harper & Row, 1980); Ted Solotaroff and Nessa Rapoport, eds., *Writing Our Way Home: Contemporary Stories by American Jewish Writers* (New York: Schocken, 1993).

We are confident you will plan your Jewish Education programming for the year around this study guide, using it for study groups, Board education, programs for meetings, or Jewish Education seminars. The topics will certainly engender a greater understanding of Israeli culture, as well as create much discussion. Our "how-to" suggestions follow.

Meetings

Choose two or three stories to discuss at a general meeting. Since the discussion questions are extensive, this could be a very successful lay-facilitated program. If, however, your chapter has access to a local professor of Hebrew or comparative literature who could lead the discussion and perhaps make comparisons to American authors, that would make an excellent program as well.

Study Groups

The optimal study group will have between ten and twenty people, and will meet regularly, perhaps every two weeks or once a month. Since scheduling time is a critical factor all our lives, consider a lunch-and-learn or dinner meeting. Your board meetings provide a good pool of attendees; the study sessions could convene before the regular meetings. It helps to have a designated study leader, and one can be chosen at the first session. Choosing someone else to handle administrative tasks makes the leader's job more palatable.

Since there are sixteen stories included in the study guide, you can divide them up according to the number of sessions you have planned, discussing more than one story at each session. It would be best for each participant to have a copy of the guide, so that the stories can be read prior to the sessions. The group may wish to rotate the leader's job of conducting the discussion, or one leader may facilitate the discussion at all sessions. In order to vary the sessions, you may want to read parts of the stories aloud or act them out before the discussion begins. Questions could even be answered by study group members acting the part of a character in the stories. Participants should review the Questions for Discussion in advance so that an easy and open exchange of ideas can ensue at each session.

At Home

Involve those you live with in regular study, using the guide. Read stories aloud to each other around the dining room table, in bedrooms and living rooms, discussing themes and issues as you go along. This affords you a wonderful opportunity to raise your relationships to a new plane.

Annual Event

Jewish Education Days and Evenings are multi-part seminars that are designed to involve the larger community in educational pursuits as well as to motivate study among Hadassah members. Consider holding your event in the evening to accommodate working women. To attract mothers with young children, you could provide baby sitting. A three-part event, consisting of two lectures (presented by either one or two speakers) combined with a workshop or an open discussion, comprises an ideal experience.

You may choose to have a professional storyteller present parts of the stories. There are networks of Jewish storytellers nationwide. Your speaker could also come from your local college or university's Jewish Studies or Comparative Literature Departments, as well as from your Region or National Speakers Bureau. You may use the study guide's questions or direct the discussion as your speaker wishes. A question-and-answer period is always in order.